LIFE ON ALTAMONT COURT

FINDING THE EXTRAORDINARY IN THE ORDINARY

TRENT D. PINES

ISBN-10: 0615837956
ISBN-13: 9780615837956

To Ken:

You changed my life in so many wonderful ways. Thank you for the magic, the dreams and your love. I am forever grateful.

To Karla:

My twin, editor, conscience and lifelong friend.

To Ken's family and our family on Altamont Court:

For not being afraid to let your crazy out, you made the ordinary, extraordinary.

CONTENTS

AUTHOR NOTES

I started writing slice-of-life short stories with the intent of sending them to the local paper on the off-chance the editorial staff would have an interest in publishing them. Stories about family, actual and adopted; stories about surviving home renovations and family vacations; and stories about food. Lots and lots of food. Universally, the room in any house where everything comes together is the kitchen so many of these amazing stories involved food. Trust me, you will get hungry while reading this book. I included some key recipes at the end for readers to enjoy. As it turned out, these "short" stories were too long for publication in our weekly newspaper: undaunted, I kept writing. The events and stories surrounding our lives on Altamont Court began to take on a life of their own. Our love of the town, the people and our families play out in the chapters that follow. There is a lot of love and laughter in these pages so please sit back and enjoy.

PROLOGUE

I am a Southerner at heart. Though I grew up in a small town outside of Columbus, Ohio, my family moved to Texas before I graduated from high school. I've spent a majority of my adult life south of the Mason Dixon Line. My career and personal lives have played out in three locations: Texas, Georgia and New Jersey. Yes, New Jersey. The company I worked for was headquartered there so I found myself living in the Garden State on more than one occasion. Living in these diverse locations allowed me to meet my share of characters: wonderful, loving people, each with their own eccentricities. Let me assure you that stereotypes do have a basis in fact. Sometimes loosely, but all you have to do is turn on a reality TV program to confirm my hypothesis.

Each one of these places had something to teach me. I learned new words and truly vivid expressions while living in Texas. Words like "fixin." Such as, "I am fixin to do this and fixin to do that." To me "fixin" sounds like I should be making dinner. Then there is the word "tumped" as in "it done tumped over." This is a mash-up of the words tipped and dumped – very creative! Texans also have great one-liners to describe simple situations. For instance, instead of saying, "You're lying to me," a Texan might say, "I can tell when someone is piss'n on my boots and telling me it's a rainstorm."

While living in the land of Scarlett O'Hara, I learned the expression, "Bless your heart." "Bless your heart" can cover a multitude of sins. You can get away with saying just about anything bad about anyone as long as you finish it with, "Bless their heart." For example, "She's as dumb as a box of hair, bless her heart," or "My, that's an ugly baby! Bless his heart." My good friend Julie, a New Jersey transplant who now lives in Atlanta, believes that the northeastern equivalent to "Bless your heart" is "F&%$ you!" For those of you who have lived in the Garden State, you know that the expression "F&%$ you" works for every situation and is used liberally.

This brings me to my last relocation to New Jersey and the reason you're reading this memoir. Some stints in the Garden State have been more memorable than others. This last move was the most memorable of all.

Occasionally in life we are lucky enough to experience a bit of magic. It's something that's hard to quantify, but we know in our heart of hearts that it's special. The stars and planets align, the saints bless you, and in effect – Kismet! This is what happened when my partner Ken and I moved onto Altamont Court in Morristown, New Jersey. We were a normal gay couple living the heterosexual life next to a bunch of eccentric straight folk who thought their lifestyles were completely normal. Boy, were they ever wrong. Little did we know they would change our lives forever. As with all good stories, melodrama and mishaps make them more interesting. So, if there hadn't been any, I would have made some up. But alas, all that happens in this narrative is true. The events that took place and the places where they happened are real. Most importantly, the people who make up these unbelievable memories are also real, "Bless their hearts!"

KEN AND TRENT

"Two guys, one cart, fresh pasta. Figure it out."

- Suzanne Sugarbaker, Designing Women

Ken and I met more than 15 years ago in New Jersey when he was working as a consultant in my department. He was going through hell, as his oldest daughter Ashleigh was being treated for childhood leukemia. We often talked about her progress. With my house only five miles from the hospital where she was being treated, we'd catch up for lunch or dinner to give him a break from the 24X7 vigil he was keeping at the hospital. Although Ken had come out to his ex-wife and family, he was still struggling with what it meant to be a gay man. He was just entering the gay dating world, which provided the two of us with hours of conversation about the interesting and unusual people he'd met. It didn't take long for us to become close friends.

Very few of Ken's first dates resulted in a second date. Many that started off promising ended with Ken running for his car. These stories often caused me to laugh so hard it hurt; Ken didn't always see the humor. My favorite was the hot, hunky, "masculine" Italian guy Ken was smitten with. This was one first date he was overly excited about – and understandably so; Nick was witty, gregarious and enjoyed a night out on the town. Ken asked me to meet him at the local watering hole so he could debrief me on his date with Nick.

Ken was in the middle of telling me what a great time they had when a guy in six-inch heels, painted nails and full Barbie drag ran over and kissed him on the cheek. "Thanks for the great time last night."

My jaw hit the table. To be fair, Ken's jaw hit the table too. As Nick floated away, I looked at Ken, stifling my laughter, and said, "So that was the masculine, hot Italian you had a date with last night?"

Ken glared at me, "Not funny! He never told me he competed in drag queen competitions!"

"So you had a date with a masculine drag queen?"

With lasers coming out of his eyes, Ken said, "Are you through?"

Hell no, I was just getting started. "Okay, so he's masculine when not wearing a gown, heels and a wig. What does he do for a living?"

Ken's jaw clenched. It was not a hard question but the answer seemed to be sticking in his throat. After a 30-second pause, he said, "He's a hairdresser."

I choked on my salad. "So you had a date with a Masculine, Hair Burner, Drag Queen last night." I paused for effect before I said, "You can't make this shit up!"

We both started laughing so hard we had trouble finishing our dinner. In the back of my mind I was thinking, *I need to call National Geographic because Ken just discovered the elusive Masculine, Hairdresser, Drag Queen in its natural habitat.*

After giving Ken such a hard time about meeting this endangered species of man, I had to tell him about the time I dated a brilliantly talented ventriloquist named Jarod. We'd made it to a second date and I was looking forward to a fun evening. As we got out of the car, Jarod said, "Oh wait, I want Ronny to join us."

Ronny? Who the hell was Ronny and why was he joining us on our date? I watched as he circled around to the trunk and thought, *Oh god, Ronny's a dog and he's been locked in the trunk this entire time!* If only that had been the case.

Ronny was not a dog; Ronny was one of Jarod's dummies. In fact, Ronny was his favorite dummy and as he pulled him out of the trunk, Jarod said, "I take him everywhere."

I looked at him and said sarcastically, "I am surprised you didn't have him belted up in the back seat."

Without missing a beat, Jarod said, "That's where he normally sits but I didn't want you to freak out seeing one of my puppet friends buckled up in the backseat." Too late, I was already freaking out. He then proceeded to say, "He wasn't happy about being in the trunk, but he knew it was for a good cause." The cuckoo clock just struck the top of the hour.

At dinner, he positioned the doll so that it was looking right at me. It was creepy as hell. I thought for sure it was going to pull a 'Chucky' and fly across the table with the steak knife and attack me when Jarod had his back to us. During dinner I could have sworn I heard that dummy whisper, "Back off, bitch, he's mine!"

At the end of my night with the 'Puppet Master,' I shook his hand, shook Ronny's hand and then I ran. As you might guess, we did not have a third date. I did get a couple of messages on the answering machine from Ronny asking when we were all going out again. I started checking under my bed just to make sure he wasn't waiting to slit my throat in the middle of the night.

After my story, Ken was looking at me like I had three heads. I said defensively, "What?"

He just shook his head. "At least my date wasn't Sybil."

"Really? You need to remember that Nick and Nicole are the same person, or should I call him Barbie?"

As our friendship grew, we realized we had a lot in common. We both had performed in several musical theater productions, and we both enjoyed traveling, movies, and restaurants. All of that sounds fairly mundane but as we shared more details about our lives and families, it seemed like more than a coincidence that we'd met.

To start with, our mothers are about the same age. What's more interesting, they are both named Sally and, scarier still, they are both the oldest of three girls. In fact, when you look at a picture of the four of us, you would swear Ken's mother is my mother and my mother is Ken's. Ken's mother is blonde, has a moderate complexion, northern Italian/Germanic features and green eyes. I am, or

I should say *was*, a blond, (male pattern baldness has forced me to adopt a buzz cut, thanks to my dad). Like her, I have a moderate complexion with Germanic looks and green eyes. My mother is dark-haired with a beautiful olive complexion and brown eyes. Ken has the exact same complexion, brown eyes and brown hair. When we vacation together, we confuse everyone who meets us. Both our mothers look ten to fifteen years younger than their actual ages. This always elicits comments such as, "You can't possibly be his mother!" and "Did you have him when you were twelve?" Ken and I just shake our heads and go with the flow. On the other hand, our mothers live for these types of compliments.

When a great career opportunity presented itself in Atlanta, I could not pass it up. Ken and I weren't an item yet, but with Ashleigh declared cancer free he decided it was a great time to make some changes in his life. He secured a job in Atlanta and the two of us left the lovely state of New Jersey behind. After a year in Atlanta we both admitted our relationship had moved from friends with benefits to something more substantial. We had evolved into a couple.

To make it official, I decided I'd better "put a ring on it" and bought us matching commitment rings, which, for two gay men, had to be more than simple bands. I purchased two platinum and 18K gold rings with four diamonds across the top of each ring. It was a total surprise for Ken as I dropped them in the bottom of our champagne glasses at dinner while he was away from the table powdering his nose. He nearly chipped a tooth as the ring tumbled down the glass when we toasted our newly cemented relationship.

Living in Atlanta was wonderful. Ken's daughters, Ashleigh and Lindsay, loved visiting for the summers. We used their summer stays as an excuse to build a fabulous pool, thus turning our backyard into a resort and summer camp rolled into one. But after seven years in Atlanta, change was afoot in our lives – careers, kids, and family had all conspired to drag us from Georgia back to New Jersey.

I was working a temporary assignment in London when we made the decision to return to the Garden State, so Ken was the first to move. He landed a great job with a successful company and took on the gargantuan responsibility of "Finding the House." Any of you who have gone through the process of home selection know that locating and signing a contract on a house that your significant other has never laid eyes on is dangerous territory – its a decision that can haunt your loving relationship for life. It's like walking a tightrope in a hurricane over a pit of snapping gators (or over a group of vicious drag queens fighting over the last pair of size eleven Manolo Blahniks on the clearance rack at Neiman Marcus)! Either way, it's not a pit you want to fall into.

If your significant other is unhappy with your choice, you could be made to pay for your decision for years, if not decades. Actually, I think that should be part of a couple's vows: "to love, honor, obey and make suffer endlessly should you make a bad decision." It would prepare you for the reality yet to come.

THE HOUSE

"Love is like a brick. You can build a house with it or sink a body."

– Lady Gaga

It was the height of the housing market in the northeast and we were unprepared for what we found. We had a substantial down payment in our pocket from the sale of our home in Atlanta and felt good about our prospects. We could not have been more wrong. Prices were double what they were in Atlanta and most homes needed substantial renovation. Even worse, we lost every house we bid on, by ten, twenty or thirty thousand dollars. The concept of offering that much over the asking price wasn't something we could wrap our heads around. I mean, who haggles and negotiates to pay more for something? It was a seller's market and we were choking on the prices.

House hunting was Ken's priority. He'd narrow down the selections; I would fly into Newark in the morning, see his favorites and take a flight out to London at night. I should note that flying makes me crabby and difficult, so hats off to Ken and our realtor, Casey, for making the best of a challenging situation. Casey is a good friend of Ken's mother– notice I did not say *was* a good friend, so yes, they did remain friends after dealing with my insanity, which I do believe was a true testament to their friendship.

Ken and Casey would pick me up at the airport and we would see twelve houses in four hours – I am a quick looker. In fact, if I didn't like the way a house looked from the outside, I wouldn't bother going in. Casey would pull up to a house; I would take one look at the outside and say imperiously (and with a touch of disdain), "Next!" Each house we looked at needed $200K just to make it livable. The thought of buying a $600K fixer-upper seemed absurd! One house we looked at was in the perfect location but was in such bad shape I thought if we shut the door too hard it would collapse on itself. I had come to the conclusion we would have to rent some shack in the woods of Pennsylvania and commute.

Just when we were reaching the end of our proverbial rope, out of nowhere, a home popped up on our realtor's radar. Casey called Ken at work and insisted he see a home she'd found in Morristown. Ken was desperate at this point and agreed to see it immediately. To be honest, he had reached an anxiety level akin to a nervous breakdown. He was twenty-four hours shy of committing himself to an institution. A crazed spouse calling you at all hours from another country can do that to you. So Ken met her in Morristown over lunch to see this "amazing" find that we just "couldn't live without."

He called me as soon as he saw it. "I found our house!" he said. "The floors and the moldings are drop-dead gorgeous. It needs a little work, but it's a great house." He described it as a center hall Queen Ann located in Morristown, NJ, with a huge porch and stunning foyer. "Casey insists we put a bid on this gem immediately." Ken and I were accustomed to homes that needed "a little work"; our last two homes had all been built before 1920.

"Trent, we need to make a bid and get a signed contract as soon as possible before someone outbids us again." Ken and I really liked Morristown. It has an amazing history. George Washington, Samuel Morris, Thomas Nast: a Who's Who of American history had lived in or visited this town. It's located fifty minutes from NYC on the Midtown Direct train line, and has a diversity of shops and restaurants and people. It was the ideal location.

We had been outbid several times on other properties so it seemed like a reasonable suggestion. No one shared with me that the house had been on the market for over a year, with no offers, during a housing boom. The only reason it showed up in our price range was due to a third reduction in the asking price. Remember the words, "a little work," gracious reader, as we will come back to that shortly.

So, sight unseen by Yours Truly, with a nagging feeling this home would need more than "a little work," we made a bid $60K below the asking price. Shockingly, it was accepted immediately. While I was signing and faxing the contracts from my office in London the hairs on my neck stood up. Was I really signing a contract on a house I had never seen? This seemed way too easy.

There had to be something wrong. But when you're desperate, jet lagged and running on empty, your intuitive instincts are somewhat diminished.

In the meantime, Ken took his mother Sally over to see the house and get her take on it. He chose not to share her reaction. I believe her exact words were, "Have you lost your mind? This is a half million-dollar fixer-upper. You need to bulldoze the place and start from scratch." Hence the reason he didn't share her feedback with me until after the closing.

On my return flight from London through NJ to Atlanta, Ken and our realtor Casey drove to the airport to pick me up and take me to the house. Ken explained on the way over that we would be living within walking distance of the Kings Grocery (a local staple in the area for great produce, fresh meat and friendly service – you're welcome Kings). In addition there were all the great shops and restaurants on South Street. I loved Kings and I loved South Street so this was an added bonus. I had worked in Morristown seventeen years earlier so I could picture the area where our house was located. If we were within walking distance of Kings and we were close to South Street then I knew there were some great old homes in that area and I was beginning to get overly (yet secretly) excited.

I was watching for the South Street sign as we were tooling down the interstate and chatting about the house, when Casey took the Morris Avenue exit instead of South Street. My jaw dropped and my heart started racing. "We don't live off Morris Avenue," I stuttered. "You t- t- told me South Street!" I was pointedly telling both Ken and Casey that this was not the way to our home, as we were to live off South Street! Mind you, I had never been to the house, and I had no idea where it was located, but I knew we couldn't possibly have bought a house on Morris Avenue by the train station. All I could think was 'druggies and hookers and pimps – oh my.' I began explaining to them, in a voice reserved for moments of horrific revelation that "I will not live off Morris Avenue" and if they'd just take me "straight back to the airport I would pretend this never happened."

I asked our shaken realtor, whose knuckles were white from holding the steering wheel so tight, if she had ever sold a home in Morristown. "Do you have any idea at all how Morristown is laid out? Do you realize how seedy Morris Avenue is? And you showed Ken a home here?" Poor Casey. She was repeatedly popping Tic-Tacs, which I now suspect were Valium.

Yes, it had been over twenty years, but my memories of Morris Avenue from the late '80s were strongly influencing my judgment. I was sure that one or both of them had lost their minds. They had obviously shared a crack pipe prior to picking me up at Newark Airport. At that point I was close to testing my Tic-Tac theory and snatching them from her to calm my nerves. I was searching the seat cushions for a Xanax or a Valium, hell at this point even a "special" brownie – minus the lint. When we exited Morris Avenue, it was clear things had improved dramatically since the 80's, but I was too far gone to care. As we pulled up to the large Queen Ann home I was shocked that we'd bought such a big house on such a small lot.

Ken incredulously reminded me that this was in-town living. In-town living? I could reach out our front door and open the door

15

of a car parked on the street. If my neighbor needed to borrow some sugar, all I would have to do is lean out the window and hand it across. Clearly this was in-town living at its worst.

The saving grace was the garage. It was an unexpected extra. This meant we wouldn't have to scrape ice and snow off our cars in the winter. Ken was over the moon about it. "This is the first time I have ever had a house with a garage," Ken boasted. I had no idea a garage could elicit such an elated response, but I went with it. He unexpectedly continued, "I know it looks like a two-car garage, but it's not. It will only fit one of our cars." Okay, so maybe I had traumatized him on the way over, but I was clearly looking at a two-car garage. Ken could tell by the look on my face that I was confused. He quickly explained. "We share both the driveway and the garage with our neighbors."

Come again? I had heard of shared driveways, but a shared garage? That was a new one. I shook my head in disbelief. "That's not possible." He pulled out the property survey that came with the information packet and there it was; the property line ran straight through the middle of the garage. Who subdivides a garage? Ladies and gentlemen, I give you - STRIKE ONE.

We started our tour by walking around the postage-stamp yard to get a feel for the property. As we toured the outside of the house I noticed we had a narrow but enormously long back yard. I was relieved. It was similar to our property in Atlanta, narrow but deep. Having just been through the shock of a shared driveway and shared garage I decided I had better ask about our property line. SURPRISE! Our property line actually ended at the lovely 1960's chain-link fence. The property beyond the fence belonged to a separate estate that faced Elm Street. Our backyard was only 40 feet deep. Our swimming pool in Atlanta was bigger than the entire back yard here. As I stared at the chain-link fence, I kept thinking to myself, *Add some razor wire and a guard tower and we'd have the prison yard at the state penitentiary* - Say hello to STRIKE TWO.

As we walked into the house to take the tour, I was met by the owners, the owners' family and their real estate agent and was immediately taken captive. Their agent looked like she had sold real estate in Morristown during the revolutionary war; I am sure she'd shown George and Martha property in the area. The agent informed us that I "could not tour the house until I had signed the original copies" to replace the faxed ones I had sent from London. The first thought that came into my head was, *Danger Will Robinson! Warning! Warning! Warning!* As I was ushered into the dining room to sit down and sign the documents I quickly found myself in a scene from a family dramedy. Ken and I were sitting with our real-tor Casey on one side of the table facing the sellers, their agent and twelve family members. One of the sellers was in total distress. She was sobbing and saying something in Portuguese that I couldn't follow.

Her brother whispered, "She thinks you're stealing her house."

There's a comforting thought. One of the sellers believed we were throwing her out into the street and stealing her home. After forty years in the same place, this was a tough transition for her. At this point my heart was pounding and my blood pressure was one notch below the eruption point of Mount Vesuvius. Were we really going to buy this house? Against all common sense, I signed the originals. Why? I don't know. Jet lag and extreme fatigue were the only rational reasons I could come up with – that or temporary insanity. I wouldn't argue with either at this point.

With my signature drying on the page, it was time to see the house. To be fair, the pictures Ken had sent me didn't do the place justice. Not by a long shot. With room darkening shades on every window, there was not enough light to provide the eye-popping details I was now seeing in vivid color. Harvest gold and avocado greens don't photograph well. As he had noted, the floors on the first floor were amazing. They were twelve-inch parquet with a cherry inlay border in each room. Heavy woodwork and coffered ceilings in the dining room were also amazing. But that's where the beauty ended. This home and its bathrooms had not seen a facelift in fifty years. The main bathroom had a pink tub, toilet and sink. That combo hasn't been around since the 50's.

I have a pet peeve when it comes to remodeling work. I hate dealing with wallpaper. I cannot express in words how much I hate dealing with wallpaper. I hate it with every fiber of my being, so I had asked Ken to make sure we did not have to deal with it. No matter what they tell you at Home Depot, there is no good way to remove wallpaper on plaster walls. It is always time consuming and always messy. No matter what "snake oil" they try to sell you, it doesn't work. And never try to paint over it because the moisture just causes it to bubble up. As I walked through the house I noticed nearly two-thirds of the rooms had been decorated with wallpaper – STRIKE THREE! All I could think about was putting my lips to a bottle of Patron. Cheers!

After this fantastically magical tour, I realized our one chance for salvation was the inspection. If the inspector found enough things wrong we would have an out. The house was nearly one hundred years old and nothing had been done to it in fifty years. As expected, the inspector found a lot of issues: bad roof, oil tank buried in the front yard, knob and tube wiring, fifty-year-old boiler, and a long list of other needed repairs. Our best way out of this nightmare was to ask for a large amount of cash back at the closing to cover the most glaring problems. By the way, insurance companies do not like things like knob and tube wiring and oil tanks buried in the yard. Trying to find someone to insure this home was a true challenge. But – "Like a good neighbor, State Farm was there" and worked with us. Twenty-five years with the same insurance company paid off. They were willing to insure the house if we contracted to have the knob and tube wiring replaced before we moved in. After three electricians looked at the house, each delivered an estimate between $20,000 to $30,000 dollars. Smiling to myself, I thought, *There is no way a seller in this market will meet my demand for $25,000 cash back at closing.* I was wrong. I had underestimated their desire to downsize. They agreed immediately. This was the second time the klaxons went off in my head – DANGER, DANGER, DANGER! I was in total shock when they agreed. My mind was spinning. We needed a house and the seller had met our demands; it was full speed ahead!

I was a total wreck at the closing. I looked like a man in the grip of the DT's, with my right leg bouncing continuously under the table. Our closing papers looked like a man in the midst of a grand mal seizure signed them. To quote my mother-in-law, Ken and I were now the proud owners of a "half-million-dollar fixer-upper." Our first stop after the closing was the nearest bar. I needed that

Patron and I needed it immediately. You might ask yourself: Where does one find a bar open at 9:30 AM on a Saturday? The answer was: Hennessey's at the bottom of the hill on Morris Avenue. As a rule, I don't think Irish pubs ever really close. The bartender didn't bat an eye when we waltzed in and asked for two shots of Patron.

After the closing and the stop at the bar, we took our keys in hand and headed for our new home. The minute we walked in, I was overwhelmed by the amount of clean-up we faced. I needed another drink, so we decided to go for a liquid lunch and draw up our attack plan for the next day. I should mention, there was more drinking than planning during lunch.

CLEANING DAY

"Cleanliness is not next to Godliness. It isn't even in the same neighborhood."

- Erma Bombeck

The next morning, dressed in our "ready-to-do-heavy-cleaning" clothes, we arrived at our home at 8:00 AM and began removing carpet, wallpaper, and rickety furniture the previous owners had left behind. This included an unusual amount of religious artwork they'd left on the walls. We worked until 8:00 PM that night and it looked like we hadn't done a thing. Exhausted, overwhelmed and now crabby as hell, we decided to call it a day. Ken tried to keep things upbeat. He had picked this house, after all, so he was trying to give it a positive spin. I believed he had a death wish. He might as well be waving a red flag in front of an angry bull.

I held up my hand and said, "Stop! Please don't say anything more. I only want three things right now: a shower, a sandwich, and 12 hours of sleep. I don't want to talk to anyone about any of this right now." At that moment I didn't feel much like being a loving, supportive and understanding spouse.

During our move to NJ, our subsequent house-hunt, and the initial renovations, we were staying with Ken's brother and sister-in-law. Warren and Heidi generously allowed us to live in their finished basement while we were in transition. Little did they know this transition was going to take six months. To be honest, it was one of the best parts of the move. Pizza and Margarita Fridays became a tradition while we stayed there – I could have used both that first night.

When we got back to my their house, I did exactly as planned. I took a *Silkwood*-like shower, grabbed a sandwich, took a Xanax and went to bed (Ok, so I wanted four things...sue me!) I dreaded going back the next day. I had a nightmare I was in a Twilight Zone episode, and as soon as I entered the house I couldn't leave. Every door led back into the house and every room was full of more carpet, wallpaper and furniture. No matter how much we removed, there was always more. It was a vortex of doom leading down into Dante's Inferno. I just wasn't sure what level of Hell I'd landed in.

To Ken's credit, he sensed that I was at my breaking point, so while I slept he put out a 911 call to family and friends. Ken has a large and wonderful family who had been extremely supportive of our move to New Jersey. He explained to everyone that we needed help badly, and if they didn't help us right away, I might try to join the Witness Protection Program and disappear permanently. His family answered the call. All twenty of them showed up the next day along with several friends and our realtor. She was making good on her promise to help strip wallpaper. Like an angry swarm of killer bees, they attacked the house, removing wallpaper, pulling out carpet, and removing stuff left behind by the previous owners. And there was a lot of stuff. So much stuff that we filled our half of the shared garage floor to ceiling, our large front porch floor to ceiling and part of the driveway with several cubic yards of stuff. We were afraid we were going to be drummed out of the neighborhood before we had a chance to buy good favor with a few strong cocktails. Our poor neighbors Pat and George, with whom we shared the garage and driveway, had to park their car next to a pile of sofas and other paraphernalia for fourteen weeks. Nothing says "Welcome home" like stepping out of your car onto a Herculon-covered sofa. I'm nominating them for sainthood; I am sure it will be fast tracked.

In addition to the furniture left behind, we had to deal with mountains of religious artwork on the walls. Actually, it was on every wall and even on a ceiling or two. I couldn't decide if this was a message from the Almighty that I needed to change my wicked ways or the house had been a convent at one point and the nuns had left their watercolors behind. As we removed the pictures from the house, we stacked them out back; no one seemed comfortable just throwing them away.

This confused our neighbors. They couldn't tell if we were moving the artwork in or out. Were we right wing religious fanatics (which seemed unlikely for a gay couple), or were we just into various forms of religious art? Ken, being a good Catholic, refused to watch me remove the pictures and dried palm leaves. He was sure I was going to be struck by lightning or spontaneously combust. To his amazement, neither happened.

While our Mongolian horde was attacking various rooms in the house, my two sisters-in-law, Heidi and Michele, were painting over the hideous color in the living room. Ken and I had picked a deep shade of olive green for the formal living room. The sample looked great, so I was certain this would be the perfect color for this room. I went with a new brand of paint because it was advertised in Architectural Digest as highly rated by various designers. I figured this was a foolproof option. So instead of going with a Pratt and Lambert Williamsburg color like I would normally do, I bought four gallons of this expensive new and improved paint. We will call it brand "M."

There are normally five finishes you can choose when you paint: Flat, Eggshell, Satin, Semi-Gloss and High Gloss. My favorite paint finishes are Flat or Eggshell for walls and Satin or Semi-Gloss for woodwork. My Grandpa Ike was a professional painter so when it comes to painting a room I am hard-nosed about quality paint, the color and detail of work.

Heidi and Michele opened brand "M's" amazing paint product and started changing the dynamic of the living room. I dropped by early on to see how it looked and it looked great. These two ladies were painting machines. I was excited because they both felt they would have two coats on the walls before we all left for the day.

While inspecting the progress the ladies were making on the living room I heard an "Oh shit!" yelled loudly from somewhere above and went bounding up the stairs. As I reached the second floor landing I saw my nephew, Warren Jr., standing in the guest room covered in wet plaster. When he was pulling down the wallpaper in the guest room, he discovered where a leak from the roof around a vent pipe had soaked and loosened the plaster. When he pulled on the paper, half the wall came with it. I was staring at bare strips of lath. Lovely. Add roof patching and wall repair to the list.

While I supervised the removal of a monstrous sofa from the third floor, my mother-in-law, Sally, dropped by the living room to see how the painting was going. Sally has a keen eye and immediately noted that the finish on the wall looked glossy. She turned and asked Heidi and Michele, "Is Trent aware he picked a semi-gloss finish for the walls?"

Heidi said, "No, this is eggshell. It says so on the can. It's probably a bit shiny because it's not quite dry."

Sally wasn't buying it. She checked one of the totally dry sections of the wall, and the finish looked semi-gloss shiny. She found Ken and let him know what was going on. Ken looked at it and said, "Mom, it's not that bad. Trent will never notice."

Sally laughed maniacally. "How long have the two of you been together? His nose and eyes are as sharp as mine. If you think he is not going to notice you're delusional."

Ken began to panic. He did not want me to have a meltdown over the shiny walls our two wonderful sisters-in-law had spent seven hours painting. As I was coming down the stairs directing our friends where to throw the next load of garbage, I noticed Ken and Sally blocking the living room with their bodies, keeping my view to a minimum. I also noticed the blinds on all six windows had been closed to reduce the amount of light in the room.

I turned to enter the living room and was astounded that Heidi and Michel had finished painting it already. The room is 15X28, so it was a huge achievement to finish it in one day. I was marveling at their work as they were rolling up the dropcloth at the far end of the room. I was about to thank them when I noticed that the wall seemed shiny. At first I thought the paint was wet, but when I examined a section of the wall that was obviously dry, it was still shiny - really shiny. My eyes grew wide and I almost said aloud, *Oh my God, we put semi-gloss paint on the living room walls. This whole room has to be repainted!*

But just as I was about to speak, Ken grabbed one arm and Sally the other. They escorted me around the living room, pointedly telling me how hard Heidi and Michele had worked to get the room finished in one day. "Look at the trim," Sally said. "They managed perfect edges."

Ken and Sally kept topping each others comments until I realized they were trying to tell me, *This is not the proper time to tell these two exhausted ladies that their work was useless and the room would have to be repainted.* Instead, I took a deep breath and thanked them for their monumental efforts. As soon as they left I turned to Ken and said, "I hate it! This room has to be repainted and I will not be using brand 'M' ever again."

Ken thought I was overreacting. We left that semi-gloss pea green color up for an entire year, so as not to seem disrespectful, and then I had the room repainted when we painted the rest of the house.

Two enormous dumpsters later, we had the house, garage, porch and driveway completely cleared. It was time to begin the renovation.

⌒

THE CRACK DEN

"Here Lies Walter Fielding. He bought a house, it killed him."

- Tom Hanks as Walter Fielding in the *Money Pit*

Our first year on Altamont Court was painful at best (from this point forward we will call it The Court). Walls were trenched, new electrical wiring pulled, floors refinished, boiler replaced, central air conditioning added, hot water heater replaced, plumbing work completed, oil tank removed - the list was endless. The words "needs a little work" were never used lightly in our home again. For all of you who are married or in a long-term relationship and have managed to survive a home renovation and remain loving partners – I take my hat off to you. Nothing tests the boundaries of your love like a home renovation, especially when you are living in that home while the work is being done.

Living in your home during a renovation is not for the faint of heart. This is something I had done before; it is not something Ken had done. He was in for a real treat.

To understand Ken's reaction to our renovation, you have to know a bit more about my partner. Ken is a neat freak, an organizational freak, and has a touch of OCD. When we first met, I was Oscar to his Felix. He folds his socks into neat squares so that each one slips neatly into place in a nice row. He's the type of guy who organizes his clothes in the closet by type and color. Everything is neatly hung and in precise order from short to long, light to dark and by color. So not just reds grouped with reds but a row of shirts moving from pink to Bordeaux. I, on the other hand, throw clothes around like confetti, rarely fold anything and never use a laundry hamper (Who needs an iron when your front load dryer has a wrinkle release setting?).

During our first three years together I traveled constantly. I lived out of a laundry basket as easily as I lived out of a suitcase. If I couldn't find a match to a sock, I would just root around on the bedroom floor or look through a suitcase until I found it. If not, I'd toss the odd sock into the laundry room and get a new pair. More than likely the missing sock was in a hotel on the other side of the globe. I am not good about thoroughly checking a hotel room to make sure I don't leave something behind. You could make a quilt from all the single socks I have. I am still convinced that washers and dryers eat socks. Every time I look at our washer and dryer they look suspiciously guilty. You can imagine the fun this created during our first couple of years.

I find that couples rarely fight over the big stuff. That's because it is BIG stuff and we all do our best to work with each other to develop a solution or at least a permanent truce. So it is the small things that drive us crazy. I like to call this "the cap and the tube of toothpaste trial." In a relationship you always have the person who squeezes from the bottom, always cleans the threads and puts the cap back on the toothpaste. Then there are those of us who don't. Yes, it's messy, and yes, we squeeze from the middle and not the bottom and yes, we annoy the hell out of our thread cleaning, cap tightening partners. I apply this metaphor to all seemingly small things that become epic battles.

Ken's "cap" issue with me was my habit of leaving my unmentionables on the bathroom floor every morning when I got into the shower. When I lived alone, I never worried about it. I just kicked them into a corner and picked them up at the end of the week when it was time to do laundry. It was a bad habit, but it worked for me. This maneuver did not work for Ken and drove him to the brink of insanity. He would pick them up every morning and put them in the hamper. At one point he stopped picking them up to see how long it would take me to notice. I didn't notice at all. As my underwear began to pile up, so did Ken's frustration. By the end of the week I got a pointed lecture about my sloppiness and complete lack of couth.

Now that you know how Ken reacts to general clutter and dirt, you can imagine his reaction to the mayhem that must precede every successful home renovation. I find this to be the exciting part of a renovation; Ken found it to be a nightmare.

When working on something as personal and challenging as a home renovation you face obstacles almost daily. You learn to sense intuitively when is the best time to drop a catastrophic batch of daisy cutters on your spouse's head. You do your best to ease your spouse into the needed conversation. You start a conversation with, "You know when we talked about moving that wall in the bedroom?" so that you can transition to, "Well, a pipe in that wall was leaking, so I figured this is the perfect time to tear it down and move it out four feet."

All couples learn to recognize that certain tone, lilt or hesitation in the voice of their loving partner that hints at impending doom. It's that special something in your life partner's voice that tells you there is a HUGE problem lurking in the hallways of your home. You know what I mean. It's the way they say your name as if it is a question - "Trent?" This has always meant disaster in our house. If I heard my name spoken in the form of a question, it meant something was leaking, spurting, spewing, hissing, blinking, smoking, popping or groaning somewhere in our home and I was being asked what was wrong with the offending item.

For a period of time it was a weekly occurrence at our home on The Court. You name it, during the first year something was always breaking. These can be defining moments in a relationship. How you handle them often determines whether your relationship lasts as long as a pop idol's marriage or whether you are in it for the long haul. Luck would have it that we moved into a neighborhood of do-it-yourselfers who had lived through these trials. Every home on the street was built before 1920, so folks on Altamont Court are downright MacGyver-esque in their ability to fix something on the fly or create a working boiler with the help of a paperclip, twine, duct tape, chewing gum, a maxipad (with wings) and a magnifying glass. In my mind, all the men and women who lived on The Court were geniuses.

The night the hot water heater blew was a classic. Literally, it was blowing water out the top like Old Faithful. Ken called me to the basement, pointed at the hot water heater and asked, "Is it supposed to be doing that?"

I watched in horror as the thing was flooding the basement and Ken wanted to know if that was a normal function of the hot water heater. Really? Is that a serious question?

I screamed, "NO IT'S NOT SUPPOSED TO DO THAT! Why didn't you just turn off the water going into the tank?"

"I didn't know which of the five valves to turn!"

"How about the one that connects to the line going into the tank?" My spouse is a brilliant man on many levels, but common sense mechanics is not his strong suit.

The complete rewiring of the entire electrical system was another classic Felix and Oscar scene. All the knob and tube wiring had to be replaced in order to bring our home up to code. Knob and tube wiring consists of ceramic "knobs and tubes" through which all the wiring in the house was connected. Wiring installed at the turn of the century was not well insulated and was very dangerous. Removal was necessary but not a pretty process. Plaster had to be busted out, walls trenched, holes punched in the ceiling, holes drilled in the 2x4s and new electrical wiring pulled throughout the house. There is nothing about this process that is neat and organized. Our electrician and his team were punching holes into every surface in the house. The walls, ceilings and floors looked like Swiss cheese.

Ken's reaction was priceless. He took one look at all the holes in the plaster and the exposed lath work and said, "Oh my god, we live in a crack house! All we need to complete the picture are some drug addicts, drunks and prostitutes!" I thought, *They used to have those on Morris Avenue.*

I thought he was being a drama queen. He picked the damn house. Did he think some gnomes and magic pixies were going to come in and do all the work in the middle of the night and tidy up after themselves? In fact, he was right; it did look like a crack den minus the drug addicts, drunks and prostitutes.

After the wiring work was complete it was time to patch up the walls and ceiling and get ready to have the floors done. This became another time-consuming project. Patching walls is no less messy than trenching walls. Drywall and plaster migrate all over the place. Can someone please explain to me the whole "dustless" sander nomenclature? It's an oxymoron – there is no such thing as a dustless sander of any kind. We had plaster dust in every nook, crack, corner and cranny. It's the equivalent of going to the beach only to come home and find sand in places you didn't even know existed on your body. Our house looked like someone had been banging old school chalkboard erasers in it for six months.

After we finally got that mess cleaned up it was time to have the floors refinished. I love hardwood floors. They add so much warmth to a home. These floors were truly beautiful and I could not wait to see them finished. I've refinished floors in multiple homes so this was an area I felt comfortable with – or so I thought.

When I brought in the floor specialists, the first three refused to touch them. Why? Because they were parquets and you couldn't use a big belt sander on them or you'd rip them apart. Additionally, floors from this period were really 3/8 of an inch of veneer on top of one-inch planks, so no one wanted the responsibility or liability to redo the floors. However, they needed to be refinished—badly. Previous pets had left their marks, so leaving them unfinished was not an option.

Done with references from other people, I took to the Yellow Pages and called Amadeus Flooring. Their Yellow Pages ad noted they specialized in antique flooring and floor refinishing. Bob from Amadeus came out and did a quick review to see what he and his team would be facing. He told us that he could do it but the job would require hand sanding to ensure they didn't pull up the parquet or take too much off the veneer. That sounded reasonable. I would simply build the amount of time hand sanding would take into my move schedule. I should have listened more closely to the amount of time he estimated to repair and finish the floors.

Though we lived in the house through many parts of the renovation, you can't really hang around while you're having all the floors of your home refinished. Ken and I left for Australia with the idea that the floors would be finished before we returned from our trip, so I scheduled our movers to deliver the furniture the week following our return. Ken went home first, as I had to stay for a business meeting. He called me in the middle of the night in Aussie land to tell me we could not move in yet because they were still working on the floors. On the other side of the globe, still in a sleep coma, I wasn't quite getting what "still working on the floors" meant. I said, "Ken, just demand that they move faster." In my mind all that was required was some stain and polyurethane and we were good to go.

When Ken picked me up at the airport he drove me straight to the house to prove to me that the floors were not going to be ready in time for the movers. Being the understanding spouse, I waved this prediction off, assuming he was being overly dramatic. As I walked in the front door my heart stopped. He was not being overly dramatic; in fact he was being downright calm. They were still sanding and repairing and were nowhere near ready to stain and poly. I had a truck full of furniture headed our way the next morning and no place to put it. I hadn't talked to Bob while I was in Australia so I wasn't aware of the amount of repair work he faced.

As we headed back to Warren and Heidi's, panic set in. It was Sunday afternoon and we had furniture being delivered to the house Monday morning. Ken and I were frantically looking for the moving information so we could stop the delivery. Since I couldn't remember the name of the moving company, I began calling every moving company in Newark. Ken kept trying to get my attention but I was totally consumed with trying to locate our movers and our stuff. I vaguely remember him saying he had all the paperwork from the move and was sure the name of the company was somewhere in the twelve-inch stack of papers he was holding. At some point during one of my frenetic phone conversations Ken shoved a piece of paper in my face with the name, address and phone number of the moving company. Show off!

No one was answering the phone on Sunday afternoon so we had to make a drive to Newark. We entered a area of the city where there were dozens of shipping and moving companies and I realized we were in an section of Newark I had previously not explored – let me state for the record that it should have remained unexplored. Fortunately, we found the company and our truck, which had been loaded that day. After a bit of begging and agreeing to a "delay of delivery" fee, they agreed to hold our stuff an additional week. My final thought as we pulled away was, *Everything we own will be sitting on that truck in this less than desirable location for a week.* I said a few Hail Mary's and Our Father's as I watched the truck disappear in my rear view window.

By the end of the week the floors were finished, and they were spectacular. The wood workers were true geniuses! Thank God Bob ignored my rantings and did the job the way he knew it needed to be done.

The day had finally come to move into our home. Ken had started a job with a new company and had limited vacation time so it was my job to get us moved in. It is important to remind you about Ken's neatness gene. I have moved multiple times so I knew this was going to be messy. On top of that we still had work being done on the top two floors – more plaster, more sanding and more dust. So I told him before he left, "Honey, it's going to be a long day and whatever you do when you get home, do not come in and start asking me questions about why I put stuff where I put it. Just take a deep breath and let it go to the universe."

When you have five guys unloading a truck and there is only one of you, you're lucky you can keep count of the boxes and tag numbers, let alone get everything where it belongs. Stuff was flying off that truck so quickly I felt like Lucy and Ethel on the conveyor at Kramer's Kandy Kitchen, but these chocolates were too big to stuff down the front of my shirt. They were coming off so fast I couldn't bark out orders fast enough. I felt like a platoon sergeant – "TOP OF THE STEPS! KITCHEN! BASEMENT! THIRD FLOOR!" When I didn't know where something went I just said, "BASEMENT!" With four levels, that was a mistake. I spent three months running stuff out of the basement to various floors. My calves have never been more defined.

It took them an entire day to unload. When they left, our home looked like a scene from the reality TV show, *Hoarders*. The boxes formed mazes that were interconnected to allow passage through the rooms. I was cursing myself that I hadn't chosen the "unpacking" option. It would have taken two days, but at least stuff would have been on the right floor. When Ken got home he spent the entire night biting his tongue. He did manage to keep most of his comments to himself, although I am sure his head was ready to rocket off his shoulders just from holding them in. A couple of times he looked at me and started to say something. One look into my psychotic eyes told him he was dealing with a man on the edge. I was so overwhelmed I flew in two of our closest neatnik friends, Bobby and Brenton, from Atlanta to help us unpack the house. I had to bribe them with a Broadway show, but it was worth every penny.

⌒⟶

A HISTORY OF THE COURT

"George Washington Slept here!"

- A sign on half the buildings in New Jersey

In New Jersey, George Washington slept everywhere. If you didn't know better you would think he was a man-whore. He came to Morristown in 1773 and seemingly never left. That's not true, of course, but his presence is strongly felt in this borough. Washington established his headquarters in Morristown just north of the Continental Army's second encampment in Jockey Hollow. The Headquarters building is now a museum and within a mile and a half of our home on The Court.

We have George to thank for Morristown's raucous Saint Patrick's Day celebration each year; he started the tradition in March 1780 as a way to honor his Irish troops. Morristonians still celebrate this holiday with great enthusiasm, starting with a huge parade. The many Irish pubs in Morristown overflow into the street on this green holiday.

Rumor and some loose bookkeeping tell us that the land Altamont Court sits on was purchased in 1913. Two brothers, supposedly Jewish twins, bought the land and created the first cul-de-sac in Morristown. At first, theirs were the only homes at the end of the long street. Two houses, identical mirror images, sat at the end of this new road. The brothers were in textile manufacturing. Some say uniforms, others say shoes; the only consistent theme is that they were in the textile business and manufactured some type of clothing.

Shortly after building their own homes they built eighteen homes along the street, two of each style. Years later, this symmetry is hard to see because so many people have made modifications to their homes, but there are still two of each style on The Court.

As the Jewish population was not always embraced by the townsfolk, the brothers supposedly created the first Jewish enclave in Morristown. All the initial owners of the homes on The Court were rumored to be Jewish. Ken and I learned a lot of our home's history from a stranger who wandered up to our house one Saturday afternoon while we were working in the yard. He told us he and his family once lived there. His father had bought the home from the original owners.

Ken and I had noticed that our home was a bit different from most of the houses on the street. Our attic seemed like it had been finished at the time the house was built rather than at some other point in its nearly one-hundred-year history. We were excited to meet someone who might know a bit of that history.

When Ken asked our new acquaintance about the origins of our home, he smiled and his eyes took on a faraway look as if he were embracing a distant memory. "I remember when my dad bought this house. He bought it from the original owner. I don't remember his name, but he was the guy who built all the homes on the street."

That made sense. The footprint of our house was about a foot bigger than the rest of the homes on the street. If I were a builder, building my own home, I would make it just a little bit bigger than everyone else's. I asked him about the attic and he said, "Oh yeah, it was already built like that. His mother used to live up there. She had a bedroom, a bathroom and a sitting room. It was a really cool place. My sister and I loved to play up there." We were touring the house and making our way to the basement when he stopped dead in his tracks in the back stairwell. He was staring at the small window by the back door. He got a bit choked up and said, "I can't believe that is still there." He pointed to a small foldout ledge under the window.

I said, "I was planning to take it off, but I never got around to it."

He looked at me and said, "Please don't. It was there when we bought the house. The builder put it in for his cat to sit on and look outside. Our cat would lie there for hours. I really hope you'll leave it."

Well, you know me, thoughtful and compassionate (don't say a word). After a story like that, how could I possibly take the ledge down?

As we walked him out the door he pointed at a small charm that was part of the doorframe. It had been painted over so many times I had never noticed it. He said, "I can't believe that is still there as well."

"What is it?" I asked.

"It's a Mezuzah."

"A what?"

"A Mezuzah," he repeated. "My father said it was placed on the doorjamb when the Rabbi blessed the home right after it was built. I don't know if that's true, but he believed it was a good omen, so even though we weren't Jewish he left it in place. Underneath that piece of metal is supposed to be a piece of paper with Hebrew writing on it. Dad didn't want to mess with it. He was afraid he might damage it."

As we said goodbye, I thought, *Others must have thought the same thing because none of the Christian families ever removed it.* Neither would I (now I am Verklempt, twalk amongst yaselves!) As I closed the door, I thought, *If it is supposed to keep evil out, maybe Ken's ex-wife won't be able to cross the threshold, or if she does she'll turn into a pillar of salt.* That never happened, but she was remarkably pleasant every time she visited.

BE CAREFUL WHAT YOU WISH FOR

"More Power!"

– Tim Allen, Home Improvement

The inside of our home was coming together and now it was time to start working on the outside. As Ken was cleaning up our Stalag 13 back yard, our two neighbors, Karla and her next door neighbor Jane, notice that the tanned, muscle tee'd, daisy duke, construction boot wearing, Italian in the back yard was a bit of a looker. Okay, lets just say he was hot. These enchanting ladies decided they'd make their way over to our backyard and introduce themselves. To this day they swear they would have done the same thing if Ken were a three hundred pound mountain troll with a beer gut, sporting a twelve-inch plumber's crack. I don't believe that for a minute. After living within a stones throw of these ladies for seven years I can say neither one is that noble. Well, maybe Jane is, but over the years I learned Karla and I are nearly the same person, like twins separated at birth, so I know she is not.

It took Karla and Jane only minutes to realize Ken and I would fit right into The Court family. Karla was expressing dismay over the mound of garbage piled on the front porch. The front of our house looked like a flea market without any of the special treasures they show on the Antique Road Show. Ken apologized all over himself for the eyesore we had created when we cleaned out the house.

Karla said, "It isn't us you have to worry about, but you really need to apologize to Leanne. She is the one who has to look at your porch every day."

Ken said, "You mean Gladys Kravitz across the street?"

Karla and Jane could not control their laughter. Leanne was The Court's own personal neighborhood watch. She missed nothing that happened on The Court. We would get a full detailed report, including a timeline, each night about various contractors who came and went from our home. So, you see, she was a lot like Gladys Kravits from "Bewitched" but it was oddly comforting.

As the three of them chatted over our chain-link fence, Ken was about to mention that we were planning to do some landscaping, but before he could tell them our plans a child appeared out of nowhere on the top of Karla's garage. He took off running and jumped from Karla's garage to Jane's garage and then back again.

Ken shouted, "Oh my god, that boy is going to kill himself!"

Karla looked over her shoulder and said, "No he won't. That's my son Davin. He does that all the time."

When Ken told me about this I looked at him in shock. All I could say was, "What kind of freakish neighborhood did we move into?"

Poor Davin. For the first year we lived on The Court, he couldn't figure out who was Trent and who was Ken. He just called both of us Kent. Karla provided the solution. She said to me, "I told Davin to think of Barbie and Ken. The guy that looks like a Ken doll is Ken. I told him there was no mistaking you for Barbie." I gave her my *I am so not impressed with your clever wit* glare and then thought to myself, *Ken did date a guy once who looked like Barbie.*

After recovering from Davin's Evel Knievel stunts, Ken finished telling the girls about our plans to cut down the overgrown bushes. The enormous yews out front were so tall they touched the gutters on the porch. From the street it didn't look like a porch at all but more like a dark cave in the woods beckoning you to your doom.

In addition to the bushes, the cedars that had been planted over fifty years ago now reached the third floor. They were so close to the house, I wasn't sure how we were going to get rid of them. Between the room darkening shades and the trees and bushes around the house, there was virtually no light coming in from the outside. It would have made a great setting for a prison insane asylum movie. Ken and I both like a home with a lot of natural light. We weren't sure how we would make it happen, but the overgrown trees and shrubs had to go.

Ken continued, "Karla and Jane said that the guys on The Court would probably help us take down the trees and bushes."

"Who are Karla and Jane?"

"Karla Tranfield, our next door neighbor. Jane is her neighbor. You know, the redhead with the big chest? Jane is the one in the bright blue house."

"The one that looks like it belongs on South Beach?"

"Yep, that's the one," he said. "Karla said her husband Rich would let us borrow his chainsaw to cut some of these trees down. She said Rich and the guys on the street might even help us cut some of this crap down."

I hate when Ken uses the ubiquitous pronoun "us." The pronoun "us" used in this context means me. When Ken told me I could borrow the chainsaw, I laughed out loud. "Just what am I supposed to do with that? I've never used a chainsaw!"

"You grew up in the Midwest, and you never used a chainsaw?" Ken said. "I thought all farm boys learned to use one."

"I wasn't raised on a farm."

"But you were in that 4H thing."

"Yes, I was. I raised vegetables and flowers since they didn't have a forestry and logging arm of the 4H in Ohio."

"I thought raising livestock was part of the 4H, too," Ken said.

I glared at him from across the room and said, "Well, I didn't keep chickens and hogs in our backyard. The homeowners association frowned on raising farm animals on your property."

First, he compared me to Paul Bunyan and next to a hog farmer from Iowa. You would think after ten plus years together and the lack of dirt under my nails, he'd know I'm not the outdoorsy type. Hell, the closest I've been to camping is a hotel without room service.

Karla shared our demolition plans with her husband, who in turn shared them with his buddies on The Court. First rule of The Court: Do not tell the Boys of Altamont Court (Also known as Rich, Todd and Jim), or their wives, that you are planning to do something unless you are truly planning on doing it — especially if it involves demolition and power tools of any kind. The importance of Rule One is magnified exponentially if said demolition requires a chainsaw. Karla's husband Rich had all the toys and he and the boys couldn't wait for an excuse to use them.

The weekend after Ken mentioned removing the cedars and bushes, we were unpacking boxes on the second floor. Since our rewiring wasn't complete, we had no overhead light fixtures. This made unpacking a challenging task. Ken and I had to carry lamps from room to room due to the lack of natural light. I suddenly heard what sounded like a number of chainsaws humming outside our house. My first thought was, *Someone must be having some trees removed.* Then, without warning, there were several loud cracks and then a BOOM! Light filled the house from all sides, literally blinding us. Had we been vampires we would have burst into flames. The boys had brought their chainsaws and a wood chipper over for a play date (who the hell owns a wood chipper, for God's sake?). In a matter of minutes our natural light problem was solved. Trees began dropping like we were in a logging camp. In short order the overgrown bushes and cedars were gone.

I came to the conclusion there must have been a logging and forestry arm of the 4H in New Jersey. Then I learned that Rich had grown up in rural New England and Todd in rural Pennsylvania;

mystery solved! Removing the stumps and roots was left for me to handle. I developed a special relationship with a pickaxe and a shovel. It would take another year for us to replace the hacked away foliage with decent landscaping. Things were moving fast on The Court. I just wasn't prepared for how fast.

About three weeks later, Ken mentioned how much we hated our chain-link fence. Chain-link fencing, actually any kind of fencing, reminded me of the movie, *The Sandlot*. Stuff that goes over a fence doesn't come back. The kids on the street hated our fence. Someone always had to climb over it to get the stray ball. Usually that was poor Davin, as he was the youngest and smallest at the time. His siblings and friends would just toss him over the fence to get the ball. If the previous owner caught him, a lecture about trespassing quickly ensued. No one wanted to get yelled at for going over the fence. It was something every kid on the street dreaded.

The fence gave the back of the house a "prison yard" motif I just couldn't embrace, so the choice was simple; add razor wire to give it authenticity or remove it completely. Remember the first rule of the court? Telling Rich and Jim how much we hated the fence was like waving candy in front of a couple of sugar-addicted schoolboys. Once Ken let them know we were planning to remove it, it was only a matter of time before it was history. I believe President Reagan coined the phrase, "Tear down this wall" – and with only a hint of our plan to remove it, the boys treated the fence like it was the Berlin Wall.

I woke up one Saturday morning to the sound of hacksaws and sledgehammers. Chain-link fencing was falling, sparks were flying, posts were being pulled and holes filled. Removing the fence posts was the biggest challenge since they were buried in holes three feet deep and filled with concrete. Leave it to these gentlemen engineers to rig a post puller with a set of pulleys and a weird looking tripod. They had solved the fence problem in a weekend. I still have a picture of 8-year-old Davin wielding a hacksaw bigger than he was; he truly hated that fence. I found stray pieces of chain-link fencing in the backyard for over a year.

After the removal of the fence, I began selectively pruning the trees and bushes in the backyard and working on the lawn. I am a lawn master, a grass god. No matter where we have lived I have created lawns that would make the head groundskeeper at Augusta National green with envy (pun intended). Back in Atlanta people knew us more by our yard than by our names. It was always, "Oh, you're the guys with the beautiful lawn." I would blush and say, "Thank you, thank you very much! Really, its nothing." I lived for this.

Our yard on The Court was small, so it took me no time at all to whip it into shape. Karla was not happy with my choice of chemicals and growth accelerants. She works in the chemical industry so I often got lectured about nitrates, ground water and red algae blooms. I learned it was easier to manage lawn care when she was away on vacation or business. When she did catch me I would tell her I was spreading lime or iron or overseeding. I assured her it was something benign that didn't threaten the local water supply. She didn't believe me at all.

I got the same lecture about pesticides. The problem is, I live with a bugaphobe. Ken is truly the biggest, most out of control bug-phobic person I know. We can't even watch a movie with bugs in it for fear he will have a panic attack. When you've spent as many years as I have in the South and particularly in Texas, you get used to bugs. Really big bugs. You always shake your shoes out before putting them on, as you never know what might have crawled into them during the night. In Texas, this could mean scorpions, so it was a real good idea to "bang your boots out" in the morning before putting them on.

Having survived more than a few heart-stopping screams from Ken when he was having a complete meltdown over a roach or a spider, I got used to spraying around the house frequently and liberally. The foundation, the windows, and any corner, crack or crevice were heavily sprayed whether they needed it or not. The first time I sprayed our home on The Court, it caused all sorts of crawly critters to pop up out of nowhere. I considered the centipedes and spiders to be the worst as they caused the loudest screams. No matter where I was in the house or what I was doing, I had to stop and kill the bug. Ken was fond of quoting Suzanne Sugarbaker from *Designing Women*, "The Man Should Have to Kill the Bug!" For the first three months I did a lot of bug killing and a lot of chemical spraying – and for that, I apologize to all of my Buddhist readers.

SATURDAY NIGHT AT THE MOVIES

"Toto, I've a feeling we're not in Kansas anymore— we must be over the rainbow"

-Dorothy from the Wizard of Oz

Removing the fence was key to bringing the neighborhood to our backyard. Who knew such a little thing would become such a hit? As neighbors, we wore pathways between the houses once the fence was down. The biggest and arguably the best thing to happen when the fence was removed was the creation of "Saturday Night at the Movies!" Now that we had the span of two backyards, we decided that Saturday night outdoor movies were the way to go. Rich, being the stereo commissioner of the street, bought a 9x12-foot screen and cobbled together a fantastic sound system. Rich is an audiophile so his "cobbled" together sound system is better than what you hear in most movie houses. THX is nothing compared to "TRANFIELD SOUND."

For everyone's comfort, before any of this could be set up, I endured Karla's wrath and sprayed the yard for mosquitos and other creepy crawlies. I didn't want Ken screaming over a bug and interrupting the movie. Mosquitos were really a problem for Ken. He attracts them in swarms. Karla would yell from the back window, "If my kids develop extra appendages from all your chemicals, you're paying for their college!"

Rich and Davin would spend the afternoon setting up the screen and sound system. When they completed this task, Rich would put on a concert DVD of "The Dave Mathews Band" and let it run while we finished setting up for the evening. While I was preparing hot dogs and hamburgers for the grill, the music would drift in through the open windows, riding on a muggy summer breeze. Looking out through the back kitchen window, I could see the kids setting up tables and chairs as Rich continued to tweak the sound. More than once I thought to myself, *Trent Pines, this is what living is all about.* It felt like a throwback to a different time. This memory never fails to bring a smile to my face. It was rather like a scene from a Norman Rockwell painting, but with our group it was more like an Andy Warhol creation.

When it was time for the movie, we would show a cartoon first, just like they did at the drive-in movies. It was always some Looney Tunes Bugs Bunny cartoon. I am not sure anyone born after 1990 would know what a drive-in movie is or was, but since all the adults were born way before 1990, we remembered the animated dancing hot dog followed by the fountain drinks, bags of popcorn and boxes of candy from the concession stand promo doing the "Advertisement Congo." Each of us took turns picking our favorite cartoons to start the evening. My personal favorite Bugs Bunny clip has the orange monster named Gossamer getting his big orange hair done by Bugs Bunny – "Oh my stars! Monsters make such interesting people." Fabulous!

When the time came to pick our first movie, the adults were reminiscing and romanticizing our past and decided on *The Rocky Horror Picture Show* - complete with props and scripts.

In retrospect, our nostalgia had clouded our judgment. The twelve adults in attendance hadn't remembered that certain parts of the movie were very graphic. A prescreening would've been the prudent thing to do, but alas, we did not have the foresight. When the movie started, the adults began shouting things at the screen, much to the dismay of our kids. In fact, Davin turned around and whispered loudly, "Be quiet! I can't hear the movie."

This got the best laugh of the evening. Once he figured out he was supposed to yell at the film, he was the first one yelling, "Where's your neck?" and "That's no way to pick your friends." It was even more fun throwing toast at our kids and shooting them with squirt guns.

But when it got to the bedroom scenes and "Toucha, toucha, toucha, touch me, I wanna be dirty," the adults were red-faced and squirming in our seats. When the kids started joining us in yelling "asshole" we realized we had crossed the line of good taste. By the end of the night, when the lawn was covered in toast and newspaper and the kids had wrapped themselves in toilet paper, we realized that perhaps good taste wasn't our strong suit.

The next day our backyard looked like Mardi Gras weekend on Bourbon Street. Newspaper, toilet paper, rice and toast littered the lawn. Watching Ken use the shop-vac to vacuum the lawn the next morning is still an occasional topic of conversation—and laughs.

Our second movie was *Dodgeball*. Ken was thrilled it did not come with props and thus would not require lawn vacuuming. I normally don't like silly slapstick films but with Ken having had his first major back surgery four weeks earlier and still struggling to get around, I figured he needed a good laugh. Karla and I thought a funny movie would help brighten his spirits and make him feel good. Since Karla is the queen of sixth grade potty humor, I let her choose. Any funny movie would have done the trick, but *Dodgeball* isn't just any funny movie; it's a hysterical movie. Since Ken and I had never seen it, we didn't know what to expect.

Like a scene from *The Beverly Hillbillies*, Rich and I moved Ken's recliner out of the basement and onto the back lawn. It was an electric recliner so we had to run an extension cord out to his chair. This would allow him to elevate his feet and make him more comfortable. When he turned the chair on it blew the breaker for the outside outlet. The chair, the film and the sound equipment were too much for that circuit. I had to admit, it looked like Lisa Douglas' kitchen outlet on *Green Acres*.

Rich got a longer extension cord and ran it from his house to power the chair. I told you the men of The Court were industrious and resourceful. I also meant to add super classy! As the movie picked up steam it caused Ken to laugh so hard we almost had to call an ambulance. We had to stop the movie and put him into his back brace so he wouldn't hurt himself. I was afraid he was going to laugh himself into another herniated disc.

Other movie nights included *Airplane, Star Wars, Grease...* all complete with burgers, hotdogs, root beer floats, popcorn and chocolate chip cookies. We made Grease the theme of my step-daughter Lindsays sweet sixteen-birthday party. I decorated the two backyards in pink and black balloons and pink tablecloths. Our friend John came up with a great idea to add a bit of nostalgia to the décor.

John is more than a friend to Ken and me; he's more like a brother. I met him at my office and we worked together on several projects. He's smart, witty, and was brilliant at taking complex issues and distilling them into one presentation slide, a skill of priceless value in the business world.

Ken and I quickly became friends with John and his partner Mark. Tragedy struck six months after we met Mark. Mark suffered a massive cardiac episode that took his life. The Court quickly adopted John as one of our own. John's Irish background provided the necessary party and drinking skills to be part of The Court family. John invented Cosmo Fridays. It was the perfect comple-ment to Margarita Saturdays and Champagne Sundays. If John had spent any more time on The Court, we would've had to host Twelve-Step Tuesdays.

John decided we should hang old 45 RPM vinyl records from all of the trees. I loved the idea. The two of us went to an old style record store on South Street and bought a large number of scratched up 45s. Rich drilled little holes in them so we could hang dozens from the trees in both yards. The trees glittered with vinyl.

Everyone arrived in their best fifties garb or as characters from the movie. Ken and I had bought Lindsay a full poodle skirt, a pink ladies jacket, cat-eye glasses and saddle shoes – she looked amazing. Karla came in curlers and a smock as the Beauty School Dropout. She looked hysterical. Her daughter Erin was so embarrassed by her costume she refused to stand or sit next to her all night. My mother-in-law came as Rizzo and Jane came as ChaCha DiGregorio, the best dancer at Saint Bernadette's, with the worst reputation. I'm not sure Jane's wardrobe choice was appropriate for a woman whose career has been promoting women's rights and defending against domestic violence. Regardless, all of these characters were immortalized in digital pictures.

The guys all came as T-Birds. It gave us a great excuse to pull out old leather jackets and grease our hair. Interesting that no one volunteered to be Eugene. With all the engineers on our block I was sure one of them would relate to Eugene. I know they all have pocket protectors. Of course, being straight men, none of them had ever seen the movie *Grease* before, so I cut them some slack. Our little party made the Morristown Weekly society pages (using the term loosely). Lindsay still talks about her sweet sixteen party as her "Most favoritist birthday party! Ever!"

With all these impromptu summer parties The Court was getting a reputation as THE place to go for good family fun. The area of town that The Court occupies is referred to as Franklin Corners – or "lesser" Franklin Corners as we Courtians affectionately called it - as there is no way to get to Franklin Street from The Court unless you sneak through someone's backyard. The folks who lived in Franklin Corners put together a summer event called Friday in the Driveway (FITD). Each Friday night one of the homes would host a FITD event from six to eight as a way to get to know your neighbors. It was BYOB and the host would serve finger foods while everyone caught up on neighborhood gossip.

Karla and Ken were tapped to reconnoiter one of these get-togethers, as Rich and I weren't always the most social of individuals. Carrying their bottle of wine, they headed off to their first FITD. They were back in less than forty minutes. Attendance hovered around 8 people with individuals coming and going during the length of the event. One of the folks from the "real" Franklin Corners suggested to Karla and Ken that the Altamont Court clan needed to step up and host a "Friday in the Driveway" event as we were part of the Franklin Corners area of Morristown. Truthfully, I believe they annexed us because they had heard about our fabulous parties. On the surface, this request seemed pretty harmless. We were used to hosting far larger crowds on movie night and with the turn-out Ken and Karla described, this would be a breeze. Karla and I decided we would do it Court style and put out tables and tablecloths; we beefed up the food selection to include grilled quesadillas, sliders, home made margaritas, the works. Rich put up the screen and sound system so we could show a concert and have music throughout the evening.

Since we knew most of The Court folks would attend, we planned for those twenty people plus twenty additional. We missed the mark by 100%. Word spread via email and flyers throughout Franklin Corners and adjacent neighborhoods. The next thing we knew over eighty people were walking around our backyards. Even more surprising, half of those folks stayed for the movie. It was a madhouse. Food was disappearing faster than we could put it out on the tables. We had the kids do a grocery run for ice and hot dogs. It truly was an insane, fun, out of control evening that we knew we'd be talking about for months. The look in Ken's eyes told me he would be vacuuming the backyard again.

The success of this event solidified The Court's reputation as the premier family party street in Morristown. During the last FITD, the count went over 100 attendees. It should be noted that the Franklin Corners neighborhood contains several multi-family dwellings. All I could think was, *What if all of Franklin Corners decides to show up? What if we start to get party crashers from other neighborhoods?* I suspected we had had some of those 'crashers' already. I just needed to make sure this party was never listed on a social media site.

PETS ARE PEOPLE TOO

"Don't wanna, Don't have ta, Ain't gonna"

- Anonymous Cat Sign

Just before we left Atlanta, our kitty Manilla, who was fifteen years old, passed away. She was quite a character and still holds a special place in our hearts. She loved sitting on our huge porch in Atlanta and watching the world go by. Manilla would sit out there for hours. She knew she was not allowed off the porch but that didn't keep her from testing her boundaries. The porch had a huge lip on it and buttresses that jutted out on both sides of the wide steps leading to the front door. She would "cat walk" all around that lip and look back at us occasionally to see if we were watching her. She would strut out onto the buttresses as far as she could go then look back at us with total disdain as if to say, "I am still on the porch so deal with it, bitches......meow!"

Ken brought Manilla to our relationship. She was a cream colored, longhaired kitty with beautiful golden green eyes. Manilla never let me forget that Ken was hers and hers alone. Sharing was not her strong suit. She would sit on his lap, follow him everywhere and when we went to bed she slept by his pillow, often falling asleep with her face buried in his hand. This changed only when Ken's daughters, Ashleigh and Lindsay, came down for the summers. The three of them would sit on the couch and watch TV while I cooked dinner. Manilla would watch them from the adjoining room, glaring the entire time. At some point, disgusted by this view, she would turn her back to them and go to our room. When it came time to go to sleep, Ken would pat the bed for her to jump up just like he always did. She'd just look up at him, let out a meow that sounded like a bitch slap, walk all the way around the bed, jump up on my side and curl up next to me. She would take one last look at him, lick me and then begin cleaning herself. This was Manilla's best attempt at saying "F$%& you" in feline parlance.

The year she passed, we had both been traveling separately on business when a heart condition took her from us. I carried guilt around for so long I am sure I have Jewish ancestry. Our poor friend Doris was pet sitting and was truly traumatized. Though we had warned her that Manilla had a heart issue, neither of us expected her to pass so suddenly. Doris had to race her to the vet while the cardiac episode was taking place. When her friends found out about it, she had to live with the stigma of "pet killer" for years.

The trip home from London was long and painful. I knew I was coming home to say good-bye. Tears ran down my face so randomly that I'm sure my fellow passengers thought I had some sort of condition. Ken flew in from NJ and landed before I did. He waited at the airport for me. Neither one of us wanted to go home and face her loss alone.

There was a small gap under our front door, so you could always see the shadow from her feet going back and forth whenever we pulled into the driveway. This time when we pulled in, there was no shadow. When I opened the front door, I couldn't breathe. She had always been there waiting for us to come home and today she wasn't. The house felt truly empty and her loss hit me deep in the heart. I felt like Sally Fields in Steel Magnolias saying, "I wanna know why!" Ken and I cried it out that night, reliving memories of her loving jealousy. We went to the vet's in the morning to say farewell to our feline diva and arrange for her cremation. She was family and I would miss her, always.

Before we left Atlanta, Ken and I stood on that fabulous front porch and said a quiet prayer while sprinkling some of her ashes in the flowerbeds around her beloved porch so that a part of her would always be there. It makes me smile to think of her sitting on the edge of that porch, guarding her realm. She truly was the queen of that castle.

Once we got settled in NJ we started talking about adopting another kitty. This time we decided we would get two so they could keep each other company when we were at work or when we traveled. It had been nine months since Manilla passed, so we were ready for a couple of fur babies. After looking at several kitten types, we settled on a breed; now we had to find a breeder.

Cat breeders are a strange lot. One woman we met actually looked like a cat. The way she swept back her hair and did her eye make-up, I expected her at any moment to lick her hand and use it to wash her face. Every surface in her house was covered with cat figurines and pictures. Her kittens were adorable but, trust me, we didn't stay long. It took a long time to find a breeder who didn't creep us out.

Eventually we found Cathy, a breeder in upstate New York who we loved. She delivered a doll-faced tortoiseshell Persian with lots of attitude (breeders call it tortitude) and a handsome male seal point Himalayan. We named them Princess Anastasia and Alexander the Great. They came to live with us shortly after we moved into the house and lived through a lot of the renovation. Their paw prints in the construction dust drove Ken nuts.

When we picked up our babies, Ken fell in love with their mother Mimi. She was a ball of personality and love and reminded him of Manilla. Ken told Cathy, "If you ever retired Mimi please call us and we will adopt her." It was about a year later when Cathy called to see if we were still interested and we agreed to adopt her without hesitation.

Once we got Mimi home, she struggled adjusting to her new environment. We kept her in the guest room so she could acclimate at her own pace. I would check on her regularly and sleep in there at night so she'd have company. This ended up backfiring on me big-time. Mimi became my kitty, not Ken's. She followed me everywhere, slept at the foot of my bed, and would sit in my lap to be brushed. All I had to do was tap the brush on the floor like beating a drum and she would come running from wherever she was in the house. She was my doll baby.

We only had her a year; tragically, she passed away due to a congenital heart issue. Losing a pet is always sad. When Manilla passed, my heart broke because I was not able to be there. For years I believed that her dying without Ken or me there was a sin of unbelievable proportion. Mimi passed in the middle of the night at the foot of the bed, in her favorite spot. I had never had a pet that was solely mine. Mimi had worked her way into my heart and her loss was devastating.

I wailed like a mourner at an Irish wake, truly inconsolable. Ken was the strong one and helped me get her to the vet so we could work through her cremation. He helped me gather her favorite toys and blanket to send with her just as we had for Manilla. It took several months for Alex and Anastasia to adjust to her loss. They would wander the house meowing and looking for her and every time I heard them cry out for her I cried myself. Even as I type these words years later, tears come to my eyes. Her loss is still with me.

I remained emotional for a long time. Cathy was overwhelmed when I told her of Mimi's passing. Mimi was one of her first females and she loved her dearly. Several months later she retired one of Mimi's kittens so I jumped at the chance, thinking she would be just like Mimi. That is when Priscilla, Queen of the Desert, joined the family. Priscilla was not like Mimi at all. In fact, she had more attitude than Anastasia. She was a show kitty and she knew it. She was all cat. Truly beautiful, but not very friendly. It took years for her to warm up. Now she is a lap kitty who demands attention on a constant basis. She and Anastasia love Ken; Alex loves everyone.

That brings me to the addition of Paisley Ann to our household. Paisley Ann is truly one of a kind. Cathy had told her friend and fellow breeder Sally how much Mimi's loss had affected me. Sally bred Persians as well and was thinking about retiring one of her favorite kitties, a blue cream Persian named Paisley Ann. Sally sent me a picture and I fell in love. Paisley Ann had markings similar to Mimi's and, from what Sally said, her personality was a delight. I told Ken I had to have her. He knew I still was not dealing well with Mimi's loss so he gave me a hug and said, "Whatever you want, babe."

Paisley Ann can best be described as Nermal from the Garfield comic strip. "Nermal, the world's cutest kitten." We jokingly call her Nermalina. It took Mimi about six weeks to adjust to the house and leave the guest room. It took Priscilla about two and a half weeks. It took Paisley Ann, two and a half days before she wanted out.

Sally was right, Paisley Ann was a doll and had a pip of a personality. She really didn't care what the other kitties thought; she was here now and ready to get her party on. Just like Mimi, she is my baby and is always with me. Our family was now in balance and complete. Trent, Ken, and our four cats. I'm surprised no one has sent us an honorary lesbian card. Maybe it's because neither of us own a pair of Birkenstocks?

HOLIDAY MADNESS

"You're too much. I can say this because, I myself, am too much."

– Suzanne Sugarbaker, Designing Women

To hear our friends tell it, you would think that we queens invented Halloween. Our friend Will goes as far as to say, "It's our Holiday!" I don't disagree but I won't go as far as saying we "own" Halloween; I can say that we queens do it better than anyone else. If you have ever been to Greenwich Village, the Castro in San Francisco, West Hollywood, or the Halloween Mecca itself, New Orleans, on Halloween, you know just how revered this holiday is for the gays. The amount of creativity is mind-boggling. There is no such thing as "too much" or "too big"; in fact, it is all about being "too much" and "too big" and putting it on display for the world to see. Queens believe that nothing succeeds quite as well as excess. When it comes to All Hallows Eve – more is more. Period.

I've had the good fortune to enjoy Halloween in each of these cities and every one of them was unique. At my first West Hollywood Halloween I saw a guy walking down Santa Monica Boulevard (where they have the annual parade) dressed up as Bette Davis from *Whatever Happened to Baby Jane*, and he was dragging a life-size Joan Crawford doll by the foot. Right behind him was a guy dressed up like Tippi Hedren from the Hitchcock movie, *The Birds*. He had wired birds around his dress suit and had blood dripping from a hundred peck wounds. As I rounded the corner I ran into a headless Jane Mansfield carrying a headless stuffed dog. Everything was movie themed.

My first Halloween in New Orleans was truly over the top. It was the year of *To Wong Foo*, and I saw at least six sets of queens dressed as the characters in the movie. They were all wearing exact replicas of those costumes; dresses, hair, jewels – the entire ensemble. It was also the year of the hoopla over Miss America and the swimsuit competition. 12 guys had dressed in one-piece bathing suits, donned tiaras and pinned on sashes. Each sash had some hysterical fictional place written across it in glitter: Miss Corn-hole, Miss Waste Management, Miss Compost.

When it comes to Halloween, as well as most other holidays, it is hard to out-glitz a queen.

It was our first Halloween on The Court and Ken wanted to do it up right. He loves Halloween. And because he loves Halloween, we have decorations of all kinds: smoke machines, screaming, howling life-size lawn ornaments, dozens of costumes and so on. He gets this from his mother Sally. She's in her 70's and still dresses in full costume for her office Halloween party. Her favorite costume is a dominatrix outfit, complete with leather bustier, spiked heels and a whip.

Growing up, Sally made costumes for all the kids each year for Halloween, forcing them to wear her imaginative creations. One year she dressed up Ken's brother Warren as the ghost of a dead female singer. Warren is as straight as they come and would have made an excellent junior Mafioso, but instead, Sally had him wearing drag. Sally swears it was Ethel Merman. Warren swears she put him in a caftan and made him go as Mama Cass. They were arguing about this at dinner one night when Warren yelled, "Mom, it was that woman who died eating a ham sandwich!"

I laughed so hard at this exchange I couldn't breathe. The thought of Warren, my uber straight brother-in-law, parading around in muumuu drag was more than I could take.

Each year I'd haul all of Ken's decorations out to the front porch for him to begin his creative process. The first year Ken began installing his decorations on The Court, our driveway neighbors, Pat and George, took one look at all the Halloween stuff and Pat said, "Oh my, you have no idea what you have started." And with a smirk on her face she kept on walking.

We had no idea what she meant until the next weekend when the Tranfields started putting up their Halloween decorations. Davin, being half monkey, was furiously crawling all over the front of the house hanging decorations and lights. Ken, who was not going to be outdone by an eight-year old, ran out and bought more Halloween décor. This caused Davin to push Rich for MORE Halloween glitz of his own. Rich only purchases holiday decorations from the bargain bin at Agway the tackier the better. The houses looked like they belonged in a Florida trailer park. At some point both Karla and I said, ENOUGH!

It had been years since we had lived in a neighborhood full of kids, so it had been years since we'd been through "Goosy Night." I would love to know who came up with the nomenclature "Goosy Night" for the night before Halloween. I always called it "Mischief Night." A little research shows that "Goosy Night" is only used in the north Jersey region and around New York City. Go Figure. On this festive night before Halloween, Ken and I were watching TV in our basement rec room, oblivious to what was happening on the street. I was heading up to bed while Ken locked up when I heard him yell, "Oh my God, we have been violated! Someone vandalized our home!"

I came running down the stairs to see what was going on. I had no idea what he meant by vandalized. All I could think was, *We'd have heard something if the house had been damaged.* As I looked over Ken's shoulder I was shocked. We had been violated – and by the ROLL. We had been toilet papered. TP'd! And not just a little mind you; it covered everything. The porch had been wrapped, the trees were streaming hundreds of TP tails and all of Ken's decorations had been thoroughly wrapped. I laughed out loud. We had just been welcomed to the neighborhood in a big way. I found myself crossing my fingers that it was two-ply, which would make it easier to pull down.

I found out it wasn't just the kids getting their "Goosey Night" on. The adults (if you can call anyone an adult on The Court) had been involved in this little prank. Karla had driven the kids to Costco to buy the 24-pack of Scotts biodegradable, septic tank friendly toilet paper. Karla noted, "Not only is it a price performer, it is also strong enough to hold up when being tossed over a roof or into a twenty foot tall tree." Lovely.

Rich had taught all three kids the proper TP technique while they were still in preschool. Rich also let me in on a Court secret. It seems they had been punking each other LONG before Ashton Kutcher had his "Pucked" show. Any time someone renovated a bath, the old pink, blue or black toilet would end up in someone's yard as a planter. When we took our pink and blue toilets out of the old bathrooms, they were stolen from the garage and ended up as a "his and hers set" in front of our neighbors', Jim and Kathi's, house with pirate skeletons popping out of the bowls. Charming!

Halloween is Ken's holiday to decorate – the bigger and tackier it is, the more fun he has. Christmas decorating is my domain. Christmas is a dignified, glorious holiday and I decorate accordingly. Karla is eye-rolling as she reads this, thinking, *BORING*. Each year when I pack away the Halloween decorations, I begin pulling out the Christmas decorations. It takes me a full month to decorate. There are three trees to dress and when I am finished each one looks as if it had been decorated by the designer for a Saks Fifth Avenues window display. Putting up three trees took a couple of weekends and the outside required just as much work. I would describe to Ken what I wanted, then he'd build an electrical diagram to accommodate the lighting layout and take charge of hanging icicle lights from the eves, wrap lighted garlands across the huge porch, and place electric candles in every window. Huge burgundy-bowed wreaths decorated all the windows. Decorating for Christmas was quite the production at our house. Once all this décor was in place the home truly looked like a Christmas house by Disney, minus the annoying characters.

If our house looked like a tasteful, picture perfect postcard that embraced the true magic of Christmas, then the Tranfields looked like something from the Great American Trailer Park Musical. The Tranfield house was the decorating haven for all the neighborhood children who werent allowed to participate in decorating their own tasteful homes. They went big. Plastic glowing lawn ornaments, disco lighting, giant blow-up Santa on the roof, blow-up Nascar Santa on the front lawn and multi-colored chase lights around the windows. There was even a lighted inflatable palm tree on the front porch. They went from tacky Halloween décor to even tackier Christmas décor in one weekend. Nothing like this would ever grace the windows at Saks!

Just after we finished hanging our decorations and had everything perfectly in place, we were vandalized yet again. One evening, a group of Santa's "not-so-nice" elves decided to do a bit of additional decorating. It was a repeat of Halloween, but instead of being TP'd, these unhelpful elves placed a twenty-foot blow-up snowman on our front lawn. It took up the entire right side of the house and was secured to the porch with multiple ropes. When we looked out the second story window in our bedroom, we were staring at a huge white bulbous head. It was my turn to scream like a girl as I stared out the window, praying I would not see "the abominable snowman" in a NASCAR-labeled stock car on the other side of our lawn.

These cretins had violated a holy holiday with this inflatable piece of trailer park trash. It had to be Toddy or Rich. One or both were always guilty of this type of mischief. I started mashing up their last names. Talarico and Tranfield became the Talifields and the Tranricos!

I was traveling the next day for business so that monstrosity had to remain in place for nearly two weeks. It was the first thing you noticed when you looked down the street. The only thing taller than Frosty was the giant Santa that Rich had attached to the roof of their porch. When I got back from my trip on Friday I got a call from someone claiming to be "Mrs. Kowalski" from the Morristown Beautification Committee notifying me that our home had been selected as the winner of the 1st ward's "best decorated home" award.

"We just loved how pretty your house looked," she said, "and the giant Frosty the Snowman really made your home pop!"

"Pop?" I said. "Seriously? You think the twenty-foot Frosty makes the house pop? Who is this really?"

"I introduced myself at the beginning of the call, Mr. Pines. I am Ms. Kowalski, with the Morristown Beautification Committee. I just wanted you to know your home won this year and that you will be receiving a $100 dollar gift card from the town. Your gift card is accepted at most Morristown shops and eating establishments."

I paused for a minute. This had to be a joke. Rich or Toddy had some friend of theirs call me and mock me in my humiliation. The only other possible conclusion was that members of the Morristown Beautification Committee were all taking some powerful psychotropic medications.

So "Ms. Kowalski," if that truly was her name, told me they would be having a ceremony at the town hall to award this certificate and present me with an etched glass award to commemorate our win. I was not falling for it. I thanked her and the Morristown Beautification Committee for their thoughtfulness and hung up the phone. No way was I trekking up to the town hall just to have Todd and Rich jump out and yell "gotcha" when I walked into the lobby.

The final joke was on me. A week later I got a note from the Morristown Beautification Committee congratulating me on our win in the 1st ward. Inside the package was the etched glass award with the $100 gift certificate and a note from "Ms. Kowalski" saying how very disappointed they were that I was not able to attend the award ceremony and be included in the picture taken for the paper. I felt terrible. I had to call Ms. Kowalski and offer my apologies and explain why I didn't show. She was not impressed or amused. After that faux pas, we were never again honored by the Morristown Beautification Committee. Rich and Todd still laugh about this; they frequently noted the reason we didn't win this award again was due to my refusal to put Frosty on the front lawn.

As we moved from Christmas to New Year's Eve, Ken and I decided to start a tradition by hosting a New Year's Eve open house for The Court. Open invitations went out to friends and family. I catered and friends brought libations. Our good friend Catherine brought one of the key libations for this celebration each year—the eggnog—a potent, delicious eggnog. It had bourbon, rum, cognac, and brandy in it, along with 2 dozen egg yolks, heavy cream, milk and fresh ground nutmeg. Catherine would make this special elixir three to four weeks prior to the party and would say, "Trent, you need your eggnog to ferment for this long in your refrigerator to allow the full flavor of the nog to develop."

Develop, my ass; it just made this shit stronger. The longer it fermented, the stronger it got. You didn't dare light a match when she took the top off of the container or the entire house would have blown.

The unveiling of the eggnog was a key part of the evening. It usually happened around 10:00 PM, so by 10:15 everyone was trashed. Each year the number of guests, friends, and friends of guests increased. This meant an increase in the batches of eggnog. Had we stayed any longer, Catherine would have had to install a walk-in refrigerator in her basement to manage the vats of this magnificent holiday concoction.

By midnight, people couldn't remember their own names. This was perfect timing as Morristown hosted a fireworks display at midnight and we could watch them from our street. One of our well-lubricated neighbors marched up and down the street while the fireworks exploded, yelling, "The British are coming, the British are coming. They're bombing the harbor! Listen to their cannons! We must resist; we must fight back. It's our liberty at stake!"

Seriously, our liberty? I was more concerned she was having an arterial flow problem or that eggnog was causing early onset dementia. Remarkably, no one seemed to notice her or the fact that it was ten degrees outside. I blamed the eggnog.

Post midnight, most open houses would begin winding down. Not on The Court. Our guests would invite additional people who were leaving other parties to drop by for a nightcap. At three in the morning we still had thirty people in our home. At one point a Colombian wearing dozens of Mardi Gras beads grabbed me, bear hugged me, kissed me and said, "HAPPPY NEW YEAR, PAPI." All

I could say was, "Who are you? Do I know you?" It didn't faze him; he and his cartel of friends were hugging and kissing everyone. To this day, I have no idea who the hell they were or why they were at our party.

At 3:30 AM, someone I didn't know was using a rubber spatula to scrape the last of the eggnog from its container. I had had enough New Year's cheer to last the entire year so I started flashing the lights and telling everyone to leave. I literally shoveled them out the front door. Since all of them could walk to their homes, I didn't have to worry about taking keys and calling cabs. Ken was mortified when he saw me pushing people out the door.

"You are so rude!" he tsked and tut-tutted. "So rude! I have no idea why people like you. I am surprised we have any friends at all."

I replied, "It's my charismatic charm and witty repartee."

"You're hopeless."

My apparent rudeness didn't matter, as most of our guests didn't remember much about the party the next day. But their hangovers told them they had had one hell of a good time.

ELDIN THE PAINTER

"Are you ever going to finish?"

- Murphy Brown, Murphy Brown

At the start of year two, we decided to paint the entire inside of the house – all five bedrooms, three baths and so on. We hired another neighbor from The Court to do the painting. Heather Talarico, namesake of Talarico Painting. She's Todd's wife and Pat and George's daughter. We're a very incestuous group on The Court.

It was a huge project for one person, but she raised her hand for the job and her pricing was fantastic. Since I had done quite a bit of painting in my youth, I knew this was going to be a lot of work. The trim alone went on for miles. Heather is a meticulous painter. She can paint an edge without tape that is so perfect you could shave with it.

We started with the living room. I had never warmed up to the pea soup colored glossy walls and it was time for them to go. Ken thought I was nuts to choose another shade of green.

"Why are you repainting this room if you're just going to paint it green again?"

"It's not green," I said indignantly. "It's King's Knight Tavern Arms Gray."

"It's green," he insisted and walked away.

Okay, it was a green, but it was a gray green. It was a color from Pratt and Lambert's Williamsburg collection. I love Pratt and Lambert paint and their choice of rich colors is truly unbeatable and I made sure the finish was flat. FLAT, FLAT, FLAT. I wasn't about to repeat the mistake I had made the first time around. There would be no slimy shine on these walls. Ken refused to admit the color was any different than what we had on the walls. He just rolled his eyes at me.

Eye rolling is something couples perfect over time. There is the "Oh, please, you are such a drama queen" eye roll, the "I would rather be having a root canal than listen to this babble" eye roll, and the all encompassing "Whatever" eye roll, which can be used often and broadly. I chose to ignore them all; If I did respond it would be with an eye-roll of my own. The "Oh, no, you did *not* just roll your eyes at me" eye roll.

As Heather began to paint the walls, the room started to change and transform. Ken noticed. "You have got to be kidding me. I can't believe how much better this room looks. How did you know there would be such a huge difference? I hate to admit it, but this color looks much better."

As our friend Will would say, "I don't know, it's a gift. I don't own it."

The living room was huge and it took two weeks to finish painting the walls, ceiling and trim. It was worth the wait. The room was gorgeous and had warmth the other color couldn't match.

By the way, who do you think comes up with names for paint colors? Ken and I believe there is a super secret room of gay men that create the names. How else do you come up with "Midnight in Marrakesh Blue", "Frothy Peach Taffeta Cream" and "Sienna Summer Afternoon?" I just know these "girls" do nothing but sit around and dream up the most outrageous, comical and somewhat dreamy names for paint colors. It is the only reasonable conclusion I can come up with.

After two weeks and the truly exceptional work Heather had done on the living room, we settled in for the long haul. First we had to pick colors for each of the rooms. This, in itself, was a major undertaking. Ken and I did a lot of compromising to get to a decision that we could mutually agree on. When we first met, Ken was a modern furniture type of guy with the Italian desire for black lacquer and chrome. He liked matching sets of furniture that could be easily coordinated. I am the direct opposite. I am more of a "search for the right piece of furniture to add to your collection" type of guy.

When I buy furniture I think of it as a big purchase for the long haul. Our Henredon bedroom set is nearly twenty years old and we are not getting rid of it anytime soon. When I met Ken, he had been trained by his mother to change looks frequently. She loves a coordinated look and tends to change out furniture for her entire house every two years. Literally! During our time on The Court, she offered us dozens of pieces. Since we had a five-bedroom home and a finished basement, her cast-offs helped furnish our home.

When it came to painting walls, my mother-in-law painted her walls white and used art, collectables, family photos and ornamental hangings to decorate her walls. On the other hand, my mother decorated with color. Lots and lots of color. And paneling. I remember a lot of paneling. My brother and I had "barn side paneling" in our room. Yes, they made such a thing and it was very popular in Midwestern suburbia. People actually paid money to make the inside of a room look like the inside of a barn. Dreadful. Add to that our NFL sheets and our NFL curtains made from aforementioned sheets and you have a redneck, straight man's paradise.

This meant that Ken and I, two men with completely divergent tastes, had to find common ground. In contrast to Ken's fondness for contemporary, black lacquer, glass and chrome, white paint and lots of things on the walls, I like neoclassic, empire style furniture, with limited artwork or photos on bold colored walls. Anytime we had to agree on a color or work of art or furniture it could take weeks if not months. Sometimes it took years. I remember going without a coffee table for two years before we found something we could agree on. Since I am not someone who'll buy something just to 'get by,' we used TV trays in the interim.

My mother-in-law thought we were insane. She tried to give us a coffee table on more than one occasion. I remember one coffee table with a top that lifted up and toward you to create TV trays. When she showed it to us I looked at her and said, "Don't even think about it."

I love dark, bold colors and limited, lighted artwork on the walls, so my goal was to convince Ken this could work. We finally agreed on a neutral color for the foyer, stairways, landings and halls and started working on deeper colors for the main rooms. Painting rooms a bold color meant using a primer and three coats of paint to ensure consistent, even coverage. Heather warned us that painting the entire interior of our home was going to take "a shitload of time." I told her, "We are in no rush, take your time." I would say goodbye to her in the morning when I left for work and hello to her in the evening when I returned. She was part painter, part therapist and part referee.

It took nearly seven months to paint all four floors. We jokingly called her "Eldin the Painter " from *Murphy Brown*. When she finished, it was a masterpiece.

THE KITCHEN RENOVATION

"When do you think this will all be done?"

– Walter Fielding, The Money Pit

"2 Weeks!"

– Curly the contractor, The Money Pit

Renovations are challenging and a kitchen renovation is the mother of all renovations. You have plumbing for both the water and the gas lines. You have heavy electrical needs for the stove, microwave, refrigerator and other major appliances. Add cabinets, granite, butcher-block center island, farm sink, floors, hardware – the list is endless. We were well into our second year on Altamont Court when I fortunately came into a chunk of money. I told Ken it was time to tackle the kitchen. After eighteen months it was time to take a hatchet to the harvest gold countertops and avocado green appliances and install the kitchen of my dreams; and I had some big dreams for this kitchen.

I consider myself a damn good cook. I won't get any gold stars from Le Cordon Bleu, but I can hold my own. Cooking is both chemistry and art. The ability to mix flavors and textures allows for a great deal of creativity. I also subscribe to the "It doesn't have to be from scratch" and "I rarely measure anything" mentality. If someone has created a fabulous cake mix, I am comfortable using that as a base. (Karla would scoff and say, "There's no such thing as a fabulous cake mix"). But really, it's what you add that makes all the difference. And with cakes, the keys are frosting and fillings. Master a fabulous butter cream icing with egg whites, sugar and butter and no one even cares about the cake. When someone asks me for a recipe I truly have to wing it. I was beyond excited at the prospect of designing my first custom kitchen.

The first step in this process was sitting down with the general contractor, a man named Jake who had the voice of a chain smoking bullfrog, and Brian, our kitchen designer. When you get that first set of drawings you think to yourself, *Oh man, this is really going to happen. This is going to be the kitchen of my dreams.* Reality set in when they started the demolition. We watched with sadistic glee as our demo team ripped those old cabinets and bad appliances from the walls and threw them in the dumpster. I knew I would never miss the avocado green appliances and harvest gold countertops.

The nightmares began when the demo team started tearing down the walls, pulling up the floor and so on. This is when we found out just how many things in our demo'd kitchen space were not up to code. We had subflooring that did not have the right underpinning, ceiling supports that had been heavily notched out and needed additional support, and a wall that was not properly tied into the foundation to support the ceiling above it.

In addition to all this, we had decided to increase the size of the kitchen by removing the maid's staircase that descended into the kitchen. All the homes on the street had been built with a secondary staircase into the kitchen. This allowed the domestic help access to the upper floors without going through the main family living area of the house. Ours ran parallel to the front foyer staircase so it seemed redundant. Besides, these staircases were steep, narrow and short. Anybody over 4' 10" had to duck to get up and down and there was no accommodating two people at the same time. After flying down those stairs on more than one occasion and nearly knocking myself out, we decided it was time to pull them out and make room for more cabinets and the refrigerator. I doubted I would find domestic help the size of garden gnomes who would be willing to work in our home and agree to use the back stairs. The whole idea of live-in domestic help felt a bit antiquated. Some of the purists in the neighborhood were less than impressed with our choice. But I was not saving a useless stairwell to keep the historically conscious happy.

When they began to tear out the staircase it was apparent we would need a structural engineer to shore up the walls and ceiling. If we didn't do it right, the guest bedroom on the second floor would collapse into the kitchen. Having a bedroom drop into your kitchen on top of a guest during a dinner party can really put a damper on an evening. These "small" changes cost around seven thousand dollars and three weeks to the schedule.

A little advice to anyone attempting a renovation: Determine your budget and be prepared to spend an additional twenty-five to thirty percent more. This is especially true in older homes because building codes have changed dramatically since the early 1900s. You also have to prepare yourself for the barrage of permits you will need to complete your renovation. I have lived in a lot of cities and done a lot of home renovations. New Jersey is by far the most permit-driven state I have ever lived in. When our hot water heater blew we needed a permit to replace it. When our boiler blew we needed a permit to replace it. I found this absurd, as you can't go without hot water or heat. Well, maybe you could, but we've established I am not the outdoorsy type, so living like Grizzly Adams was not an option.

Before actual construction could begin, I needed to get my permits. I headed up to town hall with my lists for electrical, plumbing, and construction. The list was long and uninteresting, but the process and expense caught me by surprise. Forms, forms and more forms had to be completed before we could begin. The real pain came when the clerk asked me for one thousand, one hundred and forty dollars. Really? Over a thousand dollars for permits? Where's the hidden camera? I just knew someone must have been filming my reaction to this ridiculous request for such a ludicrous amount of money for *permits*.

This number seemed so absurd you would think I was asking to shut down Main Street to host a parade. All we wanted to do was introduce our kitchen to the 21st century. All the clerk could do was shrug and say, "Yeah, it sucks, doesn't it."

Sucks was an understatement. More than once during my efforts to obtain permits I was told, "You are out of process." Once I made the mistake of asking, "Well, what is the process?" The clerk said, "I don't know, I just know you are out of it." I felt like I was in a Seinfeld episode and I'd just been told, "No soup for you!"

After giving blood at the town hall, I was off to the appliance store. Brian, our kitchen designer, needed me to pick out our appliances so he could complete the cabinet design. If you have never shopped for professional-grade appliances, it is overwhelming. I knew I wanted a six-burner stove, but the rest was a crapshoot. By the time I left we had a 42-inch fridge, a six-burner dual fuel range, a professional range hood, a built-in microwave, a wall oven, a two-drawer dishwasher, a wine cooler, a food warmer and a stainless steel farm sink. It was like a Chinese buffet and I wanted one of everything. We were now several thousand dollars poorer, but I was feeling virtuous having saved three grand buying from the scratch and dent bone yard located on the loading dock. All the dents and scratches were on the backsides of these appliances. Once inserted, we would never know they were there.

One of my fellow shoppers made the comment, "I could never buy something like that."

I said, "Like what?"

She looked at me and whispered, "Damaged," like she was saying the word "Cancer." She went on, "I would know those dents and scratches were back there. I would lay awake at night knowing that behind my cabinets someone had damaged my appliances. I know I would lose sleep over that!"

I looked at her like she had left her sanity at home and only brought her crazy with her. I asked her, "Have you ever had kids?"

She answered, "No, I have a damaged uterus that doesn't work."

Oh God! The last thing I wanted to hear about was her uterus. All I could say was, "Sorry about your uterus, but if you had kids you would know that a scratched back plate on your refrigerator doesn't rate the loss of a night's sleep." As I walked away, I couldn't help but wonder if her uterus was scratched and dented like my appliances – bless her heart.

A couple of days later Brian called to tell me, "I got all the measurements from the appliance store. Wow! You certainly made some salesperson's day with this order."

I was painfully aware that I had made some salesperson's quota for the quarter; he didn't need to remind me.

He continued, "I will have the preliminary design ready for you by Saturday."

Now that the shock of appliance shopping was over, I was getting excited again. It was time to finalize our kitchen design and order the cabinets.

WHEN IN ROME

"Julia, where are our seats?"

         -**Suzanne Sugarbaker,** *Designing Women*

"I don't know. If history teaches us anything,
mine will be next to a baby who smokes."

         –**Julia Sugarbaker,** *Designing Women*

In the middle of all of this Ken and I planned to take our mothers to Italy to celebrate their 65th birthdays. They both have Italian backgrounds and had always wanted to go there. Rome, Florence and Venice were our choices of cities, so I started the planning. I hate guided tours. Trapped for two weeks busing around Italy with a group of church ladies from Missoula was not my idea of a good time. As Ken is fond of telling me, "You don't like people."

Well, he's right, in a way. I don't like being held hostage with people I don't know for extended periods of time. I am on vacation. I want to relax. I don't want to spend my time with an over talkative bus driver or a chatty couple from Utica on vacation, all whilst singing theme songs to old television sitcoms. "Flintstones, meet the Flintstones." That was not happening.

About a year before this trip I had bought a *Bon Appétit* magazine that featured Rome, Florence and Venice, so I dug this issue out and started planning. They had done a great job of outlining things to see, places to eat, places to shop, how to secure tickets in advance to museums - you name it, they had it covered. So I decided this would be our guidebook for our Italian adventure. The editors had chosen places that weren't your typical tourist traps. They had also noted in each city where to get the best pizza, best gelato and much more. Busting out my trusty calendar, I started building our daily activities in Italy.

Before we left I reviewed the finalized kitchen plans with Brian, the kitchen designer. He presented his drawings and Ken and I just stared at the plans in total amazement. Neither one of us could believe this was going to be our kitchen. We made minor adjustments and then left it in the hands of Brian and the kitchen gods to ensure that what was on the drawings would become our kitchen. It was time to head to Italy.

We started the trip off right by renting a limo to get us to the airport complete with a bottle of champagne to toast the beginning of our adventure. We felt very fortunate to be able to take our mothers on a once-in-a-lifetime birthday trip to Italy. The fun began the moment we arrived at the airport when a power outage caused the computers to reboot. This made check-in super fun.

I have the memory of an elephant. That said, if I am distracted at any point while focusing on a task, I can set my keys down and I won't have a clue where I put them. That goes for anything and everything. As I was shepherding us to the gate, I made sure everyone had everything ready to board the flight. Tickets, passports and so on. The only person I didn't check on was myself. For someone who has traveled extensively internationally, this was a cruel twist of fate. When we got to the gate and I couldn't find my passport. I panicked. Did I drop it after security? Did I leave it in the lounge or one of the shops? I had it to check in so I had to have lost it on the concourse somewhere. Being a problem solver, my mind immediately jumped to solving the problem at hand. Ken was trying to talk to me and all I could think about was what it would take to get a new passport and meet them somewhere in Italy. I knew I could get a passport in twenty-four hours if I went into NYC and then I could rebook my flight and catch up with them in forty-eight hours. With any luck I would catch up with them in Florence. It was then I heard Ken's voice calling my name. It sounded like it was coming from a distant fog instead of three feet away.

"Trent, will you slow down and empty your shoulder bag?" he said.

"I already have," I yelled. "And it's not in there! You guys board and I will join you in a couple of days."

Ken realized there was no getting through to me so he took the bag off my shoulder, unzipped it and dumped it out on the concourse floor. I was watching the contents of my shoulder bag drop to the floor when, like magic, my passport fell out as well. So humiliating. I was so focused on solving my nonexistent problem that I had not fully searched the bag. All this activity had garnered the attention of nearly everyone waiting for the flight. Ken received a hearty ovation when he held my passport over his head and said, "We found it! Crisis averted." So much for my problem-solving prowess.

Once we were boarded, I drugged myself with an Ambien, two Xanax and two shots of vodka and woke up as we landed. Again, don't judge me. I'm a terrible flyer. Believe me when I say it's in everyone's best interest that I remain anesthetized on long international flights.

Ken shook me awake as we landed in Rome and helped me disembark from the plane since I was still in an Ambien haze. Once we cleared customs, we grabbed a taxi to take us to our hotel. As the driver rounded a corner, I saw a long set of stairs and thought, *Oh, those must be the Spanish Steps.* I made the mistake of pointing this out to everyone in the car. "Look, those are the Spanish Steps." The problem was, they weren't. They were just a long, wide set of old run-of-the-mill steps. When walking around Rome the next day, we found the actual Spanish Steps, fountain and all. The problem was that my mother-in-law had been paying attention when I pointed to the non-Spanish Steps and was now convinced we were not standing on the real ones. She kept asking Ken and me when she was going to get to see the "real" Spanish Steps. No matter how many times we told her "These are the real Spanish Steps", she remembered the first set of steps I had pointed to and, for her, those were the one and only Spanish Steps.

Our first night in Rome was incredible. The staff at the hotel was outstanding and helped us settle in quickly. We took in our first view of the city from the roof top terrace bar. It was hard to believe we were watching the sunset over the eternal city. We had dinner at a small local restaurant recommended by the hotel staff and it was fantastic. I thought, *If all our meals are going to be this good, I should have packed larger pants* – elastic waistbands are not an option for gay men. If you're gay and reading this and wearing elastic anything, please drop off your gay card at the nearest HRC office. Gay men do not wear elastic waistbands (unless we are at the gym).

We finished our evening back at the hotel on the rooftop lounge with our stunning and charming waiter, Rodolfo. This boy knew how to work a crowd. He flirted with our mothers, he flirted with Ken, he flirted with me, hell, he flirted with anything that had a pulse. As he took our drink orders he told each person, "Wonderful choice, you will love it." That is until he got to me. I asked him for Baileys on the rocks and he said, "No."

I asked, "What do you mean, no? No, you don't have Bailey's or no, you won't take my order for a Bailey's."

Rodolfo looked at me with a wicked grin and said, "Yes, we have Bailey's, but I no like, so you order something else."

I said, "Well, you're not the one who will be drinking it." I stared at him dumbfounded. Ken and the Sallys were laughing their collective asses off during this exchange.

I continued to push. "So, because you no like, I no get?"

He stared into my eyes and said, "Yes."

I laughed and finally gave in. "So, what can I order that you will say yes to?"

Without missing a beat he leaned in close, looked me directly in the eye and in a low voice that was nearly a whisper, said, "Something Italian."

Those smoldering green eyes were causing me to sweat. I was looking at something Italian but I doubted he was on the cocktail menu. Two could play this game. So I took a deep breath, met his gaze with my own smoldering stare, and said, "I'll take an Amaretto."

He leaned in closer and said, "Perrrfect, a beautiful choice," with a nice roll of the R.

I matched his tone and said, "Good, I am so glad you approve."

The stares lasted a couple more seconds and then he smiled, winked and headed for the bar. Everyone was laughing but me. I don't smoke, but I needed a cigarette after that exchange. I am glad he didn't notice I had pitted my shirt. Ken looked at me with a sly smile and said, "When are you going to learn you can't out-flirt an Italian? By the way, you pitted your shirt." I need to change deodorants.

We started our first full day in Rome with my mother-in-law blowing up her curling iron. She was using the converter/adapter kit but not the transformer that came with it. All that juice burnt the curling iron to a metal crisp. For my mother-in-law, this was a disaster of Biblical proportions. Therefore, between seeing the Colosseum, the Forum, the Pantheon, the Trevi Fountain, and the Vatican, we had to search for a curling iron. We spent three full days trekking around Rome stopping at every pharmacy and department store we came across. We discovered amazing history, beautiful sites, but no curling iron. It felt like we were on a snipe hunt. Her hair was going to remain flat while we were in Rome – bless her heart.

Following our Bon Appétit driven schedule, we had dinner at Sora Lellas, a restaurant the magazine noted as a place local residents frequent. Its located on Tiber Island in the middle of the

Tiber River. To get to the restaurant we had to walk across a bridge that had been in place since 40 BC. Watching my mother-in-law navigate the cobblestone walk in three and-a-half inch stilettos was amazing. It had to be part of her Italian heritage as she managed perfect balance all the way to the restaurant.

Just as it was stated in Bon Appétit, the restaurant was full of locals having dinner. I think we were the only ones not speaking Italian. Dinner was truly a treat. Their eggplant parmesan was spectacular. At the end of the meal Ken decided we all needed to try Grappa. This was not one of his better ideas. We knew it was an Italian tradition, but thats about it. When the waiter brought our order to the table, we toasted and tossed back this clear fluid. As soon as this battery acid of a libation hit the back of our throats, we all started coughing and gasping for air. I turned to Ken and said, What the hell did you order? This stuff tastes like paint thinner.

Ken immediately reached into his bag and pulled out our Italian translation guide phrase and looked up Grappa. "Lets see. Here it is: Grappa. Grappa, a cheap brandy made by distilling the skins, pulp, seeds and stems left over from winemaking and pressing the grapes."

I looked at him in utter disbelief. "So it's made from all the leftover crap at the bottom of the barrel?"

"Yep."

"Wonderful! It's the scrapple of the wine world."

We thanked all the wonderful folks at the restaurant and went out to the street to catch a cab.

It was late on a Friday night in Rome and there was not a cab in sight so we decided to walk to the Trastevere area of Rome to see if we could catch one from there. We were all starting to get a little concerned that we could not find a cab. Having a NYC mentality didn't help. We just expected to hail one like you do on the streets of New York. It doesn't work that way in Rome. You need to go to a Taxi stand.

As we continued our fruitless search we found ourselves passing what we assume was the Israeli Consulate as there were Israeli soldiers posted out front with AK47 assault rifles. This was not comforting. I had had enough fun for one night and my mother-in-law's ability to negotiate cobblestone walkways in stilettos was waning. I suggested we head back to the restaurant and ask for help. The folks at Sora Lella's were amazing. Two gentlemen worked two different phones trying to get us a taxi while our waiter was giving us complimentary shots of Sambuca. You've got to love the Italians. Forty-five minutes and three shots of Sambuca later we were in a taxi heading back to our hotel. Our destination the next day was Florence.

By the time we boarded the train to Florence, flat-haired Sally had moved from desperate to possessed. After a couple of conversations with the hotel manager, we found out that items such as curling irons are carried by appliance stores, not by drug stores or department stores. We were walking the streets of Florence and there it was, the shiny beacon of an appliance store. It was one o'clock and the owners were out until three. You have to love Italy; two-hour lunches are common. We need to import that. Sally sat herself down at the coffee shop across the street and refused to move until they opened. Two and a half hours later, she had a curling iron.

I was on a quest of my own. I had read about an apothecary run by monks that made soaps using the same process they used when it was founded in the 1600's. I dragged Ken up and down every blind alley looking for this place. Street addresses can be a bit hard to follow because they evolve with the town. The ancient building that housed the apothecary was not visible from the street. Over the last couple of centuries newer buildings had been built in front of and around the original structure so the actual address was not helpful. You had to go into the foyer and to the back of the lobby of one building to find the structure the shop was housed in. It was a fantastic place. However, Ken was ready to kill me when we walked out with two hundred euros worth of soap and bath oils.

On our way back to meet up with the Sallys, we came across a pottery shop that had amazing hand-painted ceramics. The next thing I knew we were going through their catalog and ordering pottery to have shipped home. Ken and I love fleurs-de-lis, so everything we picked out had a fleur-de-lis painted on it somewhere. Our trip to Florence was proving to be an expensive one. Between the linens we purchased in Rome and all the goodies we bought in Florence, I was going to have to take out a second mortgage to pay for it all.

The next day we had tickets to see the statue of David at the Academia and then a tour of the Uffizi. The statue of David is mind-blowing. This statue is massive and the intricate detail that Michelangelo carved into that single slab of marble clearly indicates it was a labor of love. The same can be said about the Pieta at Saint Peter's in Rome. The longer you stare at these statues carved from solid marble, the more you marvel at the genius that created them. The statue of David is at the Academia, which is nowhere near the Uffizi Gallery. In fact, David is about the only thing worth seeing at the Academia. That being said, it was absolutely worth the trip. A true must see.

After our morning at the Academia, we made our way to the Uffizi Gallery, a truly unique experience. It is an old Medici palace that housed enough art and statuary to keep us busy for hours. Ken humorously named the Birth of Venus, Venus on the Half-Shell. Super classy. I imagined the artist, Sandro Botticelli, rolling over in his grave.

After the tenth room of art I nearly got us thrown out trying to take pictures of the architecture. As I was apologizing to the security matron who was threatening to take my camera, I heard my mother-in-law proclaim, "You know, the Catholic Church is the master of PR and marketing. They hired all these artists and had them paint 'Madonna and Child' over and over again." She looked up at the wall in front of us, pointed at each painting and said, "Madonna and Child, Madonna and Child, Madonna and Child. These Popes could have worked on Madison Avenue." The Catholics in the room were not impressed with her proclamation.

My mother found all the naked statuary disturbing. After several dozen pieces she looked at me and said, "Did anyone ever wear clothes at this point in history? I mean seriously, Trent, I am tired of looking at all these pee-pees."

I couldn't believe my mother had just used the word pee-pee to describe a penis. I said, "Mom, there is beauty in the naked form. It allows the artist to capture the contour of the subject's body. Look at the detail; all of that was done by hand."

Mom looked around at all the statues and said, "Well, I don't like it. It's creepy. All these naked boys make me think they were all perverts."

Oh lord, give me strength. These statues were incredibly beautiful works of art from antiquity and all my mom could see were "pee-pees."

As we left the Uffizi, my mother-in-law, now that she had her curls back, was ready to shop. She could smell gold jewelry and followed the scent to the Ponte Vecchio, where she hit the jackpot. The entire bridge was covered with shops selling gold jewelry. Lots and lots and lots of gold jewelry. She had found her Mecca and proceeded to singlehandedly bolstered the Italian economy.

That night we had dinner in the hills just outside of Florence, where the countryside is absolutely beautiful. Getting up to this restaurant was a harrowing experience. We took a small taxi up to the restaurant and nearly died getting there. The small road was barely one lane wide and had sheer drop-offs that continually kissed the edge of our tires. Our taxi driver must have been a long lost relative of Mario Andretti as he was taking the curves at sixty miles per hour. His side mirrors were held in place with duct tape.

I asked about that during one of our hair-pin turns and he said, "I keep'a knockin them off'a, so I no replace, just tape'a. Easy to stick on new one. I get from, uh, how you say.... junkyard." *Oh great, that's comforting.*

The view of the Italian countryside from Omero's was spectacular, the food fabulous, and the service divine. For dessert, my mother-in-law ordered the cheesecake. It was a "no bake" cheesecake with an amazing flavor. I was obsessed with getting the recipe, so obsessed that I asked the waiter to introduce me to the chef so I could ask for it. I drive Ken nuts when I do this and I do it often. You would be surprised how many cooks and chefs will tell you what is in your dish if you compliment them by asking for the recipe. So through broken English and rough translation, I managed to get a rough idea of the recipe.

When I walked out the front door the three of them were staring at me incredulously. I said, "What? Did you think I was leaving that restaurant without knowing how he made that cheesecake?"

The restaurant provided a car to take us back into Florence. It was a new Audi sedan so our ride down was far different than our ride up − no duct tape.

The next morning we were heading to Venice to see the canals. Venice, my friends, is a tourist trap, and we bought into it hook, line and sinker. Honestly, it felt a bit Disneyesque. Thankfully there was no piped-in music to force-feed us a cheery rendition of "It's a Small World," in Italian. All we found on these islands were hotels, restaurants and shopping, lots and lots of shopping, so shop we did. Linens, masks, drawings, Murano glass − there was no way to get off the island of Murano without buying something.

Venice is definitely a walking city with lots of tiny alleys and bridges to traverse as you wind your way along. The beauty and grandeur of Saint Mark's Square is inspiring. My mother and I were totally fascinated by all the pigeons that inhabit the square. Ken and his mother absolutely hate birds. They took one horrifying look at all the pigeons and started speed walking towards the nearest exit from the square. All I heard was Ken yelling, "We'll see you back here in an hour," and off they went.

My mom and I wanted to feed the birds. Flocks and flocks of birds. Once we had our corn, those flying rats landed on our arms and took the feed right from our hands. Mom was laughing like a schoolgirl as she hopped around with a half dozen pigeons on her arms.

After we finished our "Alfred Hitchcock Presents" moment, we decided to sit down, order a large gelato and listen to the string orchestras that populated the square. We figured this was the perfect way to wait for Ken and Sally's return. At exactly one o'clock, Ken and his mother showed up, just in time to join us for a scoop of gelato and a Bellini. I have always loved Bellinis, a concoction of Prosecco, peach nectar and a small shot of peach liqueur. What's not to like? It was a surreal moment sitting in Saint Mark's Square, listening to Broadway showtunes from the orchestra, drinking Bellinis and eating gelato. I could have gone to heaven in that moment.

Right at the height of my euphoria, the waiter showed up with the bill. My mother insisted on treating and picked up the folder. Her face went pale when she saw the amount. Four Bellinis and one large scoop of gelato came to a hundred and twenty-four Euros, the equivalent of about one hundred and sixty US dollars. We should have read the sign. There was a seven dollar per person cover charge to enjoy the orchestra, a five dollar per person service charge for waiting on you, and a three dollar per person city fee, for who knows what. So before we ordered a thing we were at sixty euros!

It has become my mother's favorite story to tell. "Remember when I paid one hundred and sixty dollars for a scoop of ice cream and a few cocktails?"

Before we left Venice, we had to take a gondola ride. Many of the gondoliers were Italian gods. Ken and I had been teasing our mothers that we would let the two of them pick a Gondolier of their choice. It didn't really work that way. We simply got the next guy in line and in our case he looked more like Joe Pesci than an Italian god. A gondola ride in Venice is a lot like a horse drawn carriage ride through Central Park. It's very expensive, relatively short, very pretty, but is a one-time gig. I did enjoy viewing the architecture and seeing where Cassanova and Marco Polo once lived. At least that is what the Gondolier told us. Who really knows after five hundred years?

On the train ride back to Rome we were all exhausted. We had two more days in Rome before our mothers went home and Ken and I would head to Mykonos to recover. When we pulled into Rome's version of Grand Central station, Ken and I told the Sallys to stand on the platform with the luggage, and we would get it all unloaded. We hauled the big bags off first and set them by our mothers and ran back on the train to get the rest. As I looked out the window I could see our bags sitting on the platform—minus our mothers! My mother had climbed back on the train to help us unload and Ken's mother had wandered off to find a trashcan. I turned to Ken and said, "Oh my God! Where the hell did our mothers go? Our bags are just sitting out there on the platform!"

Ken said, "Oh, shit!" and started getting off the train. As we were rushing off with our remaining bags, I looked down the aisle and saw my mother boarding the train at the other end of the car.

I yelled down to her, "Mother, get off the train. It's loading up to pull out!"

She gave me a flustered look. "But I wanted to help you with the bags."

I was dumbfounded. I threw the bags out to Ken and ran down the car to get my mother off the train before it left with her on it. As I escorted her to our bags, Ken's mother popped up out of nowhere from her trash run. At the same time Ken and I said the exact same thing to our mothers, "What were you doing? I told you to wait by the bags." They both thought they were being helpful, while all I could imagine were our bags disappearing and the locals showing up the next day wearing our clothes.

Our first night back in Rome was actually my mother's birthday. I'd made reservations at a very special restaurant that Bon Appétit rated five stars. Being Americans, our reservations were on the early side, as dinner for authentic Romans doesn't start until 9 PM or later. When we arrived, we had the restaurant to ourselves. This restaurant was everything Bon Appétit said it was. The food, service and atmosphere were all amazing.

What I didn't know when I booked our reservation was that this was a restaurant for the rich and glamorous of Rome. It was fashion week and everyone in this restaurant looked like they'd just stepped off a runway. Six-foot glamazons in four-inch stilettos were gliding through the restaurant escorted by their equally stunning male counterparts. In fact, everyone in the restaurant was stunning, even the wait staff. The headwaiter and his four assistants looked like they'd stepped out of the pages of GQ. In retrospect, the food could have been mediocre and we would never have noticed with all this eye candy floating around the restaurant. At the end of the meal, the headwaiter brought out gift bags and gave our mother's each a bottle of wine with the bill. My mother whispered to me as we were leaving, "So how much was my birthday dinner?" I refused to tell her. We were celebrating my mother's birthday in Rome. It was a once-in-a-lifetime experience. It didn't matter how much it cost; it was well worth it.

Our final day had arrived and Ken's mother wanted to treat us on our last night together so I picked a restaurant known for its view. This place had floor to ceiling windows that looked directly out at Saint Peter's Basilica. The food was mediocre, the service was weak, but the view was spectacular. We watched the sun go down and the lights flicker to life on Saint Peter's.

The waiter, who looked like he had been waiting tables since WWII, told us an amazing story about all the lights on Saint Peter's and in the square on the grand colonnade. He said, "Prior to electricity being installed, it used to be lit with candles."

I looked at him and said, "Seriously? Candles?"

"Yes," he said. "It used to look like ants crawling all over the square as workers swung from ropes. Scary job, very dangerous." I could only imagine.

Our dinner lasted over two hours simply because we didn't want to leave such a magnificent panorama of the Eternal City. My mother-in-law and I have always played a good-natured game of one-up-men-ship when it comes to paying for dinner. It was a running joke during our trip. She let me get a peek at the receipt and damn if she hadn't bested me with our last dinner in Rome. I just laughed and said, "You win."

The next morning our mothers went home and we went to Greece. We couldn't board our plane fast enough. We were heading to a whitewashed, terraced hotel on the Aegean with a gorgeous pool and stunning views. And that pool had a bar. For four days Ken and I lounged by the pool, soaked up the rays of the Mediterranean, and let the pool staff at the hotel wait on us hand and foot. To me, this is what vacation is all about. Lie around, read, soak up some sun, drink and eat more than you should and enjoy the sights. Not once during this trip did I have to sing a theme song from a television show. Heaven!

GI JOE AND GI JANE

"Schizoid behavior is pretty common thing in children.
It's acceptable, because all we adults have this unspoken
agreement that children are lunatics."

- Stephen King

During our time out of the country, the kitchen remodeling was in full swing. The kitchen area was hermetically sealed off from the rest of the house to keep the dirt on one side and the cats on the other. Our mothers arrived home first and we had forgotten to give them a key. They were staying at the house for the night so my mother-in-law could take my mother to the airport in the morning for her trip back home. I had told them Karla had a key so her kids could let themselves in to feed and clean up after the cats. Of course, Karla was running a conference call and could not break free. She also couldn't remember where she put our key so she sent her youngest son Davin to help. My mother-in-law is a resourceful and persuasive woman. She got a stepladder, jimmied the back kitchen window, and convinced Davin to do a bit of breaking and entering. She and my mother managed to toss Davin over the threshold. Davin was accustomed to being tossed over things. Add to that his Spiderman-like climbing skills, and this little adventure was a walk in the park for him.

The second problem they faced was the sealed off kitchen. The ladies had to hack through several layers of heavy plastic and duct tape to get to the rest of the house. The cats were going crazy on the other side of the plastic and shot through as soon as the opening was cut. I wish I had a video of these two women herding our cats back through the plastic and fending them off while they retaped the seal.

Sadly, we don't have video of these ladies chasing cats, but there was a video made in our home during our absence. While Ken and I were enjoying our decompression time in Mykonos, Karla's children, Davin, Erin, Victor and three or four of their friends were entertaining our kitties. They also made an epic home movie of their own.

One of the advantages of living on The Court was having built-in pet sitters right next door. We now had four cats that basically allow us to live in their presence. When we acquired the first two, Anastasia and Alexander, Erin and Davin were still in grade school and Victor was just starting high school, so they were always looking for a way to make a few dollars. When Alex was standing on his hind legs he was as tall as Davin. The two were fast friends from the moment they met. With four floors, the kitties had lots of space to entertain themselves. The same could be said for our kitty sitters. It was a great arrangement – they would come over every day, several times a day, and play with the kittens, take care of the litter boxes, provide food and water and so on. Little did we know during our trip to Italy that our home had become a sound stage for a major motion picture.

During their occupation of our home they decided to make an epic war movie with our house as ground zero for invasion. Using a digital home movie camera, they ran from room to room, avoiding the enemy forces that were attacking Altamont Court. They used the decorative bed pillows as grenades and bombs, and wrapping paper tubes as rifles. All of this activity was going on unbeknownst to Karla or Rich. They knew nothing until one of the kids had a slip-of-the-tongue within earshot of Karla. Something along the lines of "Trent and Ken's bed is so cool! You can run, jump and dive on it and still have room to roll across before you drop on the other side."

Karla's head just about spun off her shoulders. The kids' faces went white when she seemingly appeared out of nowhere. "What in the world were you doing in Trent and Ken's bedroom? There's absolutely no reason for you to be in their room. I want answers, you three, and I want them now!" Karla continued to drill the kids on their activities in our house like a dentist doing a root canal. By the time she was done, she was mortified that over a two-week period, the kids had filmed "Invasion on Altamont Court" using our home as the command center. She dragged them all back over to the house and went room by room, straightening the beds, fixing pillows, and generally tidying up so we would not see the level of carnage that had taken place at the hands of our esteemed kitty sitters.

When we arrived home from Greece, I noticed things didn't seem quite right. The beds were made, but not quite like I had made them before we left. I just assumed it was the cats or a left over from the nights the Sallys stayed.

Karla called that evening and asked, "Do you have a few minutes to come over? The kids have something they want to tell you."

This sounded ominous. All the kitties were alive and breathing so I couldn't imagine what was so dire that I needed to go over to their house as soon as possible to talk to the kids. "Sure," I said.

When I got there, the kids were a pale, ashen color and were sitting side by side on the couch. Davin was looking at the ceiling, Victor at the floor and Erin was looking at her mother like she was about to puke.

Karla took a step towards them and said, "Okay, you three, spill it! Tell Trent what you were up to in their house while they were on vacation. Explain to him what you three were doing when you were supposed to be watching their kitties."

You could have heard a pin drop. Everyone was holding their breath, including me. After about 3 seconds, Karla said, "NOW!"

That "NOW" caused all three of them to levitate off the couch. Hell, it caused me to take a step back from Karla – if I had a handbag, this is when I would be clutching it.

I couldn't imagine what they had done that could possibly have been so bad. They were great kids. I thought, *Maybe she caught them snooping and going through drawers or they made themselves snacks and left a mess in the kitchen or they hosted a dinner party without parental consent.* Seriously, the house looked fine except for the beds looking a bit disheveled.

Erin was the brave one. She stood up and walked over to me with her eyes never leaving the floor. "While you were gone, we made a movie in your house."

I stood there a bit mystified, thinking, *I am jet lagged, exhausted and this is what Karla wanted me to hear immediately? What had she been smoking before she called me? This was not urgent.*

Karla looked at Erin and said, "And?"

Erin continued, "Well, it was kind of a big deal. We had other friends in the house and we were running from room to room. It was a war movie and we were evading the enemy."

Okay, now this was getting interesting. Before I could ask a question Karla said, "And?" with a bit more intensity.

"And we were doing dive rolls across the beds and throwing all the pillows like grenades."

At this point I nearly laughed out loud. Pillow grenades, how cool.

Karla added one more, "AND?"

Erin said, "And we are really sorry that we had other people in your house and we did not treat your house with more respect."

Okay, Karla had to have given Erin the word respect. No ten-year-old uses the word respect in a sentence.

At this point Karla was expecting me to admonish the kids for their behavior and thorough disregard for our personal property. I knew what was expected of me, but I was having the hardest time trying not to smile, not to laugh, not to make a wise-ass comment. Before I could stop my mouth, I said, "Pillow grenades, huh?" I could feel Karla's eyes on me like two laser beams cutting through the side of my skull.

I said, "Probably not one of your better choices. I would have gone with some of the cat toys, as the squishy balls are more the size of grenades. I would have used the pillows as bunker reinforcement."

Erin looked up at me with a sly grin and the boys laughed under their breath.

As soon as the word reinforcement came out of my mouth, Karla smacked me in the back of the head. "You're not helping their situation – or yourself!"

Okay, so the kids should not have invited other kids to join them in the house. That was a no-no, so I decided to focus on that indiscretion. "Okay, guys, you didn't have permission to bring other kids into the house. Who all was involved in this epic war movie?"

Erin looked back at the boys and said, "You two are not being very helpful!"

I believe that was followed by "stupid dumb asses" but it was said under her breath so I can't be sure.

I told her to "get used to it because men are never that helpful."

Karla smacked the back of my head again.

Erin took a breath and started naming names. "Stevie, Ricky, Christen, Gabby and Becca all helped make the movie."

These were all kids from the street who had been in our house on more than one occasion and like these three, loved to drop by and play with the cats. Not one stranger among them. She went on, "Becca shot the film, Stevie, Christen and Gabby were soldiers and Ricky was the nurse. He had a white cap and everything."

Ricky as the nurse did not surprise me. He was a great kid, smart as hell, but I was pretty sure, even at the age of 11, Ricky was probably gay. Every other word out of this child's mouth was "FABULOUS." I remember one summer he was playing hide and seek with all the kids on the block. I was on the front walk weather-proofing outdoor furniture, watching all the kids run around, yelling and laughing when Ricky ran up on our porch and said to me, "Don't tell them I am up here. They will never look for me here."

I said "okay" and kept working. He quickly became bored and decided to quit the game and sit and talk to me while I worked. He said, "This house used to be the scariest house on the block. No one ever wanted to come near it. I used to walk on the other side of the street so I didn't have to walk in front of it. But now," he continued, "it is just fabulous. I can't imagine anyone who would not find it divine! And this porch is fierce! The whole place is really a hot mess." His eyes got wide and he continued, "Oh, hot mess means really cool. This designer on *Project Runway* made up that saying."

Ding, ding, ding – a straight guy may use the word fabulous once in a blue moon. No straight guy uses the word divine (unless he is a priest), and he would never use the word fierce or the expression 'hot mess.' So Ricky as the nurse was the most believable part of the story.

At this point I was not sure what to say. I feared Karla's wrath, bodily harm, and the potential of the kids getting an even harsher punishment if I didn't do something. I said, "It sounds like you guys had a bit of an adventure while we were gone." Still trying to swallow the hysterical laugher hiding behind my teeth, I said, "So here's what we are going to do. Ken and I are planning on traveling over the holidays. Normally I would pay you for kitty sitting, but this time you will do it for free. Is that fair?"

The kids let out a collective sigh and rapidly agreed. Karla let out a huff loud enough to clearly indicate that she felt the punishment did not fit the crime. I went back home, poured a large glass of wine and explained the whole thing to Ken. At the end of the story he looked at me and said, "So Ricky played the nurse? White hat and all?"

I looked at him and said, "That was the best part of the story."

After I finished my glass of wine, Ken and I went upstairs to unpack our clothes from our trip. I kept staring at our bed and thinking, *It really does look like you could do a dive roll across this bed and come up on your feet on the other side.* And without a moment of hesitation, that's exactly what I did.

Ken walked out of the closet just in time to see this spectacle. "What the hell are you doing?"

He was less impressed when I started launching pillows off the bed at him while yelling, "Grenade!"

MEANWHILE BACK AT THE RANCH

"Ah, home crap home."

- Walter Fielding, The Money Pit

Now that we were back from Italy, reality set in. The kitchen had been completely demolished and the real work was about to begin. The first couple of tasks were simple and went smoothly. The plumbing and electrical had all been run so it was time to close up the walls. First they had to level the ceiling and lay the floor. Both went in without incident. I am not sure the guy who leveled the ceiling would agree that it 'went without incident,' as it took him a full week to complete the task. His exact words were, "This room is so warped its like a old LP (vinyl record) that was left in a hot car." At that point we had a room—an empty room—but a room nonetheless.

Next it was the carpenter's turn. These are the guys who install the cabinets and all the trim. Our house was back to looking like an episode of Hoarders as all the cabinet boxes, wood trim and the entire contents of our kitchen were now sitting in our dining room, the foyer and the living room. I was really ready for these guys to get started. I vividly remember the day the carpenter showed up with his assistant to begin installing the cabinets. I opened the door and there stood two extremely good-looking men. Anthony was a 5'8" Italian who was seriously built, and the other, Jay, was a 6'1" Midwestern boy who was equally well built.

In New Jersey and New York, the name Anthony is very popular. It is the pronunciation that I find peculiar. Its like the "th" or better yet, the "ho" are missing from the pronunciation. When he introduced himself he said, "Yo, Mr. Pines, right?"

"Yes," I replied.

"Great, my name is Ant'ny, and this is my partner Jay." The "tho" sound was completely nonexistent – say it with me, Ant-knee (There is also "Ant" for short). I'm not sure how that pronunciation evolved, but I'm sure it didn't start in Italy. "Yo, we're here ta install your cabinets and put up da trim."

Yo? Where did the Yo come from? All I needed now was a "How you doin'?" and I would have had Joey from "Friends," at my door. What really caught me by surprise was the way Anthony (we will respectfully call him Ant'ny from here on out) was dressed. He was wearing a one-piece flight jumpsuit. Yes, a jumpsuit. This is Jersey, so of course it was sleeveless. The zipper was unzipped halfway down his chest and he was going commando. The man had a hell of a body and ample equipment so it was like I had stepped into a porno flick from the 80's. Jay was a blond Viking from the Midwest and was wearing cut off denims, nearly short enough to be "Daisy Dukes," construction boots and a tank top.

Ant'ny showed up every day for three weeks to install the cabinets and trim. His jumpsuit uniform was consistent; the height of the zipper was not. Sometimes that puppy was zipped just below his navel. It was truly hard not to stare; the man was a Roman god. One Saturday morning I came down the stairs to Ant'ny working on crown molding. Jay had the day off so Ant'ny was flying solo. He had copied a page from Jay's wardrobe handbook and on this particular Saturday was wearing cut-off jeans and a tank top. The only difference was that Ant'ny's jean shorts were truly "Daisy Dukes." I was talking to him while he was standing on his ladder when I realized I was staring straight at his package. This was unavoidable for two reasons; actually three reasons. The first, he was standing high on the ladder so his crotch was level with my eyes. Two, he may have changed from a jumpsuit to shorts, but he was still going commando. His entire "package" was falling out of the left side of his shorts. I should note he had impeccable grooming. Three, I'm a gay man; of course I am going to notice! Here's an analogy for straight men; this would be like walking in on Pamela Anderson in her Baywatch days, braless, in a wet tee shirt, while she's on all fours caulking tile. All renovation work should be so visually enjoyable.

Ken was out the door each morning before these two carpentry gods showed up for work. I had described them to him in great detail, but he didn't actually believe me. It wasn't until the second Saturday that An'tny and Jay showed up for work that Ken first saw them in their full glory. I was standing in the kitchen talking to our gods of woodworking when Ken entered drinking coffee he had brought back from the bakery. He looked up and saw An'tny and Jay dressed like twins in their cut-offs and tank tops. Ant'ny was going commando as usual. An'tny said, "Yo, you must be Ken." Coffee blew out Ken's nose and he went into a coughing fit. He quickly excused himself to change his coffee-stained shirt.

Ant'ny asked, "Yo, he alright?"

"Yes" I said, "He's easily startled." I went upstairs to make sure Ken was still breathing.

When I walked into our room, Ken said, "Why didn't you tell me they were built like gladiators and dressed like strippers?"

"What do you mean I didn't tell you? I have been telling you that every day for two weeks. Haven't you been listening?"

"Of course I was listening. I just assumed you were exaggerating."

"Gee, thanks," I said. "Next time you need to trust what I'm telling you."

I left our bedroom, went downstairs to check on our "Gladiator Strippers" and then went outside to do some yard work. About forty minutes later I walked back in to find a totally 'freshened' Ken wearing shorts and a tank top, chatting up our carpenters. As I walked by him in the kitchen, the only word I said was "Shameless." Later that night I reminded him, "You do know they are both straight men?"

"Yes," Ken said, "but that doesn't mean I shouldn't look my best." Like I said, shameless.

The following Saturday we sadly said goodbye to our two Chippendale carpenters; the work was completed so we had to let them go. We could not legally keep them locked in our basement. I had to remind Ken that kidnapping was a federal offense. It was now time for the plumber to connect the gas lines for the stove and the water lines for the dishwasher and sink.

Monday, Frank the plumber arrived. Frank was nothing like the carpenters. In fact he was the polar opposite. He looked more like Rubeus Hagrid from Harry Potter than a Chippendale dancer. Frank also sweated like some kind of farm animal in labor. His body odor was heavily tainted with Jack Daniels and cigarettes. Alcohol-laden smokers' sweat is truly nauseating. Thank God his work was done in less than a week. Every time I dealt with that man I had to put Vicks VapoRub under my nose. His work was excellent, but I could not wait for him to finish, Bless his heart.

After the walls, trim, cabinets and plumbing were complete, it was time for the electricians to install the appliances. Our three-month project was running closer to five, and we were heading toward the finish line. The electricians were neither Chippendale dancers nor half-giant trollish wizards. They were the guys who had rewired the entire house so I was glad to see them. As they moved the appliances from the living room to the kitchen, I noticed an issue. The spot for the microwave, wall-oven and warming drawer looked much too small to fit all three appliances.

I called Brian the kitchen designer and he assured me, based on the paperwork he was looking at, that all three appliances would fit in the cabinet. I said, "Brian, unless you have some super secret miniaturization ray stashed in your cabinetry laboratory, this shit ain't gonna fit. You ever heard anybody say, 'It's like trying to stuff ten pounds of crap in a five pound bag?' Well, that is what we have here." He still sounded doubtful so I said, "Fine, then you can take the call from the electricians tomorrow and explain just how to install these appliances."

He finally realized he was dealing with a man who had lived without a kitchen for five months. I was down to my last gay nerve and he was stomping all over it. He agreed to come out first thing in the morning to look at the "potential problem" and attempt to scrape me off the ceiling.

When Brian walked into the kitchen, he took a look at the cabinet, and then at all the appliances slotted to fit in that space. His face went slack, his eyes bulged and he said, "What the hell? That shit ain't gonna fit!"

Really? Thank you for your expert analysis of the obvious. He pulled out his drawing and sure enough, to his credit, he had ordered the correct cabinet. The manufacturer had made and delivered the wrong piece. Bob could tell I was in no mood to dance on this so he called the manufacturer to figure out how to get the correct cabinet. I was pacing back and forth during the entire conversation. These were custom cabinets so I knew the lead-time would be weeks. Ten weeks, to be exact. I said, "No! Brian, I am not waiting another two months for this kitchen. It'll be cut from a different lot of lumber so who knows how well it will match."

Brian gave me a pleading look. "How can I make this right? This is our manufacturer's fault and we need to get this right."

As much as I am a hard ass, when someone steps up and owns an issue they created, I am extremely merciful as long as they continue to work to solve the problem and don't try to abdicate their responsibility.

I looked him in the eye and said, "This sucks. I really wanted that warming drawer but I'm not waiting 10 weeks: nor am I willing to take a risk that the wood colors won't match. Here's how this is going to go. You will call the appliance people at Karl's, where they have a policy of 'no returns', and get them to pick up this warmer free of charge and credit my account."

Brian said, "Done."

"Second," I said, "you will call the cabinet company and tell them that neither you nor the client will be paying for a cabinet that we did not order. They will deduct it from your total and you will credit me for this piece of cabinetry."

Brian said, "Done."

And I finished with, "If you cannot get them to credit your account, you will still credit me for this incorrect cabinet."

Brian said, "Absolutely."

"Then I would say we have a deal, Brian. Take it and run!"

After that fiasco was solved and the cabinets and appliances were in, it was time to finish the hardwood floors. I made a grave mistake with the hardwood floors. Instead of going with the brilliant team at Amadeus Flooring, I used the subcontractor my general contractor selected.

I wanted the kitchen to look like the rest of the house. I wanted provincial colored stain and an oil based poly. I had multiple conversations with this contractor about how the poly should be applied. Instead of looking like the rest of the house, they applied a super high gloss finish that made the kitchen floor look like a bowling alley.

I called the floor guy and told him we were not planning on using the kitchen as a bowling alley, so get it "fixed." The contractor apologized and had one of his guys come out and throw on a coat of satin-finish poly. This made the floor look like it had a bad skin condition. It was blotchy with high gloss spots showing through the satin finish. I didn't know whether to call the floor guy or a dermatologist. Another angry call to this subcontractor netted me another coat of satin. I lost count on the number of layers of polyurethane we put on that floor. I should have called the guys at Amadeus Flooring and started from scratch.

To add insult to injury, I found an empty container of the poly they were using to correct their mistakes and it was water based. Our kitchen floor never did look quite like the rest of the house. An oil-based poly would have added a rich hue to the stain. What we got was a watered-down cocktail instead of the brand I ordered. The floor contractor refused to fix the mess he had created and I refused to make the final payment. Ken lived in fear he would find me sanding our floors in the middle of the night, prepping them for a 'do-over.'

FOOD: THE UNIVERSAL GOOD NEIGHBOR

"The only time to eat diet food is while you're waiting for the steak to cook."

-Julia Child

"If I've learned one thing in my life, never fry chicken when you're naked."

- Charlene, Designing Women

Sunday is a day for rejuvenation. The week is over, weekend errands are complete and I am ready to relax. Relaxation for me comes in many forms. I am a person with a lot of energy. In fact, I drive Ken nuts. Sitting still is not my thing; I'm a bit of a Jack-in-the-Box. Coupled with the fact that I need some personal quiet time over a weekend to get myself ready to face another week, living with me can be a challenge. Okay, so Ken should get a humanitarian award for dealing with me day in and day out.

On Sundays I like to cook. Not Sunday dinner mind you, just cook. I don't always know what I'm going to cook until the day arrives. Roast chicken, fresh pasta, ravioli, stuffed shells, a crown roast, risotto balls, molten chocolate cake, or a brand new dish. It's all about making the food, being alone with my thoughts and losing myself in the preparation. It is a totally different experience to cook for the sheer joy of it. Don't get me wrong, we enjoy the fruits of this labor, but there's no pressure to get something ready for dinner. We just eat whatever I create – and yes, on occasion, we have chocolate cake for dinner. I can feel judgment coming from the Paleo Diet gurus.

With my new, chef's style kitchen, my cooking on Sundays became a well-known activity on The Court. The smells that were pumped from my stove onto The Court via that high-powered range hood caused noses to twitch and stomachs to grumble. I have no sense of proportion when I cook, which leads to massive quantities of food so I would just send out my creations to my neighbors. Little did these folks know they were trying my first-time dishes.

I truly believe that food is the key to making lasting friendships. Send someone a roasted chicken with stuffing and you have a friend for life. Since I never answer the phone when I am in the cooking zone, Ken fields the calls. On one of my extra creative days I took some samples out to our neighbors. Moments later, Ken took a phone call from one of the recipients and yelled from the living room, "Honey, what in the world did you just send next door? Pat just called to tell you that your balls were divine!"

The Chianti I was drinking shot out my nose. My balls were divine? A new dish was born - "Trent's Divine Balls." Who knew risotto balls stuffed with Fontina cheese could get such a reaction?

Occasionally, the timing of one of my surprise deliveries would cause a totally unexpected reaction. Our neighbors across the street, Jeanne and John, have toddlers who are a handful. John travels a lot on business so Jeanne holds down the fort when he's on the road. One Sunday afternoon I was making cheese ravioli to freeze and a wild mushroom and chicken risotto for dinner. I remembered that Jeanne was home alone with the kids; John was out of town on business. This left Jeanne with their five-year-old boy who has boundless amounts of energy and a cranky six-month old girl with a cold. Risotto must be served the moment it is done or it just turns into flavored sticky rice, so I quickly wrapped up these goodies and ran them across the street. When she answered the door, she had the wild-eyed stare of a cornered animal ready to bolt in any direction to escape.

She looked down at the food, then at me, then back at the food. "That's for me?" she asked. Her eyes began to well up with tears. I think this was the first time my cooking had ever caused anyone to weep openly. Wait, strike that. There was a chili dish I made once that brought grown men to their knees and caused molars to melt. I do remember some tears from that.

When I handed Jean the ravioli she wept tears of joy. All kids love ravioli so there would be no fight over what to cook for dinner. When she took the risotto from my hand, she said, "This one is mine." I ran home to get a bottle of wine to compliment her dinner.

I knew from experience she would need it once the kids were asleep. Besides, few meals on The Court are consumed without wine.

Nothing makes a cook happier than to know their food is loved and enjoyed. That said, it makes a cook ecstatic to know that you will throw your best friend under the bus to get to said cook's food! Jane and Karla are the best of friends and have been neighbors for nearly twenty years. Karla's was my first stop on food deliveries because she had three hungry kids and an eagle's eye view of my back door. Jane rarely got a chance to taste whatever I happened to create. But, if I knocked on Karla's door and no one answered it quickly, Jane would pop her head out the window and say, "I don't think anyone is home."

I would reply, "Both cars are here."

Jane would quickly say with an innocent smile, "I believe they walked up to town. You can leave that with me."

I knew full well the moment it disappeared into her home, it was not coming back out until it was empty. Jane gave Karla the thirty-second rule. If she didn't answer in thirty-seconds, Jane would rush over, pick up the culinary offering and rush back into her home.

There's probably such a thing as "too familiar," but that rule was seldom applied on The Court. If Karla's kids knew I was making something they liked, they would drop by just to "see how the cats were doing," and walk off with some goodies. Since our back doors were rarely locked the kids would come and go at will; we wore quite a path between our homes. Erin, our faux goddaughter, showed up one afternoon and wanted to know what I was a cooking. She said, "I don't like the left-overs mom has. When I told her

I didn't like anything in our fridge she said to come over here and see what you had in yours."

I laughed out loud. I could totally hear Karla saying this sarcastically (just as I would have) not expecting Erin to take it literally. I knew what Erin wanted. I had just made a big batch of my semi-famous chicken salad and she was addicted to it. My stepdaughters love it. Anyone who tastes it loves it. I made her a container to take home for lunch. Karla was mortified. Only on The Court would your neighbors' children walk into your home and ask you what you have in your fridge for lunch.

The first real test of the new kitchen was a brainchild of Karla's, my separated-at-birth twin. Each year the social club to which most of The Court belonged would host wine tasting events paired with slightly above average dinner or hors d'oeuvres. As if living on The Court were not social enough. Karla had noted to other club members on The Court that the cost of the wine tasting events at the social club was getting out of hand and, in her opinion, there was an unrealistic expectation of decorum so we should just "host our own wine tasting."

Rich and Ken, who are the winos (I mean wine aficionados), thought this was a great idea. They'd promised to connect with our neighbor Joe, a former food and wine editor in NYC, to come up with wine pairings for each dish. Joe couldnt attend the winetasting event as it conflicted with a scheduled booty call in Bogotá, Columbia. Karla circulated the idea, and it was decided. What they failed to tell me was Ken had agreed to have it at our home and had volunteered me to cook for the evening!

As you already know, I like to cook and if truth were told, I love to cook, but this situation was different on several fronts. First and foremost, people would be paying ninety-five dollars each for a three-course meal with wines and dessert. I was a wreck. Karla volunteered as sous chef and the older kids offered to serve for the evening. Heather removed her painter's hat and took charge of cleanup for the event, which was a monumental undertaking. Karla, Heather and Ken have dubbed me a slob in the kitchen. I accepted this designation gladly. My creative genius was reserved for cooking – not cleaning.

Second, these friends are all discriminating about how they spend their hard-earned money. These six couples, all gathered around our makeshift square dining room table, would be demanding a quality experience. I knew Joe, our designated sommelier, would work with Ken and Rich to select fabulous, affordable wines so the food had to be perfect. If not, said wine consumption would lead to wisecracks about the queen of the kitchen. I was not going to give up the spotlight to another gay man, regardless of his professional knowledge of food and wine.

Dinner parties can be a lovely thing, unless you happen to be chief cook. Timing is key, and if you're the cook, this can get tricky. Food has to be prepared, plated and served in a well-choreographed way that allows your guests to enjoy your hard work while food is fresh and hot. It also means you are the last to sit down to choke down the course with them and the first to help clear the table, all while stressing about when to plate the next course. It's a real challenge to stay engaged in conversation.

A helpful hint to the folks sitting at the table: Do not say to the cook, "Honey, you need to sit down and enjoy this wonderful meal with us. You are missing the whole evening running back and forth to the kitchen."

When someone says this to me I want to strangle him or her with their embroidered napkin. I often wonder if the person who says this thinks a group of leprechauns is magically cooking and plating the food.

Karla and I were in charge of the menu, so I grabbed a batch of cupcakes I'd made earlier in the day and headed over to her house to work out the details. I spotted Davin as I walked in the back door. I looked at him and said, "Hey, Davin, I brought you guys some cupcakes."

He gave me a deadpan look and said, "No, thank you, I don't like cupcakes."

I was stunned. What kid doesn't like cupcakes? Maybe that's why the kid only has 2% body fat.

Rich was sitting in the kitchen and overheard the conversation. Horrified, Rich said, "Davin, that was rude. When someone gives you a gift, you say thank-you."

Without missing a beat and with great sincerity, Davin turned to me and said, "Thank you for the cupcakes, Trent. I am sure they'll be delicious," and up the stairs he went.

I truly love this boy. He's as honest and sincere as they come and I never have to guess what he is thinking.

After the cupcake exchange, Karla and I started working on our menu. To begin the evening we would start with light munchies and champagne. This called for Gougers (small cheese puffs) and shrimp cocktail. I love this combo. It looks and tastes fantastic and requires a minimal amount of effort. For an appetizer we decided on orzo carbonara made with pancetta. The salad for the evening would be spinach with feta and dried cranberries with a white balsamic vinegar-raspberry reduction.

The main course was a challenge, but we finally agreed on a standing rib roast, twice baked potatoes with sour cream and cheddar cheese, green beans and carrots sautéed in a garlic, onion and butter sauce, and a bit of pickled red cabbage for the center of the plate. I was against the red cabbage. I hate pickled anything other than cucumbers. Karla insisted the cabbage would help cut the richness of the rest of the meal. To her credit, everyone loved the pickled cabbage. Mine stayed on my plate.

Last but not least was dessert – not that anyone would even notice the dessert once they were liquored up from "tasting" wine all evening.

I was known for making cakes. Fantastic cakes. Orgasmic cakes. In fact, my caller ID on Karla's cell phone is a photo of a fresh-baked chocolate cake. Everyone assumed I would make some spectacular cake and call it a day. When I make a cake for a group this size, it can take an entire day to bake, cool, layer and decorate.

I looked at Karla and said, "That ain't happening. I'm having a minor psychotic episode over making a gourmet dinner for twelve. I am not adding the stress of making a cake. Any ideas?"

She said, "Do something chocolate. Everyone loves chocolate. No one will care what it is or what it looks like as long as it is chocolate."

I knew what she was hinting at. "I am not making my chocolate cake!"

She glared at me. "Spoilsport." Then her eyes got big and she said, "What about those gooey chocolate cakes you make for Erin?"

"You mean the molten chocolate cakes?" I asked.

"Yes, those."

Actually, that was a great idea. They are individual, poured into ramekins and baked for 10 minutes. Add a dollop of fresh whipped cream and a few fresh raspberries and serve. All the work is in the prep and it can be done a day in advance. I was sold. I looked at her and said, "Done!" and made a mental note to make enough for our serving staff (aka, the kids).

Once the meal preparation started, there was no going back. Karla and I started furiously chopping and mixing, followed closely at all times by Heather and her dishrag. She was following us so closely some of that dishrag may have ended up in one of our dishes. That girl developed a serious case of dishpan hands by the end of the evening that even "Madge" and Palmolive couldn't control.

Ken took charge of making the dining room look as fabulous as one can make it using Costco folding tables. Thank God for the embroidered linens we picked up in Italy. To his horror, Ken realized that we didn't have enough matching china and crystal for our sophisticated evening. What to do? Then Ken remembered Karla's set of Waterford stemware was the same as ours, so he gave her a quick call and asked her to bring over a couple of sets.

When Karla arrived, she said to Ken, "I also have china for 12."

Ken looked at her and said, "Seriously?"

I was behind Karla and shaking my head no, no, no. I love my twin, but style is not her strong suit. Its not that she's hopeless, she just doesn't care – bless her heart. I was planning on using our plain white dinnerware but Ken just ignored me and said, "Great, bring it over."

As Karla went next door I glared at him. "I was happy with the plain white plates."

"How bad can it be?" he asked.

I gave him an eye roll and went back in the kitchen.

When Karla arrived with her china, Ken opened the box, took one look and said, "This is your china?"

"Yes, it's my china. You think I went and stole someone else's china? We picked it out when we got married but don't use it often. I pull it out for birthdays and such. Why?"

"I like the pattern. It's contemporary yet very tasteful. Not something I would expect you to have." Ouch. When I heard this, the first thing I thought was, *Ken has lived with me for too long. He has taken on some of my less attractive qualities.*

Karla joined me in the kitchen while Ken was unpacking the china. Ken yelled from the dining room, "You weren't kidding when you said you didn't use this stuff often. Half of it still has stickers on it!"

"I told you we don't use it often. Half of it has never been opened. Don't worry about it, no one will notice what's on the bottom of their plate."

I looked at Karla and started shaking my head no, no, no. She mouthed the word "What?" and then I heard Ken say, "Do I look like Mini Pearl to you? We are not leaving the price tags on this china."

I mouthed back, "I warned you."

Ken spent 30 minutes peeling and scrubbing off stickers. In the middle of his sticker removing frenzy Karla said, "Just stick them in the dishwasher and they will eventually fall off."

This elicited a gasp from Ken. "Do not tell me you put your good china in the dishwasher!"

Karla snapped back, "I use the china setting." She looked at me and continued, "After a birthday dinner I am too 'in-the-bag' to reliably wash them by hand. I figure they're safer in the dishwasher."

I thought she had a point, but Ken was not impressed.

Finally the prep was complete and it was time for me to shower and receive our guests. To slake my thirst I hit the champagne hard and popped a couple of cheese puffs into my mouth as I headed up the stairs. My food-to-alcohol consumption ratio was off because the rest of the evening was a blur to me.

I remember that Heather coordinated the kids whisking dirty plates away into the kitchen while Ken and Rich took turns introducing the wines using Joes script and running the tasting. They must have been delicious because by the end of the evening the guests were heckling Joes carefully scripted speeches. Too bad he missed out on the abuse. I wasnt willing to call it into Bogotá.

I tore around the kitchen finishing side dishes and plating food like Julia Child on crack. Now I understand why she always had wine on hand while taping her television show. Karla popped in occasionally to lend encouragement and steal a taste but made the executive decision that the kitchen was too crowded and she needed to help manage the wine tasting. Traitor!

By the time dessert was served my energy reserves were exhausted. I vaguely recall lots of raucous laughter, loosened pants and rosy cheeks so I assume the horde was satisfied. The group patted me on the head, assured me that I had done a spectacular job and mercifully sent me off to bed. The glowing reports on Sunday confirmed I had been fabulous, but I had already decided that I would never again allow myself to be suckered into such an event. I would stick to orchestrating backyard barbeques.

Sunday afternoon, still struggling with a mild wineover (coined after my first wine hangover), I decided to heat up some leftovers for lunch. I went to put a baking sheet of food into the oven and noticed the oven already had something in it. My first thought was, *What the hell did Ken leave in the oven?* I reached down, pulled out the baking sheet and found myself staring at the twice-baked potatoes with sour cream and white cheddar cheese. These puppies never made it to the plates – bless our hearts.

A CORNUCOPIA OF FUN

"Insanity is doing the same thing over and over again and expecting a different result."

– Albert Einstein

Generally, ideas are good things. They can lead to innovation, change and progress. But more times than not, an idea can take on a life of its own. What starts out as a small idea often becomes a snowball rolling down a mountain, gaining size and speed as it rolls. And sometimes that giant snowball rolls down the hill and shoots off a cliff into midair with no parachute attached.

This particular idea actually started one year prior to coming to fruition. It was Thanksgiving 2006 and I was cooking in the kitchen while watching the Macy's Parade on TV. My high school band was marching that year and I looked forward to seeing those purple and white uniforms marching down Broadway. I knew it would bring back incredible high school memories of my time in the band. The phone rang and it was my Aunt Sandy who still lives in my hometown of Pickerington, Ohio. She wanted to know if I had the parade on so I could see the band.

We started talking about Manhattan and reminiscing about her last visit. I told her she should visit us next Thanksgiving so we could all go into the city and see the parade in person. There it was – THE IDEA! I had innocently planted a seed that would burst through the ground in the spring of 2007 and go from an idea to an out of control snowball rolling down the side of a mountain. It was April when the first call came in from my Aunt Sandy. She wanted to know if I was serious about my invitation to her and her husband to visit for Thanksgiving.

"Of course," I said. It was April; November seemed an eternity away.

Sometime in June my cousin Dana called and said, "I hear Mom and Dad are coming for Thanksgiving. How would you like to have a couple more?"

"Sure," I said. "You, Doug and Ella are more than welcome." November still seemed like a land far, far away. But the snowball was getting bigger.

News of these plans made its way to my parents. So I got a call from my mother, who asked, "Why didn't you invite Dad and me for Thanksgiving?"

"You know you are welcome anytime, Mom," I replied. "You don't need an invitation." Whew, that was a close call. The snowball was now a boulder.

Another couple of months went by and my cousin Troy called. "I hear that Mom and Dad, Dana, Doug and Ella, and your parents are coming to your house for Thanksgiving. Would it be okay if Amy, Gracie and I joined them?"

"Of course," I said. It was September, and we still had a few months; I was still feeling pretty confident I could pull this off.

Along came October first. I woke up in a cold sweat from a nightmare about killer turkeys chasing me through a pumpkin patch toward a large group of famished people at a table with no food on it. I had not been tracking the head count. I had no idea how much food we would need to feed the horde that was about to descend on our house. There it was – the snow boulder just launched off the cliff, and was falling directly onto The Court.

That morning I sat down with Ken and we began to count. First we started with his family. Mother, brothers, sister, spouses, kids and so on. Over twenty-five people. We added Ken's girls and my family and we were over forty. Oh brother! I had forgotten we'd invited Karla, Rich and the kids to join us as well. All totaled, we had invited forty-eight people for Thanksgiving. This by itself was daunting, but add to it the fact that neither Ken nor I would ever use plastic or paper plates for Thanksgiving, that meant we had to come up with linens, plates, glassware and silverware for forty-eight people. Our Altamont Court family and my sister-in-law Heidi came to the rescue. They generously lent us all types of dinnerware, stemware, and glassware, so we had that requirement covered.

The first to arrive were my parents. My mother, father and their dog, a Chinese Pug, uniquely named Pugsley, drove all the way from Dallas. From the moment Pugsley trotted into the house, all he wanted to do was chase the kitties. They were less than impressed with this yapping intruder. I watched as Puglsey chased and barked at the cats and the cats swatted and hissed at Pugsley. This was going to be so much fun.

Pugsley became a hit on the streets of Morristown. He received hugs, petting sessions, cookies, meatballs — you name it, he got it from the local town merchants. Because of all this attention and free swag, he barked at my father multiple times a day to go for a walk. At home Mom and Dad were lucky if they could get him to lift his thirty-pound body off the chair to walk to the mailbox. By the end of the week, he was practically dragging my father up and down South Street to stop at each of the businesses where he knew the owners would give him a free hand-out. Pugsley was one smart dog.

On Wednesday the rest of the family arrived. With five bedrooms and a finished basement, each family had their own room. I rushed to get everyone settled so we could leave for NYC to see the balloons being inflated for the Macy's Day parade. I figured this was the next best thing to actually seeing the parade. New Yorkers always rave about this pre-parade ritual. More than one person could be seen on the news saying, "Oh, this is a must-see for me and my family every year. It's just magical. We never miss it."

Wrong! It was not magical; nor was it a must-see event. It was so crowded we could barely walk down the streets to see the balloons. To keep the balloons in place, netting was draped over them and pulled tight to the ground. The balloons were so distorted you had to be a contortionist to decide what they were. Disney World is magical too until you're trying to exit the Magic Kingdom after the fireworks with fifty thousand cranky adults and twenty thousand worn out children all with the same goal in mind - escape. We didn't last long before we called it quits and went to a deli for a bite to eat. Thanksgiving was the next morning so I was happy to head home early and start cooking. We all agreed on the train ride home that we would be watching the parade on TV from the comfort of our living room. Some ideas should remain ideas.

In situations like this, there must be a little extra drama to make things super fun. Our fun involved a steam pipe that had rusted through. The pressure from the steam blew a hole in the side of the weakened pipe, spitting steam and a nasty brown, rusty residue all over the basement. With only twenty-four hours before additional guests arrived, I was in a panic. We had no central heat, twelve houseguests and thirty-six others joining us for Thanksgiving. Knowing our ambient body heat would not be enough to warm the entire house, I called the ever-supportive Altamont Court Boys Club for some help. Jim and Rich took on the task of replacing the rusted section of blown-out piping. With little time to spare, they went to work. I heard the banging, sawing and grunts of effort coming from the basement all morning. When I went down to see how they were doing I noticed they had opened the basement windows and the air in the basement had an oily look to it. I assumed it was just from all that sawing and banging. WRONG! A few days and a couple of glasses of wine later, I got the real story.

Steam pipes are treated with an oily residue to prevent rusting. The guys pulled a rag soaked with paint thinner through the pipe to clean out this residue to prevent the odor from permeating the house. The idea is to keep your house from smelling like *Jiffy Lube* when you crank up the heat. It took a couple of rags to get the pipes clean and ready to install.

Here's a shop tip for you do-it-yourselfers: Properly dispose of rags soaked in flammable liquids outside and away from any area where you will be using an acetylene torch. When the guys started soldering the pipe over their heads, hot material from the solder dropped from the pipe, hit the rags and WHOOSH!

Rich did not see this happen. All he said to Jim was, "Damn it's getting warm down here."

Of course it was getting warm. Rich had flames jumping waist high up the side of his pants.

Jim exclaimed, "It's warm because you're on fire!"

Jim and Rich looked like psychotic Flamenco Dancers as they stomped out the flames. Other than a few toasted eyebrows, everyone was fine. Choosing to tell me at a later time was the right thing to do. I was in no shape to hear about the towering inferno in our basement while trying to baste three turkeys.

It's amazing how quickly forty-eight people can consume three turkeys, fifteen pounds of Yukon Gold potatoes, ten pounds of stuffing, stuffed shells and sauce (it's an Italian thing, shells and sauce go with everything, even turkey) and countless side dishes. Add Thanksgiving favorites from every household, thus causing the dessert table to 'runneth over' and you get the picture. At this meal it was Karla's cranberry/lime relish that was the forgotten dish. We actually found a more creative use for this forlorn dish. It served double duty as the base for "Cranaritas." I personally am not a fan of her cranberry/lime sauce unless it is used to make a "Cranarita."

All our guests seemed to have a wonderful time at this over-sized Thanksgiving. Or at least that is the way I remember it now. My memories are a little hazy – kind of like the air in our basement.

If the worst idea for our Thanksgiving family weekend was the pre-parade balloon inflation, the best idea was securing tickets for my immediate family to see Jersey Boys. This show features the music of my parents' and my aunt and uncle's generation and we were going to see it on Broadway. The show was fantastic. It was hard to keep my father from singing along with Frankie Valli and his buddies. I had to remind him that the people around him had paid over a hundred dollars a seat to hear the folks on stage, not the person sitting next to them. My father is a person who talks to his TV. You can hear him shout, "Don't go in there!" or "He's behind the door!" so it is hard for him not to provide running commentary. The music was infectious and I quickly noticed dad wasn't the only one singing along with the performers. This show is about the original Jersey Boys, so the word F$%& was used liberally. As I noted, it is a staple of the New Jersey dialect. Thank God my father did not participate in the dialog.

After the matinee we had reservations at Isabella's, just north of Columbus Circle. It was a crisp, clear, late fall night so we decided to walk to the restaurant. The city was already decorated for Christmas, and the streets were glittering with lights. Arm-in-arm, we walked all the way.

As we approached the restaurant, my father asked loudly, "Is this place expensive?"

"Dad, it doesn't matter," I said. "You're not paying, so hush already! Besides, it's all relative. Compared to Rockwall, Texas, everything here is expensive." Hell, Ray's Original pizza would be considered expensive.

Dad huffed a bit and we continued walking.

When we got to the restaurant he looked in the window and said loudly, "It's got table clothes and cloth napkins! I knew it. I knew this place was going to be real expensive."

My mother elbowed him and said, "Jack, hush or you can go wait at the train station." Parents are so much fun.

It was the perfect ending to an amazing Thanksgiving weekend. As I sat there at Isabella's I couldn't help but look around at the twelve of us who attended the show and then think about the forty-eight people who had shared our feast on Thanksgiving Day. All of those people in our home laughing, smiling, loving. Talk about a cup that truly runneth over; mine seemed to be on free refill. I was reminded just how blessed Ken and I truly are.

CHRISTMAS!

"Our holidays were always such a mess."

- Clark Griswold (Chevy Chase)

"Oh, yeah."

- Clark Senior (John Randolph)

"How'd you get through it?"

- Clark Griswold (Chevy Chase)

"I had a lot of help from Jack Daniels."

- Clark Senior (John Randolph)

Christmas! That one word can fill you with warm memories of love and laughter or with dread and despair. It all depends on your experiences. Movies such as *Christmas Vacation* or *Four Christmases* may be stereotypical, but stereotypes exist for a reason. They're more factual and real than people like to admit.

Ken and I have gay friends who can't go home for Christmas because they're not welcome. They've had to build new families, so for them this is a bittersweet holiday. It's hard for me to imagine what that would be like. Feeling unwelcome and unwanted at Christmas is truly a burden no one should ever have to bear. Anytime I feel a bit overwhelmed by my family during the holidays, I remind myself that it's a burden I am blessed to carry.

Personally, I love Christmas. I consider myself a Christmas junkie. I love Christmas decorations - my "Saks Fifth Avenue" window-ready display trees, sending beautiful, hand painted Christmas Cards, finding that one-of-a-kind gift no one expects. And lights. Lots and lots of little white lights. They make everything seem a bit more magical.

Christmas on The Court was an interesting affair, as we had a strong mix of Jewish and Christian people on our street. For every home decorated for Christmas, there was one with a menorah in the window. Whether Jewish or Christian, I enjoyed the lights that came from everyone's homes.

I opted for artificial trees, which Karla said were "unnatural" and "produce toxins when they're lit that cause brain damage." They were perfectly symmetrical, all three of them. Our first year on The Court, I excitedly called Karla over on a Sunday evening to unveil our first perfect Christmas tree of the season. Despite her migraine she trudged over to see the spectacular sight. Imagine her dismay when she witnessed a perfectly coiffed, seven-foot-tall cone of green petroleum by-product. Trying to be tactful (not Karla's strong suit), she responded to my enthusiasm with some weak acknowledgment of my decorating prowess. Karla returned home to Rich, who was unraveling endless strings of gaudy colored bulbs, and to her oldest son Victor, who was doing his homework, and announce sarcastically, "I saw the tree and I think Ken and Trent are gay." Victor just looked up from his math problem and said, "Ya think?"

The Tranfield's didn't believe in symmetrical trees. In fact, Karla went out of her way to find really big, fat, bulbous trees that could fill a room. Rich would have to prune this monstrosity into an unnatural shape that would squeeze into a corner of the living room. They have permanent eyelet screws affixed to their window-sills to shore up this annual fiasco. One year their tree was so big and fat that it shattered the wrapping tube at the tree farm and Rich tore out part of the doorframe getting it into the house. When it was unbound, the damn thing took up half the living room and no one could walk down the main stairs. When the kids were little, only the bottom half of the tree was decorated. I asked Karla about it once and she said, "It's the kid's job to decorate the tree and I don't let them use a ladder. I love seeing how much farther up the tree they decorate each year."

There was a certain logic to her argument—warped Tranfield logic—but it worked for them. I guess it was much easier to repair the damage when the cat invariably knocked the tree over.

Over the years Karla and Rich had developed a last minute habit of shipping all the family gifts to our house for wrapping. Once the pile was neatly stacked in the basement, one of them would stay home on kid duty and the lucky one would bring over a couple bottles of wine and we would start wrapping. I introduced them to our tradition of watching *A Tuna Christmas* every year over the holidays. In this comedy, two men play all the characters, men, women, and kids. It's truly a hilarious bit of theater. Karla nicknamed it, "A Drag Queen Christmas." No matter how many times I told her it wasn't a drag show, she refused to call it anything else. Unfortunately, the funnier the skit, the worse the wrapping job. At least that was Rich's excuse....

The kids would make their way over after the wrapping was complete, the gifts were hidden in trash bags, and the adults were enjoying a moderate buzz from the wine. They would show up just in time for the *Saturday Night Live Christmas Special*. The first time we all watched this together, the kids had never seen the "Schweddy Balls" skit. At first Davin's pre-teen face showed shock. Was he really hearing this right? Were they really taking about sweaty balls on TV in front of his mother and his gay neighbors? Then, like a light bulb going on, he got it. When Pete Schweddy said, "No one can resist my Schweddy Balls," Davin choked on his Christmas cookie, and laughed so hard he fell off the couch on top of my head. He went around for weeks saying, "No one can resist my Schweddy Balls." Erin was impressed that they came in their own Schweddy Ball Sack. Good times! And in keeping with the spirit of inclusivity on The Court, the evening would end with a showing of Adam Sandler performing his Chanukah Song. O.J. Simpson – still not a Jew? Karla and the kids have this jewel loaded on their iPhones.

Christmas on The Court also meant a special delivery of Karla's Christmas Caramel Corn. This stuff is like crack. Since Karla didn't believe you should put anything unnatural in your body, she made it from scratch. Popped the corn, used real butter and sugar to create the caramel, and had a bunch of brown paper bags to shake up the popcorn to ensure there were no old maids when she was ready to mix the popcorn and the caramel. When the heavenly smell of caramel corn made it to my back door, I knew Christmas had arrived. I would steal extra bags off her dining room table and hoard it. Ken never knew how many bags were actually in the house at any given time.

My family and Ken's family celebrate Christmas in very different ways. During the years before I met Ken, I was always on the road with my job so I would fly into town for a couple of days before heading off to my next destination. As my brother and I got older, exchanging gifts became a thing of the past and getting together as a family became even more difficult. When we did get together Mom always made it special by cooking Italian on Christmas. It's one of my favorite memories. As she put it, "It's the one day a year I actually cook." Dad would always mumble, "She ain't kidding about that."

My parents are very independent people. If I didn't call and schedule a visit home in advance, I would most likely show up to an empty home. They are golf-crazed retirees who would spend seven days a week on the golf course if their bodies would let them. And the answer is, "Yes, who hasn't?" when asked the question, "Have they ever golfed on Christmas Day?"

Christmas with Ken's family is completely different. All of Sally's kids had their children back to back. Over a six-year period, my mother-in-law became a grandmother ten times. Each Christmas there were more kids at the table as Sally and her brood grew exponentially. By the time I arrived on the scene, the tradition of spending Christmas at my mother-in-law's was well entrenched. My mother-in-law is the quintessential Italian matriarch. She is the official head of the family and all who call her mother or grand-mother or mother-in-law know that Christmas is her domain.

When we moved to NJ, I had to get used to her calling on Saturday or Sunday to say, "I made a pot of sauce, you'll come for dinner." If Ken answered the phone, we were doomed. None of Sally's children can tell her no. If we had other plans, we had to change them because Sally had "made a pot of sauce." Sally lived forty-five minutes from us, so this was not a simple request. From previous experience I was well aware that a call to come to dinner was not a two-hour affair. This was a whole day affair starting with appetizers at one p.m. and dessert at eight p.m.

Ken would take one look at the caller ID and say, "Trent, it's my mother. Do you want to pick it up or should I?" I would lunge for the phone since I had a much better chance of keeping us free from an all day dinner affair. The conversation would often start out the same way it did with Ken, but the request was softer.

I would say, "Hey, Sally, what's up?"

She would respond with, "Hi, Honey, just called to tell you I made a pot of sauce, and wanted to know if you guys were free for dinner."

You see the difference? This felt more like an invitation. Instead of, "I made a pot of sauce, you'll come to dinner," it was now, "if you guys were free for dinner." Those raised by Italian matriarchs know the wording may be different, but the implication is the same – you'll come to dinner.

An eight-hour day with my in-laws eating way too much food and drinking way too much wine was not the way I intended to spend every weekend. After moving out of Warren and Heidi's basement, I figured we'd escaped the weekly family dinners. I figured wrong. During one of these invitation/command appearance phone calls, I said, "Thanks so much for the invite, Sally, but we have plans this evening." I might as well have taken a hammer to a hornets' nest.

"Plans, what plans? What are you guys doing?"

"We are going to the movies tonight," I said, as unassuming as possible.

"What time tonight?" she asked with more force.

"The movie starts at 6:45, why?"

"6:45? You have more than enough time to come to dinner."

Well this was going to be fun. I felt like Alice falling down the rabbit hole. "Actually we have reservations for dinner before the show."

"Where?" she asked in a very Jersey tone.

I was thinking, *Why does it matter where we are going?* But trust me, it matters. I said, "A place locally, why?"

"So what you are saying is, you would rather eat out than come up here and eat my food?"

Oh my God. When did this get personal? Ken and I had planned an evening out that included dinner and a movie and that turned into 'you hate my food and don't want to see me.' God give me strength. Ken was sitting on the couch snickering. I was going to pay for this.

I realized it was time to draw the line on spending every weekend out on "Walton's Mountain." That's what I nicknamed the area where she lives because it's in the middle of no-where.) So I said, "Sally, this has nothing to do with you or your food and everything to do with the fact that I made these plans for Ken and me a week ago. We rarely get any alone time, so tonight I am taking him out for a nice dinner in town and after that we are going to the movies. A two-hour round trip for dinner is not in the cards tonight."

Without missing a beat, Sally said, "Geez honey, why didn't you say so earlier? That sounds really nice. Are you free next weekend?"

I was cornered. There was no escape. I said, "Yes, we are free next weekend."

"Wonderful, next weekend I am making a huge pan of Paella so you can come for dinner!" Before I could respond she said, "Have a great time tonight. See you next weekend."

And with that I heard the click of the receiver. Paella? I hate Paella.

If weekend dinners were huge, Christmas dinner was ginormous. It was a two-day affair from which there was no escape. It started with Christmas Eve. Sally hosted a dinner for family members who were orphaned on Christmas Eve. It was a different group every year based on alternating commitments. Ken's girls alternated Christmas Eves between Ken and me and his ex-wife. On Christmas Eves when we had the girls, if Sally was not hosting other family orphans, she would join us for dinner on The Court. Oh, the joys of the modern split family.

I loved her Christmas Eve dinners. It was always a small, intimate group, and her menu was spectacular. She served whole lobsters, King Crab Legs, and tenderloin, the kind of outrageous artery-clogging food you can cook when you are not feeding the Twelve Tribes (I know this is a Jewish reference but it seemed appropriate). The real endurance test was Christmas Day.

Gift giving in Ken's family is both an art form and a lesson in capitalistic excess. It is not just the quality of gift, but the quantity. They love gift giving. They love gift receiving. Most importantly, they love gift unwrapping. Every year, everyone arrives at Sally's around 1:00 PM, and everyone is carrying gifts. Lots and lots of gifts. It takes twenty minutes for each family to unload their car full of gifts. First the area around the tree fills to a point that the gifts are level with the star on the top. From there, they began to fill the room around the tree, on the couch, and on the coffee table. In fact, by the time the last family arrives, no one can enter the room where the tree is standing.

While the various pack mules unload their treasures, Sally acts as air traffic controller, keeping track of where each family's gifts were placed. As Sally plays Santa, she has a system that only she understands, and it works. When it comes time for gift giving, she knows exactly where she has directed each group of gifts. How? I have no idea.

This Christmas was a typical day of excess indulgence, so we had to pace ourselves. Appetizers started at 1:30 and my mother-in-law had the day timed down to the minute. She is the only person I know who can manage to keep a steady stream of ever-changing food moving from her ovens, refrigerator and stove top. Gordon Ramsay would be impressed by her cooking skills. The range of appetizers was staggering. Shrimp cocktail, crab stuffed mushrooms, rosemary lamb chops, kabobs of all types, wings, lemon scallops, lasagna rollatini, baked brie and an antipasto platter that could feed a small nation. After the first round of grazing was complete, all I could think was, *I wonder if Sally has a bottle of Ipecac.*

Ken's oldest brother had an unnatural need to watch *It's a Wonderful Life* every year on Christmas Day. At some point during the day I would hear Jimmy Stuart's voice coming from the living room, making its way through the mountain of gifts. Just prior to dinner being served we were treated to a live performance, complements of our nieces and daughters. I am talking full lip-synched Broadway numbers with choreography. It would have made RuPaul proud. We're not talking about some lovely carols from *White Christmas*. No, it was always something not quite appropriate for the holiday. Nothing says Christmas like a group of girls, ages five through twelve doing, "The Cell Block Tango" from *Chicago*.

After the live performance, dinner was served. My jaw dropped the first time I experienced the unveiling of dinner. I thought the appetizers were over the top, but Sally's Christmas dinner was something out of a medieval feast. She had three different meats: a ham, a turkey, and a full tenderloin. This was accompanied by hundreds of meatballs, Baked Ziti, Chicken Parmesan, Manicotti crepes....I gained fifteen pounds just looking at the food laid out on the table. After finishing dinner, which was a two-hour affair, we would begin our slow migration to the living room. Stamina was needed to survive what happened next.

Gift giving in Ken's family was completely orchestrated by Mother Christmas, aka, my mother-in-law. She would hand out each gift based on the names on the tags. First, she would read the name of person giving the gift and then the name of the person getting the gift. Each person had to unwrap his or her gift to the accompaniment of delighted squeals from the entire family. To put this in perspective, you have to do the math. Twenty people times twenty gifts. This was four hundred individual unwrapping's every Christmas. It took over four hours to complete the process. Since Sally was Santa, she always went last.

This was a truly amazing scene to watch. Like the gift of the Magi, each grandchild and each adult would bring their gift forward and place it in front of Sally. As I watched, I thought, *Any minute now, one of them is going to kneel, kiss her ring and genuflect when they back away.* She looked like a bejeweled Madonna. All we needed were some frankincense and myrrh; she was already wearing plenty of gold.

At the bottom of the third hour, my sister-in-law Heidi and I would escape to put the coffee on and set out the desserts. As soon as these Christmas crazies finished opening gifts I wanted dessert ready so we could eat and go home. After dessert was completed, I would start sneaking our gifts out the back door and down to the car. I always parked it on the street so we'd have an easy escape route. The moment I finished my last bite of pumpkin roll, we'd make our mad dash for the car.

Every year was the same until our last year in the house. Ken's back had become so bad he had to have another surgery three weeks before Christmas. Sally was very understanding when I called to tell her there was no way we would be able to come to her house for Christmas, as Ken was not allowed to ride in a car. Sally graciously said, "Oh, honey, that's no problem. I will call everybody and let them know we're bringing Christmas to you."

I was in shock. She was moving the family Christmas to Altamont Court? I quickly looked around the room to make sure we were not in the middle of the second coming. I said, "Sally, I am not sure what to say. I know this is a hike for everyone. Are you sure everyone will be okay with this?"

"Don't worry about that," she said. "I will call everyone and let them know what's going on and ask if they are okay with having Christmas at your house." I thought, *Ask them or tell them?* With Sally, it was the same thing.

So Sally brought her style of Christmas to The Court, and I was anything but prepared. My first thought was, *Where will I put all of the gifts?* My amazing mother-in-law pre-prepared all of the food, so it was ready to put in the ovens. She never missed a beat. She told me, "The only thing you have to do is rearrange the furniture to accommodate the gifts."

That was the year "The Rich who Stole Christmas" put a Seinfeld Festivus Pole on the front walk to spite me for not putting up his giant Frosty the Snowman. It was a single pole with a sign on it that said "Festivus for the Rest of Us." We left that thing up all through Christmas. I made all the kids do a "Christmas Story" picture, sticking out their tongues as if they were going to lick the pole. It's one of my favorite pictures from Christmas on The Court.

That was our last Christmas in the house. Funny how that changed things. All the details that had caused me to squirm and roll my eyes, my typical impatience with the gift giving process, these traditions Sally held to; it all seemed right. I found myself looking around during dinner, watching people eat, drink, laugh, tell stories. Normally, I am one of those people who "runs" the table. Telling stories, engaging people in conversation. That Christmas, on The Court, I just listened and watched. It was mesmerizing.

More than once I found myself misty-eyed. The sheer volume of love in our home, on that Christmas, was overwhelming.

I relished every gift opening, every ooh and aah, every smile and laugh. And in that single moment in time, I fell in love with it all.

PORCH THERAPY

*"I know God won't give me anything I can't handle.
I just wish he didn't trust me so much."*

— Mother Teresa

The front porch is an American institution. My Grandma Gert had a great front porch. My brother Tod and I would visit her in Zanesville, Ohio, and sit out there for hours playing "Your car, my car." It was a game we made up where every other car was his car or my car. Sometimes you got a great car, sometimes a clunker, or sometimes a truck. Trucks were worth the most points. It makes me smile to think about all the time we spent on her porch. I can still hear my grandmother shouting across the street to her neighbor Adelaide. They would discuss the news of the day by yelling back and forth to each other from their front porches (long before cell phones and text messaging, yes, the good ole days).

Our house on The Court had a large porch just like my grandmother's and just like our place in Atlanta. When we first bought the house, we didn't even realize there was a porch. The yews and cedars covered it completely. Sitting on the porch then was akin to sitting in the middle of an overgrown briar patch. After the boys finished their play date with the chainsaws voilà! We had a porch.

With its four-foot overhang, we could sit out and enjoy the sights and fresh air in any kind of weather. We added a couple of outdoor fans to increase our comfort on humid summer evenings. Our electrician tried to convince us we wouldn't need porch fans. "Aren't you two from Atlanta?" he asked. "You're used to some pretty hot weather. It never gets that hot here."

One word came to mind – Bullshit! I had lived in NJ often enough to know that it could easily get to ninety-five degrees during the day with eighty-five percent humidity and no breeze. This kind of heat is as bad if not worse than Atlanta heat. I'm not one who likes to repeat myself to someone I hire to do a specific job, but I looked at him and said, "Add the fans. Now!"

That summer we had twenty-two days over ninety-five degrees and the humidity never dropped below eighty percent. Our porch was the only place on the street you could sit outside without melting.

Once we added some wicker furniture and a round table and chairs that seated six we were ready for entertaining. I quickly grew to love this space as much as I did the porch in Atlanta. During the spring and summer months we could people watch, catch up with neighbors, and listen to live music as it glided down The Court from a rental property at the head of our street. That rental unit always had interesting residents. The entire time we lived on The Court, it seemed as though only musicians rented it: a pianist, a violinist, and an electric guitar player. Every summer The Court was treated to a new style of music. It all felt very Bohemian listening to their music drift down our street while we sat on our porch and sipped wine. I guess I should be thankful they were all talented. Had they all been musical hacks with no talent, it would have been like nails on a chalkboard.

The porch began to develop mystical properties, drawing everyone who walked past up to its steps to stop, chat, have a glass of wine, gossip, and confess sins – you name it, it happened on the porch. People from the street could not walk by without stopping for a minute or an hour or an evening. On those occasions when it turned into an evening, a call to Milano's Pizza would supply the food. But the porch was strictly BYOB unless I was up to making a batch of margaritas or Ken made cosmos. In the summer a couple of pitchers of white Sangria could magically appear. Now that's a party!

During the summer, Friday and Saturday nights became a kind of impromptu celebration. We didn't need much of a reason to celebrate on The Court. A soccer win, a good day in the office, someone mowing the grass, someone walking the dog – you name it, we would celebrate it. In fact, you had to be careful when you left the porch because you might lose your seat. What would start as a couple of drop-ins often turned into fifteen or more people sitting on our steps and porch railing. Several bottles of wine would evaporate throughout the evening. Adults, kids, and pets – all were welcome. We didn't even have to be home for the porch to be used by our neighbors.

Ken's Mom would occasionally come down off "Walton's Mountain" and spend the night with us in Morristown. We would sit on the porch and eat dinner, drink wine, and have a wonderful evening. She loves in-town living and sitting on the porch gave her a chance to catch up with our neighbors. The mystical properties of the porch, assisted by two or three glasses of wine, would lead to fascinating conversations.

As we get older, the appropriateness barrier that exists between parent and child begins to crumble. It's subtle at first. It usually happens around the first funeral you attend as an adult. Your Mom drops a bombshell like, "Uncle Frank loved to dress up in women's clothes. It's so nice to see him in a suit for once." At first you're not sure you heard it right and then you realize it is one of those many secrets your parents kept from you as a child. In retrospect, I now realize why we never stayed the night with Uncle Frank. I am sure if Uncle Frank had his way, he would have been buried in a Dior gown and a pair of Jimmy Choo pumps.

Just before my dad's mother passed away she dropped the ultimate family secret. She told Dad that his father, my grandfather, might not really be his father. Dad dropped this tidbit of family drama during a holiday gathering at Thanksgiving or Christmas. He casually mentioned Grandma's deathbed confession as if he were discussing the weather.

My grandmother on my father's side was truly a brilliant woman. After thirty years of marriage and raising kids she decided to sell real estate. In a matter of ten years she became the top realtor in her city. She eventually went on to become a broker and establish her own firm. I have no doubt if she was in the work force today, she would be a CEO.

From the story dad tells, it seems my grandmother was considered a bit of a wild child in her day. She was Scotch-Irish with flaming red hair and a temper to match. She was way ahead of Liz Taylor in the marriage game, having married five times, twice to the same man before Liz made it to her fifth husband. Her third husband, my father's father, Grandpa Ed, had died several years before so she felt free to spill the beans on our lineage.

As the story goes, Bea's second husband, Wayne, did not want to have kids and Bea wanted more children desperately. On top of that, Wayne's father was a doctor and was not happy with his son's choice in a bride. These two tension points finally led to divorce. Just prior to Bea marrying Ed, Wayne called to tell her he was shipping off to the Pacific and begged to see her one last time before he left. It was World War II and most guys weren't sure they'd be returning. Bea met him for one last romantic interlude the day before he shipped out.

Bea then married Ed two weeks later. Nine months after the wedding Jack, my father was born. Bea wasn't sure if Dad was Ed's child or Wayne's but at this particular point in time, she was convinced that her son was Wayne's. At first Dad thought it was just a bit of a fantasy, as Grandma was in and out of lucidity during her final days at the rehab center. On one of her more lucid days she insisted that Dad look for a picture of Wayne she had kept all these years in her "panty drawer." I can only imagine what was going through my father's mind while he dug through his seventy-nine year old mother's unmentionables. Working his way through orthopedic support hose and granny panties, lo and behold, there was a picture in that drawer. Dad said his heart skipped a beat when he looked at the picture. Wayne had the same physical defect I had when I was born. The cartilage in our ears was malformed causing our ears to stick out like two open car doors. Mine were surgically corrected when I was five. Wayne's never were. When he went back to the hospital, Bea could tell by the look in Dad's eyes that he had found the picture.

All she did was smile and say, "I told you I wasn't making it up, Jacky"

"You know, Wayne got to see you once when he was on leave. I was pushing you in a stroller when I ran into him on the street. He took one look at you and said, 'That's my son. That's my boy, Bea! When I get back from the Pacific, you're going to leave Ed and marry me!'"

Bea continued the story. "But he never made it home....he died in the Bataan Death March. I've always missed him. He was the love of my life, Jacky. He's still waiting for me. I saw him in my bedroom the night before I went to the hospital. He said he would see me soon."

I had to choke back tears as I finished my wine. At the end of this story I asked my sister-in-law for a refill. I was girding myself for potential additional revelations.

I tell this story to set the stage for another conversation that took place on our porch, specifically, a conversation with my mother-in-law.

I am not really a people person and I am the last person you'd want to ask for advice, as I will tell you straight out what I am thinking. No sugar coating. For some reason, everyone I meet seems comfortable in telling me their most intimate thoughts and asking for my opinion.

This mystifies Ken. "I have no idea why people feel the need to seek your opinion or approval. You are not nice about it, you tell them things they don't want to hear and they still want to be around you. Hell, you don't even like people!" He said he wanted to submit a request to Johns Hopkins' Division of Social and Behavioral Sciences to do a case study on this phenomenon.

One evening, my mother-in-law dropped in for dinner and beat Ken to the house by an hour. We opened a bottle of wine and were working our way through said bottle while enjoying the spring evening. Sally is a brilliant woman who has overcome major obstacles in her life to become a successful executive. Her one unresolved issue is her track record with men. Sally likes bad boys. She likes a guy who has a bit of an edge to him. This has led to some poor choices over the years.

One of these questionable choices was a Tom Selleck wannabe whose hairstyle and mustache never left the 80's. First time I met him was at some family social event. When I saw him talking to my brother-in-law, I turned and asked, "Ken, who is that asshole?"

Ken grabbed my arm and quickly escorted me to the other side of the room. In a harsh whisper he said, "That's my mom's husband!"

Sally, currently in one of those on again, off again relationships, had decided it was time to talk to me about her men issues. After three glasses of wine she began expressing frustration over the current contestant on her version of "The Dating Game." It seems their relationship started out hot but had cooled somewhat and Sally wasn't sure what to do to spice things up. My mind was doing somersaults. Where in the world was she taking this conversation?

Sally is a very direct woman. She put it all out on the table. "You know, Trent, I thought all men liked a good blow job. I mean, what's not to like? We do all the work and they just lie there."

I was doing my best to keep my brain from jolting into an epileptic seizure. The idea of discussing, in intricate detail, the proper way to give a BJ is not a conversation I was prepared to have with my mother-in-law (especially since all I could think about was her asking me to peel a banana and demonstrate.) I am rarely at a loss for words, but this one caught me by surprise. In a single, long swig, I gulped downed the remainder of my glass of wine knowing that when I hit the bottom I was going to have to answer her question. I looked at her and said, "Sally, my perspective is a bit different than yours. We know what we like so it is easy to reciprocate." Oh my God! I did not just say that to my mother-in-law!

She didn't miss a beat and said, "I never thought about it before, but you guys have a distinct advantage." This conversation was NOT happening.

I found myself continuing, I couldn't help myself, "In my experience, most men enjoy a great blow job. Maybe you're just out of practice," I said. I was going to burn.

Sally tilted her head and with a wicked sparkle in her eye, said, "I would say it's like riding a bike. You never forget how to give good head, but the analogy of riding a bike takes us to an entirely different conversation."

The hell with wine, if we were going to continue this conversation I needed a shot of Patron. The "Golden Girls" had their cheesecake; I have my Patron! Viva La Golden Girls – and Viva La Me for not buying any phallic shaped produce this week.

So a shot or two of Patron later, the two of us dove into the topic of copulation.

Sally said, "I just miss having a man next to me at night. I hate sleeping alone."

Whew, this was better. We were talking about a sleeping companion.

"There are some mornings you just want to wake up to a big hunky man climbing on top of you, you know what I mean?" she asked. Okay, not a sleeping companion.

All I could say was, "Amen, sister," and offer a toast. Now that the Patron had kicked in, and all barriers to appropriate conversation had fallen, She said, "I love morning sex. It's a huge turn on." With a glint in my eye I looked at her and said, "that's why I keep breath mints in the night stand." We clinked our glasses and through back a shot. L'Caim! Now I knew for sure I was going to burn. I'm not Catholic, but I made a mental note to go to confession.

"Have you ever considered reading some trashy romance novels?" I asked. "You could live vicariously through the characters in those books."

Sally looked at me incredulously and said, "If I ain't gettin it, I ain't readin' about it!" I truly love my mother-in-law.

Ken pulled into the driveway a few seconds later, as he walked up the steps he took one look at us—two totally inebriated adults—and walked into the house. I heard the words, "I don't want to know" as he walked by. Truer words have never been spoken.

This porch of ours had a therapeutic effect on folks who came by and indulged in one glass of wine or four. I kept telling myself it was the porch and not the wine. Ken and I found ourselves being therapists for the street...drug abuse, infidelity, alcoholism, rogue children, money issues, crazy ex-spouses, remodeling stress—you name it, we tackled it on the porch. It was Dr. Phil meets Oprah meets Jerry Springer, all wrapped up in a quaint setting on The Court.

At the same time that Ken's back began to seriously fail, Karla's husband Rich began to struggle with serious intestinal issues that were totally debilitating. In addition, Rich was developing excruciating blood clots in his legs. Karla and I spent a lot of time on that porch discussing the stress of being a caregiver, chief cook and bottle washer, laundress, and breadwinner.

During the worst period of Ken's back failure, we were forced to live out of our basement. It was semi-finished and had a bathroom, entertainment center, refrigerator and microwave. Since Ken couldn't handle the stairs very well, the basement was the only place that had all the things he would need on one floor. This meant I ran the stairs morning and night. Take dinner down, bring the dishes back up. Bring the dirty clothes down, take the clean ones up. Bring the vacuum down, carry it back up. You get the picture. Though it was a nice basement, it was like living in a *Hobbit Hole*, but less charming. We couldn't wait to move up into the light.

Thank God Heather, in between her painting jobs, would drop by to see Ken for an occasional game of cards and idle chit chat or he would have been alone in that basement 10 hours a day. She was a God send.

Recovery after his third surgery was going really well when tragedy struck. During a physical therapy session at the rehab center, the exercise ball the therapist was using exploded while Ken was sitting on it, dropping him straight to the floor. With no ability to catch himself, he landed full force on his surgical site. The staff called an ambulance and he was immediately rushed to the hospital. I received a frantic call from his therapist and left the office immediately to drive straight to the hospital. Over the years I have spent many a night in the emergency room with Ken, so it's a familiar place. I have become an expert at wrangling the ER staff to get things done.

I pity the patients who don't have a family or friend to be an advocate for them while in a hospital. I realize ER staffs deal with extremes and if your case is not life threatening you're not the top priority. I have met some true heroes in this profession - brilliant men and women who truly make a difference, putting the patient above all else. But there are some that become desensitized to patient complaints and demands. I find these individuals less responsive to a patient's demands than they are to a lucid patient advocate who refuses to be placated until their, or in this case, my demands are met.

Ken's pain was off the chart. Due to the number of painkillers he took to manage his day-to-day pain and the length of time he had been on them, he was resistant to the low doses they were giving him in the ER. Dosages that would put down an elephant have only minor effects on Ken. The pain was so bad he was crying out and tears were streaming down his face as he begged for help. My heart was breaking and I was getting angry. As I was reaching my boiling point, a nurse rounded the corner with an orderly and said, "The doctor is concerned about his heart, so he is sending him for a stress test."

What? A stress test? I looked at her and said, "Are you serious? The man can't stand up. He's in excruciating pain. Are you sure you have the right person?"

She glanced at her chart and said, with attitude, "Yes, sir, I am. And he doesn't have to be able to stand. We can do a stress test by inducing increased heart activity with medication, so will you please move." Her statement was more of an order than a request. MISTAKE!

I am a demanding person in the best of situations. Anyone who knows me knows I expect a lot from myself, and the people around me. In this situation, I became a man on a mission—a general on the field of battle. I looked at little miss know-it-all and said, "You have mistaken me for someone with one brain cell if you think for one minute you're rolling him out of this room for a stress test." I continued, "Have you looked at his vitals? Can't you see that his blood pressure and his current heart rate are exceptionally high? Right now, with the amount of pain he is in, he's a living stress test!" She started to interrupt me and I cut her off. Three and a half years of surgeries, ERs, hospitals and being a primary caretaker had taken its toll. I wasn't interested in what she had to say. "He's in this hospital because a Swiss ball at the rehab center, owned by this hospital, exploded, causing him to drop on the surgical site of his spinal fusion. I am this man's partner and caregiver. Decisions about his healthcare rest with me. So you can take that order back to the doctor who wrote it and tell him to discuss it with me directly or my next call is to a lawyer." I didn't have one in mind, but I was sure I could find a hateful ambulance chaser lurking around the ER.

Nurse Nan was shell-shocked. She looked at her order, then at me, then at her order. I can only assume that she decided that facing the ER doctor who ordered the test was easier then dealing with me. When the ER doctor stormed into our room he took one look into my crazed eyes and rethought his strategy. He started with, "Mr. Pines, I don't think you understand how serious your partner's condition may be."

Really? Ken had had five surgeries in two years. His latest spinal fusion had taken place just six weeks ago. He had just fallen, dead weight, on his tailbone causing an untold amount of trauma to the surgical site. I think I understood more than the doctor did how serious this might be. I took a breath and said, "Dr. John, I want you to listen carefully to what I have to say. I want you to hear every word. When I finish, feel free to tell me I don't understand."

The doctor took a breath, and with great reluctance said, "Okay." I walked the ER doctor through the events that led to our arrival at the ER. As I spoke, I watched the color drain from his face. When I finished, he said, "Oh my God, he needs an MRI, not a stress test! Why does it say on his chart that he was having cardiac issues?"

"It's the pain," I said. "His pain caused his heart rate to go up, and he was experiencing chest pain. My guess is that the hand-off from the EMS team was not as informative as it should've been." After several apologies, Ken was rushed off for an MRI.

It was 11:30 PM when I left Ken in his room at the hospital in a comfortable drug induced haze. Eight hours of outrageous stress had left me drained. I was sitting on the porch drinking an obnoxiously large glass of wine when I saw Karla returning from her nightly walk with Buddy. Buddy is one of the most lovable but odd-looking dogs I have ever met. He was rescued off the streets of Manhattan and quickly took to the streets of Morristown. He is a lovable goofball and a perfect dog for the Tranfield's.

Karla looked at me, then at my glass of wine, and said, "Why didn't you just stick a straw in the bottle?"

I glared back at her and said, "Are you judging me?"

She laughed and said, "Hell, no, I'm jealous. Do you have a similar size glass you can share with me?"

"I don't know, but I am sure I have a chilled bottle and a straw." I brought out Karla's mega glass and settled back in my seat.

Karla looked at me again and said, "Sweetie, you look like shit. What's going on?"

Karla had just been through her own scare with Rich. Rich had developed a propensity for blood clots in his legs. Add this to his intestinal issues, and she had been having a rough time herself. At one point Rich was hospitalized on Long Island with a dangerous clot and it had taken Karla ten hours to get there.

I took her through my day, blow by blow.

At the end of my story she looked at me, lifted her glass and said, "We live to fight another day!"

I clinked her glass and said, "Here's to surviving the ER and not needing to call you for bail money."

She didn't know how close I came to being detained by hospital security. As we were gulping our wine, we both noticed that Buddy had moved from the porch to the front yard and had spread himself out on the lawn. He had decided the grass was more comfortable than the slate on the porch – bless his canine heart.

As Karla and I watched, Buddy rolled over onto his back with all four paws in the air. He lay there for a couple of minutes as if he was looking at the stars. Then for no apparent reason he began rolling back and forth in the grass while issuing gruff happy sounds.

"Karla, why is your dog rolling around like that in the grass?"

"How the hell should I know? But it seems to make him really happy." Karla turned and looked at me and said, "You know what we need to do?"

"Yes. Win the lotto, move to Aruba and open a flip-flop shack on the beach."

She slapped me on the back of the head, "No! We need to roll in the grass with Buddy!"

I looked at Karla like she had just been released from the mental ward at Bellevue. "What? Why in the world would I roll in the grass with the dog?"

"It seems to make him happy," she said, "so let's give it a try."

Karla put down her glass of wine, jumped up out of her chair, made me put down my glass of wine, grabbed my arm and dragged me down the front steps and onto the front yard.

"Karla, this is ridiculous!"

"DO IT! I am not taking no for an answer."

So we both stretched out on the grass with the dog. Buddy saw this as play time and started jumping and rolling all over us, which in turn caused us to roll in the grass. I started to giggle. Buddy just wouldn't be denied. The more I rolled around in the grass the harder I laughed. The harder I laughed, the harder Karla laughed. We were giggling and laughing so hard, lights began to come on in homes across the street.

Realizing we were waking the neighbors, Karla, Buddy and I ran around to the back yard while giggling like schoolgirls. The three of us sat down in the grass, laid back and looked at the full moon.

I heard Karla say, "Feel better?"

"Yeah, I do." I had just learned a lesson from a dog. Buddy taught me that no matter how bad it gets, you need to take a moment, forget yourself, and roll in the grass for a few minutes. Just let it go. It will all be there when you come back to face it. But in that moment, you gain the clarity and strength to move forward. Pretty heavy stuff coming from a stray mutt.

Tomorrow was another day. After my roll in the yard with Buddy and Karla, my head was clear, and I was able to focus on getting Ken back home, safe and sound.

"SECRET SQUIRREL"

"A squirrel is just a rat in a cuter outfit."

- Sarah Jessica Parker

Squirrels have a long and dubious history on The Court. The in-town areas of Morristown are heavily wooded, making it a squirrel's paradise. New York City subways have jumbo sized sewer rats; we have squirrels. Squirrels seem relatively harmless until you get an infestation in your attic. Once they get in, getting rid of them and keeping them out is a considerable challenge.

One fine spring day, our neighbor Jim discovered that a squirrel contingent had taken up residence in his attic. Fully aware of his status at the top of the food chain, Jim had few qualms about employing every anti-squirrel weapon in Morristown Lumber's arsenal. However, he didn't realize he would have to answer to 9-year-old Erin. One afternoon after a particularly successful live-trap haul, Erin wandered over from playing in the cul-de-sac and discovered that Jim had imprisoned a baby squirrel. A true naturalist (unless one considers spiders to be part of nature), Erin did not embrace the nuclear anti-squirrel options that Jim was considering. Erin made it quite clear that euthanasia was NOT an option and that she would be checking his progress frequently and randomly.

Jim survived the infestation and Erin's scrutiny by developing a special trap and release system to remove the squirrels from The Court. He'd trap them at his house and release them at a local park. That worked fine for a while, but eventually it seemed as if every time Jim relocated a squirrel a new one would take its place. Several weeks later, Heather and Karla were standing at the corner bus stop next to the Red Cross building when a man parked a car and exited carrying a rodent cage. Typically Heather spent her time at the bus stop futilely attempting to caffeinate herself into a new day while Karla stood guard in her most shapeless and dowdy office wear, tapping her foot with impatience. Karla is always tapping her foot with impatience or twiddling her thumbs; her signature moves.

The girls seldom took interest in the morning arrivals at the Red Cross office. However, a man carrying a rodent cage was new and exciting stuff for the bus stop crowd. Heather inquired about the cage only to discover that, unbeknownst to Jim, this Red Cross employee was trapping squirrels at his home and releasing them on Altamont Court. No matter how many squirrels Jim caught, he could not keep up with the number being released. This resulted in an uncomfortable conversation between Jim and the Red Cross employee.

The most annoying part of having a large contingency of squirrels on The Court was their screeching during mating season. Get a half dozen of those furry rodents wound up and it sounded like a group of high school girls screaming at a Justin Bieber concert. The noise they make is just awful. Every once in a while we would get a power outage caused by a quarreling, toasted squirrel in the middle of what I can only imagine was their mating ritual.

Pat and George, our driveway-sharing neighbors, were always fighting to keep the critters out of their flowerbeds. They had created a picture-perfect yard. Their house was a cottage cape with a picket fence and arbor, beautiful pavers leading to their front door and a backyard right out of Architectural Digest. They worked each and every weekend to keep it looking that way. When you walked by on Saturday, the two of them would be working on the lawn and beds, looking like they had just stepped out of an LL Bean catalog. No matter how long or hard they worked, they never looked messy. George still had creases in his slacks and not a hair was out of place on Pat's perfectly highlighted head. At the end of the day they looked as good as when they started. How was that possible? I wondered whether either of them had sweat glands.

I pride myself on the beauty of my landscaping, but when I work as hard on my lawn as they do, I am soaked with sweat and covered head to toe in dirt and lawn clippings. I think George and Pat just piddle around the yard for show and a secret stealth group of woodland elves show up in the middle of the night and tend their estate. That's the only possible answer because their lawn always looked tidy and neat, even during the summer when they spend their weekends at the shore. Someone else must have been doing the heavy lifting.

During one of these trips to the shore, Pat and George experienced a home intrusion. Not a typical home intrusion, but one involving a furry, four-footed thief who managed to get into the house through the vent screen on top of the chimney. The intruder couldn't get out the way he came in and he was not big enough to set off the alarm. The squirrel was trapped for the weekend.

So, if you were a squirrel trapped in a house with no way out, what would you do? You'd go squirrely! Which is exactly what happened. That squirrel got into every crack of the house looking for a way out. It chewed and tore at the window casings, hoping the invisible barrier to the world outside would fall. It foraged for food and water, tearing into cereal boxes and spreading the contents all over the kitchen.

With the inside of their house as neat and tidy as their lawn, our two picture-perfect neighbors were in for a shock when they got home. Ken and I were walking back from town and saw George and Pat's car in the driveway. "Looks like George and Pat came back early from the shore," I said. As we walked in front of their house we saw a woman who looked like Pat running around the living room wielding a broom like a samurai sword. She was swinging hard and fast. Her eyes were wide and her coifed blond hair was standing on end. Then we saw George enter the same room with another broom, swinging just as wild and fast. We were watching all this unfold in the front bay window as if it were a live action diorama. I turned to Ken and said, "It looks like they are playing indoor field hockey with brooms."

Ken just gave me that patronizing look we reserve for toddlers and the elderly and said, "Really?"

Knowing that Pat and George were not indoor field hockey enthusiasts, Ken and I went around back to see what was going on. As we rounded the corner to their back door, a half crazed screaming squirrel shot out of the house right between the two of us with Pat and George hot on its tail - literally.

Never during our five years on The Court have I seen Pat and George so winded and disheveled. I looked at Pat and said, "Rough day?" She blew the hair out of her eyes and said, "You have no idea," turned on her heel and went back inside.

Pat had the house fumigated, rugs and furniture steam cleaned and a chimney specialist properly seal the chimney cap. She was not going through this again – or at least that's what she thought. While shopping for a twenty-five pound bag of cat food for our herd of kitties, I came across a life size squirrel toy for a dog. It was truly life like. I knew it was evil but I couldn't help myself. I bought the damn thing on the spot and when I got home I asked Heather, their daughter and painter extraordinaire, to let me into her mother's house. I placed that stuffed toy squirrel in their bay window, face pressed against the glass as if it was trying to escape the house. When Pat and George got back from the shore I heard Pat's scream from the driveway. It took months for her to forgive me, but it was worth it.

Every time I think of Pat and George playing field hockey with that squirrel, the words to a Ray Stevens song come to mind:

"The day the squirrel went berserk in the First Self-Righteous Church in the sleepy little town of Pascagoula, it was a fight for survival that broke out in revival. They were jumping pews and shouting Hallelujah"
– Ray Stevens

THE PERFECT DRESS

"It's better to look good than to feel good"

– Billy Crystal as Fernando, *Saturday Night Live*

"Well, one does need a hint of color."

- Nathan Lane, *The Birdcage*

Girls are fun to dress. The options are unlimited. Guys have a fairly finite set of wardrobe options. Getting dressed up for a guy is putting on a suit or tux. He might add a watch, cufflinks, a great tie and shoes, but then he's done. On the other hand, women have shoes, dresses, shoes, earrings, shoes, purses, shoes, clutches, shoes, necklaces, shoes, bracelets, shoes.....you get the picture. When Ken came into my life he brought with him two beautiful young daughters, Ashleigh and Lindsay. It was a dream come true. I now had two daughters and I never had to change a single diaper.

Lindsay was four and Ashleigh eight. Dressing them became an obsession.

I learned a lot about women's clothing from dressing these two young ladies. First, know your colors. The wrong color can be deadly. A dress or suit could fit you like it was tailor made, but if it's the wrong color it will make you look washed out or anemic or ashy (ashy is another term for gray and no one wants to look gray). No matter how good the fit, you'll look awful in it. Know if you look better in earth tones or jewel tones or pastels (personally I hate pastels and I don't think anyone looks good in them – but to each her own) and stick to the palette of colors that works for you. The right color can do wonders for your look. The wrong color is down-right tragic.

Second, ladies, stop looking at the numbers. Whether you are a 0, 2 or 4 or a 10, 12 or 14, make sure you have the right fit. There is nothing worse for a woman than to pick out a dress that is two sizes too small just because she has always been a size 4 and now refuses to admit she's an 8. If you're an 8, wear an 8. If your top's a size 10 and your bottom's a 6, buy separates. There are many women's designers who produce beautiful formal wear in separates. What is most important is the fit. Just because the fabric has some give doesn't mean you should fill it out like you're wearing sausage casing. You'll spend your entire evening with your dress puckering all over your body. With the amount of pulling and tugging you will be doing to smooth said puckers you will look like you have fleas – or worse...you may start showing a dredgie (that's a dress wedgie).

Puckering, tugging and pulling are all very unattractive. You're better off buying the next size up and having it altered by a seamstress. This will make your clothes fit like they were made for you. It's the closest most of us will ever come to having something custom made. Custom altered, off-the-rack clothing can be extremely flattering.

My dear friend Susan at Neiman's in The Mall at Short Hills will tell you I have sold more than one dress to her clients by simply stating the obvious. I told one customer, "Try the 6 and have it fitted to your frame."

She said harshly, "But I am a size 4!"

I looked her straight in the eye and said, "Not in that dress." I'm so tactful. As I walked over to the rack and picked up a 6, I continued, "That 4 is puckering. It draws attention to the wrong areas and you are not going to be comfortable in it." I held out the 6 and said, "Try the six. Trust me, you will be much happier with the way it looks." She blinked a couple of times and then, hesitantly, took the 6 from my hand.

I winked at her and said, "Good for you, sister!"

She smiled, giggled a bit and went to the dressing room. When she came out of the dressing room she looked stunning. She was so happy she was bouncing up and down when she asked Susan to call the tailor. The sleeves needed a little work. To look good, you have to feel good, no matter what Billy Crystal says.

The same can be said for men. Age appropriate, fitted clothing looks far better than stuffing your fifty-year-old saggy ass into a spandex-like fabric with your shirt open to your navel. Once you pass forty, this needs to stop. For some of us, it should have stopped in our late twenties. Just because a Dolce and Gabanna model looks stunning in an outfit does not mean you can pull it off; only one percent of the population can pull off that look and most guys who wear this stuff are not in the one percent.

This brings me to complimenting your significant other (from this point on we will call him or her your SO). Here are a few helpful hits on how to answer that all important question, "How do I look?" When your wife, girlfriend, boyfriend, husband or SO asks you how they look, you're already in trouble. The most important person in your life should not have to ask you how they look after spending two hours getting ready for dinner. They should feel like the most beautiful person in the world when they are in your presence and if they don't, then shame on you for not telling them often enough.

Should you make the mistake of not complimenting your SO before they ask; don't double down and add fuel to the fire by verbalizing the ultimate insult, "You look fine." This kind of lackluster compliment is like bringing a ham to a Hanukkah celebration. "Honey, you look fine," translates to: 'You look boring and unattractive and I wish I didn't have to be seen with you in public.' The next step up from "You look fine" is "You look great." This will keep you from getting castigated by your SO, but it won't win you any points. Your SO believes he or she looks great, given the effort they've put into it, so you need to deliver more.

Lets start with multisyllabic words. Fabulous, fantastic and phenomenal all work. When your SO walks into the room, the following statement will make you a superstar: "WOW, Honey, you look fantastic!" If you miss your cue, you can recover with, "Honey, you always look great, but tonight you look phenomenal." Straight men, stay away from the word "fierce"; it won't work for you. If you tell your woman her shoes are fierce, she is going to wonder if you have switched teams.

Another key to winning your SO's heart is complimenting a body part, especially their ass. There is not a man or woman alive that doesn't like to be told they have a fine ass. Make sure you compliment the body part first: "Baby, you have a fine ass, but I have to tell you, in those jeans it's just sexy as hell," or "Damn, baby, your ass makes that dress sexy," or "Those shoes make your legs look sooooo hot!" Saying that a dress, suit or pair of jeans makes your SO look fantastic will put you in good standing, but stating they already have a great body and that a new piece of clothing really shows it off, my friends, is priceless and will most certainly get you laid.

I have been a Neiman Marcus shopper for years. Their sales are amazing. My fondness for Neiman's increased when I realized I could get designer girls dresses during Last Call at bargain basement prices. Seriously, I once paid twenty dollars for a children's Nicole Miller dress for Lindsay. When our daughters were young and came to spend the summers with us in Atlanta, I would do a little shopping beforehand so they had fabulous clothes to wear when we went out for dinner. To mark the end of the summer holiday we would go shopping to select stunning outfits they would wear to a Broadway tour show at the fabulous Fox Theater. They turned heads no matter where we went. This was always the highlight of the summer. Yes, I am one of those God-awful parents who believe I have the most beautiful daughters in the world.

Ashleigh's birthday is in July so was easy to celebrate during their visit. On her thirteenth birthday Ken planned a daddy/

daughter date night that included dinner and a show at The Fox. Naturally, that called for a new dress, so off to the mall we went. We found her a great little black dress that made her look amazing. While shopping, we came across a dress that Ash fell in love with but I knew would never pass her father's threshold of acceptance. The price of this dress had been slashed by eighty percent so I bought it for her anyway. This dress was made of a black and silver spandex material, which clung to her body. It was a strapless, form-fitting, mermaid design. Ashleigh had developed curves since the previous summer which neither Ken nor I had noticed. When she walked out of the dressing room in this body hugging dress I literally fell off my chair. She looked stunning. Thirteen-year-old daughters are not supposed to look stunning; they are supposed to be cute, even pretty, but not stunning.

I was going to have some fun with this at Ken's expense. I could not wait to see his reaction when she modeled the gown. I knew when Ken saw her dress I would need to be ready with the defibrillator paddles. When we go home Ashleigh wanted to do a fashion show for her daddy. The girls made this a summer tradition. Every time they got new outfits, Ken and I would sit on the front porch allowing the girls to make an entrance from the house to model their clothes. The porch became their runway. When Ashleigh walked out in her mermaid dress, Ken's jaw dropped, his eyes bulged and he just stared at her. He truly could not find words. He was in complete denial that his baby had grown up.

After staring at his daughter and stuttering through a compliment, his eyes narrowed at me and he said, "You better be sleeping with one eye open tonight."

After I told him that the dress was just for fun and not for their night out, he let out a huge sigh and told her again, without the stutter, how pretty she looked. Ashleigh giggled and ran in to change into her date-night dress. Ken, with tears in his eyes said, "How could you do that to me? I am not ready to admit my babies are growing up. I nearly had a heart attack! When did she develop curves?" Thus my need for defibrillator paddles.

Lindsay and I gave him a second heart attack on her thirteenth birthday when we picked out a rhinestone studded, satin and lace bustier "Stevie Nicks" knock-off handkerchief dress. He refuses to talk about that one.

As the token gays on The Court we were crowned the defacto fashion gurus. I'm sure I should say something about how offended we were for being grossly stereotyped as "Gay Fashionistas", but we loved it! (and who doesn't love a crown to go along with such a fierce title?)

The first challenge we were presented with was Jane's wedding dress. Karla recruited us for this very important and personal task for her best friend. Jane was getting married on a beach and wanted something formal that would work on a beach in bare feet. Ken and I hit the ever fabulous and never outdone Mall at Short Hills, where we did a stealth pre-selection run, narrowing our choices down to three dresses. Jane has substantial cleavage, a small waist, and spectacular red hair, making dress selection a real challenge. The dress we finally decided on was an off-white formal number that showed off her best assets but had a fun, frivolous air about it. She looked and felt great. The dress was a hit.

This solidified our position as fashion experts on The Court. Our next challenge came when Karla and Heather asked us to go shopping for formals for the gala at the social club. Karla and Heather are the T-Shirt and sneakers type who are most comfortable in a gym or hanging out in the backyard. They also put us on a strict budget, thus increasing the complexity of the challenge. Karla was offering us dinner and martinis at Legal Seafood, one of the nicest restaurants at this posh mall, so there was no turning them down. Offer a couple of martinis to a queen and you seal the deal.

Our first stop was an eye-opening experience for all involved. Ken and I were pulling multiple dresses and sending them back for the girls to try on. Ken was determined to get Heather out of her "Eldin the Painter" drag and into something stunningly feminine. I was hell bent on getting Karla into a dress. Any dress. The girls, laughing hysterically, would parade out and model them for our critique. These two ladies had completely different body types. Karla had no boobs and Heather was all boobs.

Everything Karla tried on looked like the top half of the dress had been deflated. I started pulling at the back of the dresses, trying to get the top parts to work. Finally she grabbed me by the shirt and said, "Bitch, how many times do I have to tell you I have no boobs?" She leaned forward and the entire front of her dressed just dropped open. I was staring at what looked like a training bra. She wasn't kidding. No boobs. We were going to need something with spandex in it.

On the other hand, Heather was spilling out of her dresses. Heather's "girls" were so cinched up she had more cleavage showing than our three hundred pound plumber. Heather and Karla were good sports and tried on everything we threw at them, even when we gave Karla a dress that made her look like a kielbasa and asked Heather to try on a solid bead dress with enough crisscrossing straps you could play tic-tac-toe across her back. While sitting in the waiting area we could hear the two of them arguing about which way the straps were supposed to be positioned.

"Under my arm?" asked Heather. "If I put this one under my arm, it's going to cut across my boob and my nipple is going to pop out!"

"I don't see where else it could go unless we pull it over your head and put it on the other side," Karla said.

"Ouch, bitch, you just pinched my boob," said Heather.

"Oh, shut up and deal with it. At least you have boobs!" I should have had a martini before we started this little adventure.

When Heather came out of the dressing room, the dress covered her body like a papier mâché school project. As she stood there I could hear beads falling off the dress and bouncing on the floor.

"That's it!" I said. "We are heading to see Susan at Neiman's. This sales rack shit ain't cutting it." I was done dealing with budget friendly department stores. I needed to get back to my mother ship.

Before we continued the painful process of dress selection, we stopped for a midday cocktail to ease the stress. After proper lubrication, we headed down to Neiman's. We were there all of fifteen minutes before we found two absolutely perfect dresses. The first dress we found was for Heather. It was a muted snake print chiffon with just the right amount of cleavage, had a slit up her long leg and gave her a fabulous waistline. We all agreed; this was her dress. With Heather all set, it was Karla's turn. When she walked out in a beautiful blue and white chiffon bias cut print, I was stunned. She looked fantastic. In fact, Karla had never looked so feminine.

I said, "Oh my god, Karla, you look like a woman."

She glared at me, "Thanks, Shania Twain."

"You're thinking, 'Man, I feel like a woman'," I replied.

"You took the words right out of my mouth!"

This bitch needed food.

When Karla looked at the price tag, she gasped, "Trent Pines, I have never, nor will I ever spend four hundred dollars on a dress."

"Sweetie, you look amazing. It is worth every penny. Be thankful I didn't pull out a pair of Jimmy Choo's to go with it."

"Not happening!" she said.

God give me strength. We were in our fourth hour and she was wearing the gay right out of me.

"Fine! We have one last place to try and them I am done. You can wear a potato sack to the spring gala."

"At least it won't cost four hundred dollars."

Someday I was going to make her eat those words.

One last dress shop was all we had left. We were out of options and had one last place to strike pay dirt. After four hours of shopping we found Karlas dress at Caché on a sales rack in three minutes. I wanted to slap that smug I told you so look right off her face. It was a boring black cocktail dress that I grudgingly admitted looked good on her. More importantly, it didnt require too much padding to make it appear as if she had boobs.

It was time for cocktails. Legal Seafood was calling. Three martinis and a bowl of clam chowder and everything was right with the world. Bless our hearts.

GIRLS GONE WILD WEEKEND HIGH SCHOOL REUNION

"While watching that movie with Trent, he said to me,
'Laura, I would never ask a woman to do that to me!'"

– Laura Byrne Klebosky, high school friend

It was early spring when I got a call from Linda, my closest friend from high school. Linda and I grew up together, crying and laughing our way through junior high and high school. She was my sister in every sense of the word. We lived across the street from each other so we walked to the bus stop every day, hung out on weekends and played in the band together. Hell, just like Mickey and Judy, we even put on a show one summer for our families at our block party. Every song was lip-synched but we had fabulous choreography. We shared everything with each other, well almost everything. I kept that one little detail about my sexuality to myself for far too long and before the weekend was over, she was unexpectedly going to make me pay for that.

Linda and five of her girlfriends, each a close friend of mine, get together every five years for a "Girls Gone Wild Weekend" to celebrate their milestone birthdays. They had been to Vegas as well as other locations across the US and were planning their next adventure. Linda called to inform me they had agreed on NYC to celebrate their 45th birthdays and would be staying with Ken and me for the week. Linda and her family had just spent spring break with us so she knew the train station was within walking distance of the house. NYC was only fifty-five minutes train ride away.

Linda said, "We have all been talking and decided we are staying with you. I hope you don't mind." She then added, "We've all missed you and it would be great to get some quality time together after all these years."

I am such a sucker. There was no way I would decline their self-invitation. I just had to break it to Ken.

Ken is a far more gracious host than I and couldn't wait for them to arrive. He'd heard me talk about these special ladies on several occasions and was eager to meet them. I believed he had alternative motives for being so wonderfully accommodating. Ken was looking for high school "dirt" on me and he figured our guests would know where all my skeletons were buried. Ken was convinced I had a deep, dark, sordid past and these ladies would provide a glimpse into my previous life. Ken was right, of course. I do have a deep, dark, sordid past, but it didn't happen till after I graduated from college.

So Linda, Laura, Tracey, Anita and Sue came to stay with us in Morristown and made us honorary Girls Gone Wild Weekend members. Being queens, our honorary status seemed appropriate. In fact, Ken extracted a promise that we could be honorary girls gone wild members for future trips. In return, they'd become honorary Altamont Court Girls.

Now that I had all these high school darlings descending on our home, I had to come up with a plan for the week. Living so close to NYC, our activities would include lots of trips into the city, but I wanted to plan a special night to celebrate our birthdays that included a Broadway show.

Our long weekend together was going really well. The Ladies were enjoying NYC and we were enjoying our evenings together. On Saturday we all headed into the city for dinner and a show. I had secured tickets for us to see *Young Frankenstein*. Andrea Martin and Megan Mullally were still performing. These two ladies are comic geniuses. I knew it would be a riot.

We went into The City early so the ladies could do some shopping near Chinatown. Purses were the name of the game. To get to the really good knock-offs you were shuffled off to back rooms. To see these gems, you had to be escorted. As we were shopping, Ken realized we weren't too far from his stepbrother and sister-in-law's city apartment in Tribeca. He called and learned they were nearby and he agreed we'd meet them at Nancy Whiskey, one of their favorite local haunts.

We got our clan together and started making our way towards the bar. In hindsight, I should have prepared my high school girlfriends for my sister-in-law. As a general rule, I would describe most northeasterners as tough customers. They never mince words, and they let you know exactly how they feel about you whether you ask them or not. More disturbingly, they are not afraid to tell you the most intimate details of their life at the drop of a hat.

To give you an example, I remember sitting next to a woman on the train to New York City whom I'd never met. She decided to share with me how her recent hysterectomy was affecting the quality of her train ride. She said, "Oh my Gawd, this train ride is killing me! I just had a hysterectomy and it feels like my insides are being pulled out with a garden rake."

Oh lord, I thought, *I really don't need to hear this.*

But she continued. "Men are so lucky they don't have this plumbing. At this point I wish I had been born with a penis. Uteruses suck!"

I choked on my Diet Coke. Not uteruses again. I don't want to hear about her uterus! I told her how sorry I was to hear this. Then she decided to tell me about the births of her three ungrateful children and her one hundred and twenty-six hours of combined labor.

Knowing how vivid northeasterners can be and knowing my sister-in-law, I should have prepared my clan for the woman they were about to meet. When Sheryl entered the bar she yelled out, "Well, it's about f&%#ing time we got together! Where the F&#% have you been? The commute in was F#$%ing horrible due to all the F#$%ing assholes on the turnpike. Some people shouldn't be allowed to F#$%ing procreate! What a bunch of F#$%tards!" She took a slight pause and said, "So, how ya been?"

CHARMED! My group of girlfriends were shelled shocked. It was like watching an episode of *Mob Wives* without the bleeping.

These ladies aren't faint of heart and their ears aren't virginal, but I don't believe they'd ever heard the F-bomb dropped so frequently inside of ten seconds. Sheryl made Madonna's appearance on David Letterman look like story telling time at the New York City Public Library.

Sheryl is one of those people who is so comfortable in her own skin she doesn't care what you think. Love her or hate her, she is who she is and makes no apologies about it. Hence the reason I love her. You can say that about most New Yorkers. While Linda, Sue, Anita and Tracey decided to "get some air," Laura stayed back at the bar; she was totally fascinated by Sheryl. Laura had been living in Scottsdale, Arizona—aka White Bread Central—for the past decade. But Laura's family was from New Jersey so she thoroughly enjoyed Sheryl's colorful commentary.

Over the next ninety minutes Sheryl told Laura and me about the trials of her treatment for skin cancer. She'd been battling cancer for over a decade and had so many things sliced off for biopsies that she felt like a slab of deli meat.

After a couple of drinks, she said, "Hell, I have to go in for another test next week! The doctor wants to biopsy something on my F#$%ing ass. Not just my ass; my asshole. Jesus, Mary and Joseph, who the F#$% has stuff sliced off their assholes?"

I slammed down my shot of whiskey and asked for another.

Laura was mesmerized. She started asking Sheryl details about her struggle with cancer. Next thing you know Sheryl was telling us about things she'd had removed from her lady parts and she wasn't using lady-like language to describe them. She sounded more like a longshoreman. If I used such language, I would have been arrested for lewd behavior. I started staring at the front entrance and praying that the other ladies would return soon so we could head to dinner.

We said our goodbyes, and as we walked out the door, Laura said, "I had the best time. Your sister-in-law is a trip – I love her!"

I thought to myself, *Yeah, sure, it was good for you, but I am going to need therapy for the next twelve months.*

Now that we had the gang together again, we took the subway to our dinner spot. I like the subway because it's quick, efficient and cost effective. Riding the subway gives you an opportunity to view a wide variety of characters that inhabit the city. Ken hates it. Being a germ-a-phobe, he always looks like he is ready to run to the nearest decontamination center when we come up out of the subway. As soon as we get above ground he starts passing around the hand sanitizer. On the way to our train we saw performing musicians, jugglers, rappers, singers of all kinds. Some are really good and you have to stop, listen, and even throw a few coins in their cases. Some are so bad you can't get away fast enough.

We got out at Columbus Circle and walked up to Isabella's. When I worked in New York and New Jersey twenty years ago, I managed events and knew most of the good restaurants and venues throughout the city. Making reservations for large business parties and hosting these events was part of my job description. My name still pops up on various reservation systems as a "very good customer." Since I was traveling internationally, I asked our friend John, the man who invented Cosmo Fridays, to help me plan the evening. With dinner, the show and dessert, each in different locations, I was afraid I would screw things up trying to arrange everything from an airport in Singapore.

When John first called Isabella's they told him there was 'no room at the inn' and they could not take his reservation. They simply could not accommodate a party of seven at 6:00 PM. John called to give me the bad news. He said, "Trent, they have nothing available at six. Do you want me to try another restaurant?"

I was surprised. I asked John, "Are you serious? What name did you use for the reservation?"

He quickly said, "Mine."

Well, no wonder he couldn't get a reservation. I said, "John, call them back immediately and give them my name, and they will find a reservation."

John called me back ten minutes later and said, "I can't believe it! I gave them your name and a table 'suddenly appeared' – that's discrimination. How can they get away with that?"

I thought, *Oh John, my naive young friend.* I teasingly call John my left-wing, pinko, commie friend because he leans so far left. He's as devoted to NPR for news and commentary as the political right is to Fox News.

"John, money talks," I said. "They saw my name in their booking system so they know how often I've been there and how many people I normally bring. Think of it as a frequent buyer perk."

John said, "Well, it's still wrong!"

I would have laughed but it was 2:00 AM in Singapore. Then it hit me. "Didn't you tell me you were going to be in the city that weekend?"

"Yes," he said.

"Why don't you up the reservation to eight and join us. The girls would love to meet you."

John paused for a moment, then said, "I have always wanted to eat there but I could never get a reservation." This put him on the horns of a dilemma. Should he stand by his convictions and boycott this restaurant that would not accept his reservation, or go and enjoy a great dinner with my friends. He chose the latter.

I said, "You're a traitor to your people."

He laughed and said, "Well, I need to experience the place so I know what I am protesting about."

I laughed. Now that was creative. I called him a traitor one more time and hung up the phone.

John did join us and dinner was a hit. After our wonderful meal we said our goodbyes to John and walked to the theater. Our seats for *Young Frankenstein* were exceptional. There were two stand-out musical numbers that night; Andrea Martin's "He was my boyfriend" and Megan Mullally's "Deep Love." These ladies truly know how to deliver a song and their comedic timing was impeccable. *Young Frankenstein* is not the best musical I have ever seen on Broadway, but it made us laugh out loud. The monster's "Putting on the Ritz" number is a classic. Before we headed to the train station and back to Morristown, we stopped at "Chez Josephine" for dessert. It's one of Ken's and my favorite restaurants, established and run by John Claude Baker, one of Josephine Baker's children. She was a world legendary performer whose amazing career ran from the 1920's through the 1960's.

John Claude, always a consummate host, greeted us at the door. He loves Ken so he was quick to grab him by the arm and escort us to our seats. This is a New Yorker's restaurant, which means the locals eat here several times a month. The atmosphere is spectacular. John Claude used his private collection of his mother's stage and movie poster art as well as paintings from famous artists around the world to decorate the walls. This created a surreal environment that makes patrons feel lost in time. The red walls, tin ceilings, crystal chandeliers, and baby grand piano work to complete this special world he created as a salute to his mother, the queen of a different age. The ladies were duly impressed when John Claude sat down and chit-chatted with us, creating a unique and magical end to our evening.

With our night in New York at an end, we began to make our way back to Penn station. We were enjoying ourselves so much that we'd lost track of the time. Anita was looking at her watch when she asked, "What time did you say the train leaves for Morristown?"

I looked down at my watch. Oh, God! We were going to miss it if we didn't pick up the pace, so we started jogging down Seventh Avenue. If we missed it, we'd have to hang out in Penn Station till 12:30 AM and then change trains in Newark; that was NOT happening. The idea of standing on the Newark train platform at 2:00 AM was not appealing. We raced down the escalators to Track 1 and onto the train thirty seconds before they closed the doors. Exhausted, we collapsed into our seats for the ride home.

On the train ride home, Laura asked if we had ever thought of leaving New Jersey for another part of the country. Let me go on record as saying that I loved living so close to New York City, but the cost of living is murder. I liked my job as well, but I really wanted to work in a different area of the business, expand my knowledge base, and do something new. I told her, "Our preference would be to move back to Atlanta or possibly to Dallas. My company is head-quartered there."

Laura looked at Ken and asked, "I know you love Atlanta, but do you think you would be happy in Dallas?"

Ken replied, "Hell yes, I could DO Dallas."

Laura's eyes shot wide open and she looked over at me. It took me less than a second to know what she was thinking and my eyes opened wide as well. Linda, who misses nothing, immediately looked at both of us and asked, "What was that? What just happened?"

Now everyone was looking at the two of us and asking the same questions.

Laura looked at me and asked, "Should I tell them?"

I said, "What the hell, it happened two decades ago. It's about time we shared that little secret." Everyone was now sitting on the edge of their seats.

My family moved to Texas in the middle of my senior year. I stayed and finished high school, then moved to Texas right after graduation. Laura wanted to take me to dinner as a send-off gift and wish me luck as I started college in my new home state. We had planned to go to the Nationwide building in downtown Columbus, Ohio and have dinner at the restaurant at the top of the building. It had a glass elevator on the outside of the building that went straight to the top where the restaurant was located. We were deep in conversation as we boarded the elevator and pushed the button marked "Restaurant". When it got to the top and stopped the doors didn't open. After ten seconds, the elevator started back down. Being a couple of high school students who were not accustomed to dining in fancy restaurants, we tried this process twice more. Up and then down. Up and then down.

Finally, we stepped out of the elevator and told the guard at the desk, "That elevator is not working. It won't let us off at the restaurant. It just keeps bringing us back down."

With an expression on his face that said, *You two aren't very bright,* he pointed to the sign in front of the elevator that said, "Restaurant Closed for Renovation." So embarrassing.

Laura took over the conversation at this point and told Ken and the girls what happened next. We got in her car and started driving around looking for somewhere to eat. Long before there was GPS, we got our directions backward and ended up on the wrong side of the tracks, so to speak. We were driving past the Westside Drive Inn movie theater, which had fallen on hard times. This theater no longer showed family oriented films; it showed only pornography.

Since we were both over eighteen, I flippantly said, "We could always go to a porn movie to celebrate my last night in town."

We laughed when we saw the title on the marquee: *Debbie Does Dallas.* Since I was moving to Dallas it seemed like an appropriate send-off. Trent and Laura went to their first porn movie.

We had no idea what to expect and were in for the shock of our young lives. First of all, the acting in porn movies is horrible. I know this is a shocking revelation. Only a gay man going to straight porn would notice the acting, but let me assure you it

195

was really, really bad. Second, the two of us were turning every shade of scarlet as we watched people do things with their bodies we didn't think humanly possible. On more than one occasion we yelled, "Oh God, that's disgusting" or "How the hell can she do that standing on her head?" We caught ourselves tilting our heads in the same direction, trying to figure out how the 'actors' were achieving their contorted positions. We thought about leaving, but it was like watching a train wreck; we couldn't take our eyes off it. All I wanted to do after the movie was take a hot shower with Borax and a Brillo pad.

As Laura was telling this story, Ken and our friends were in complete shock. They could not believe we managed to keep this secret for over twenty years. The more we shared, the harder they laughed. As the story reached its climax (pun intended), Laura dropped the line of the evening. She said, "Trent, do you remember what you said to me during the movie?"

I said, "No, I don't. I am still emotionally scarred from watching straight porn."

More laughter.

"You looked at me and said, 'Laura, I would never ask a woman to do something like that to me.'"

This had Ken and my friends rolling in the aisles.

I said to Laura, "And to my credit, I have NEVER asked a woman to do ANY of those things to me!"

We were all laughing so hard we were hyperventilating. The conductor, who lacked a sense of humor, showed up and said, "All right, people, you need to calm down. We do not allow loud drunken behavior on our trains. If you don't calm down I will have to put you off at the next station."

The scary part; we were all sober. More importantly, the next station was Newark and, as I said earlier, I didn't think it was a good idea for us to be stranded in Newark at 2:00 AM. We spent the remainder of the ride whispering and giggling like high school kids on a school bus. The conductor continued to look less than amused.

When we finally got back to the house after our memorable evening in New York, I poured us all a nightcap to toast our fabulous evening. I thought this was the end of our evening. I could not have been more wrong.

THANKS, DAD!
LOVE THE GENES!

"Sweetheart, are you a top or a bottom?"

– Jeffery's Mom, *Jeffery*

We were sitting in the living room winding down and saying good night when Linda turned to me and asked, "So, when did you know? I mean, when did you know you were gay? And why'd it take so long for you to tell us?"

You could have heard a pin drop. Sue had already gone to bed, and Anita and Laura were about to head upstairs. Their forward momentum stopped; they turned around and rushed back to their seats. I had just started to answer Linda's questions when Tracey walked into the room to say good night. She announced to everyone, "I just wanted to thank you and Ken for a great evening and say good...."

Linda immediately said, "Shh! Trent is about to tell us when he 'knew' and why it took so long to tell us."

Tracey promptly sat down and said, "Oh my. Sleep is so overrated. I want to hear this."

One word came to my mind – TRAPPED! I had managed to avoid telling this story for over two decades and now I was cornered with no room to maneuver. I thought, *Am I really going to walk through my painful, crazy, event-filled past, or could I just give them a sugarcoated version and try to skate by?* My mind was racing with trying to find the right words. Suddenly I had an epiphany. My closest friends from high school had invited themselves to our home to stay with us for the week. In their company I was surrounded by love and laughter. I was safe. I owed them the truth.

Let's see, when did I know I was different? I can honestly say it was very early in my life. As Julie Andrew's sang, "Let's start at the very beginning, a very good place to start," that's what I did. I took a couple of deep breaths and told my story.

Anyone who tells you that people aren't born gay and that it's an acquired or learned behavior is truly delusional. I remembered noticing guys when I was five or six years old. Nobody taught me to feel that way and I certainly didn't choose it. When you are that young you don't understand what that attraction means. For me, it was an attraction to the male form. If we were on vacation at the beach, I only noticed the guys. Girls were fun as friends, but I never felt a desire for anything more than *friendship*. It was like the character Greg said in *A Chorus Line* when he was describing his first time with a girl, "And then there was the time I was making out in the back seat with Sally Ketchum. We were necking and I was feeling her boobs and feeling her boobs and after about an hour or so she said, 'Don't you want to feel anything else?' and I thought to myself, *No, I don't!*" I've truly never felt an attraction to women sexually.

I continued. As I approached puberty, sexual feelings started to kick into overdrive and my attraction to men became harder to mask. Teenage hormones are a bitch. My father kept some porn magazines on the top shelf of his closet, which I am sure he would say he bought for the "articles." Who wouldn't want to read political commentary between pictures of women's breasts? When I was alone at home, I couldn't wait to get a look at those magazines. I would pull them down and quickly look through them to find pictures that showed both men and women. I wanted to see the men. I can only admit this in hindsight as I'd convinced myself at the time that I wanted to see both.

I started fooling around with other boys really early, around nine or ten. Just two kids playing doctor. By high school I realized these feelings were something I needed to suppress. I'd been called faggot more than once during my time in high school; if I didn't want to get the crap kicked out of me, I had to keep my head down. This was the Midwest and as white bread as it comes. No one was "out."

During my high school years I stayed on the 'straight' and narrow path. Lots of desire and urges I just kept to myself. The same can be said about college. I went to a Christian university where being gay could get you expelled and I was still fighting with myself over who I was. Society at the time dictated marriage, two and a half children, and a home with a white picket fence as the norm. To be honest, none of that appealed to me.

I struggled to reconcile my biological and emotional desires with my religious beliefs. I've had a strong belief system since I was very young. Choosing a Christian college seemed the right thing to do to help me manage my desires. To say I experienced no sexual encounters in high school or college would be a lie. Over that eight-year period I had more than a couple of experiences. I let my very intense audience know I would not be providing names.

I jokingly received a few, "Aw, you're leaving out the good stuff."

To which I replied, "Outing someone is serious business and something I truly don't agree with. I believe in living an authentic life, but it is a personal choice whether you share that with your friends, family, or co-workers. It is your choice and no one should take that from you. " It sounded a bit high and mighty, but that is what I believe.

I continued my story. I didn't come out in college out of fear of expulsion. I continued to suppress my feelings. The first time I had a conversation about my sexuality was during my junior year in college and it was with my father. I was home over Christmas break and Dad said he wanted to speak to me about something important. We were in the living room and he asked me to "sit down." This seemed ominous. My grades were good so I could not imagine what he wanted to talk about. He started out with general questions. "So how was school this semester? How do you think you did in your classes? Are you dating anyone?"

This had never happened before so I suspected there was something else on his mind. Even his tone was a bit too Spanish Inquisition-like for me. I finally said, "Dad, where are you going with this?"

I guess my tone rubbed him the wrong way because he jumped out of his chair and started pacing. "I want you to know that I know. I know what you are doing at college."

What? What was I doing at college? I wasn't drinking, I wasn't doing drugs, my grades were good. The man wasn't making sense. My father had been an alcoholic for about ten years of my life. He went on and off the wagon more times than I can count. It had been years since he'd had a drink but I was beginning to wonder if he had been hitting the "Jack."

Living with someone who is battling the alcohol demon makes you grow up fast. You either develop a strong backbone or you try and avoid confrontation. My younger brother closed off from all of this. He remembers very little about dad's drinking. What did I do? I grew a brass set of balls during those ten years.

I looked at him and said, "Dad, what do you know? What exactly do you know? I go to a Christian university. I don't drink, I don't do drugs, I haven't smoked pot, hell, we're not even allowed to dance at school as it might encourage lewd behavior, so please, for the love of god, tell me what I am doing that has you so worked up."

Dad said, "I saw the magazines and I KNOW!"

Magazines? I was truly lost. I was clueless. Where was he going with this? I yelled back, "What magazines and what is it you KNOW?"

"Are you denying the magazines are yours?"

I felt like Helen Keller at the water fountain trying to figure out the word water. I was beginning to wonder if my father had suffered a nervous breakdown while I was at school.

"Dad, you are losing it! I have no idea what you are talking about so get to the point. I am tired of being yelled at for something I don't know I did. You're not making any sense!"

He was furious. Finally, after 20 minutes of this dancing around, he said, "When we came out to see you in that musical show, I needed a pair of dark socks. I found gay porn magazines in your sock drawer and I am not paying for you to go to college to major in gay!"

I looked at him like he had three heads. First of all, I hadn't totally admitted to myself I was gay and my father was telling me I had a stack of gay porn magazines in my sock drawer. I was totally stumped. Then it hit me. My roommate had bought some porn magazines to play a practical joke on our orchestra conductor. Senior orchestra members would cut out the faces of performers from the show program and paste them on top of the faces in the porno magazines. This was the 1980's version of "Photoshop."

This group of musically gifted nymphs would insert these modified pictures throughout the musical conductor's score. There's nothing quite as funny as the sweet face of a cellist pasted on a porn star's body. My roommate told me the seniors did this every year and never picked the same night so it was always a surprise. I found it very funny at the time, but since my father was treating me like a prosecuting attorney treats a murder suspect, it had totally lost its humor.

I was pissed. More than pissed, I was furious. First, I didn't believe for a minute that he needed socks; he was snooping. He had gone through our drawers, not just mine, but my roommate's, and that was just wrong. Second, he questioned my sexuality and then tied it to paying for school. After all the bad decisions I had watched him make, he was going to judge me? Hell, no.

At this point, the four ladies listening to me were leaning forward and completely involved in the story. I couldn't blame them; I was getting intense. I was standing at this point and began pacing as I continued.

I stood up eye-to-eye with my father and what came out of my mouth surprised even me. "First of all, Dad, those were not my magazines, but that's irrelevant. You had no business going through those drawers. You could've just asked me for a pair of socks. You went in my roommate's drawer and what's in his drawer is none of your business."

Dad opened his mouth to say something but I cut him off.

"And I don't care if you don't pay another dime for school. Period. I will take out the loans and do it myself. I don't need you. I don't need your judgment and as long as I am making the grades, your views on my personal life mean nothing to me."

Dad's face turned beet red. I could tell he was ready to blow but couldn't find the words.

I didn't stop. "I've put up with ten years of you and your drinking and making bad decisions that have caused this family more heartache than you'll ever admit, so don't try to lecture me on my life. I'm not interested. I have enough money to get back to school on the bus if you decide I can't take the car. I will finish my degree with or without your help."

My father just stared at me, then he turned and walked away. I let out a huge sigh and collapsed on the couch. I realized I had to keep my momentum if I was going to turn this around. He was sitting at the table when I walked into the kitchen and called the bus station. Once I had the departure times, I went back to my room and started packing. I don't believe in making idle threats. This is something I learned from my father. If you state you're going to do something, do it. Don't vacillate, as it makes you look weak.

When Dad came back to my room he walked straight up to me and grabbed me in a bear hug; there were tears in his eyes. "I'm sorry," he said. We hugged for a long time.

"Can you please tell me what the hell that was all about?"

He said, "I'm afraid."

I looked at him through my own tears and said, "Afraid of what, Dad?"

"Afraid of what your life would be like if you were gay. Afraid of how you would be treated. How hard your life would be. No father wants his kid to experience that kind of stuff. I've been so afraid for you."

Our conversation had taken a huge turn. "Dad, I'm not afraid. I have your mother's ego, your determination and work ethic, and my mother's charm, so you know what? I'm not afraid. I'll figure things out as they come, whatever happens in my life.

"How did you get so tough?" Dad asked.

We were standing in my room in front of the dresser mirror. I turned him toward it and said, "Look in the mirror. Good or bad, you created this."

We both laughed a little. One more hug, and the whole thing was over. Looking back, it still feels like a twilight zone moment.

It took years for me to come out to my parents and when I did it was a complete non-event. I had tried therapy, anti-depressants, you name it I tried it. None of those things changed the way I felt towards men. I'd been out of school and working for about eight years before Dad and I circled back to the topic of my sexuality. I was home for Thanksgiving when he causally asked me if I had met anyone special and "was I dating" someone seriously. I could tell he was fishing. He had never met any of my "dates"; nor had I ever talked about a special someone. He'd met several of my guy "friends" over the years, but I had never admitted to anyone I had a boyfriend.

He was bouncing my nephew on his knee. He could tell I was thinking hard about what to say. Finally he said, "I was just wondering if there was someone we haven't met and if you ever thought about having kids someday?"

Kids? I was thirty years old and kids had never crossed my mind.

Dad continued, "That is, if you lean that way."

"Lean that way?" I asked.

"Yeah, you know, lean towards women."

Uh-oh, I was caught! I looked over at him and said, "No, Dad, I don't lean that way. I've never been interested in women."

"Really? Do you have a boyfriend?"

"I've dated, but no, I don't have a boyfriend."

He continued, "Well, when you have a boyfriend, will you guys still come to Thanksgiving dinner?"

Stunned, I said, "Of course we would. Why wouldn't we?"

Dad smiled and said, "I just wanted to make sure you knew you were welcome here anytime no matter what side of the fence you're on."

After what had happened in college I was expecting my revelation to have more impact. The overly concerned, overly emotional, crazy man from my college days was no longer there. Dad was more concerned about my feeling welcome at home than he was my sexuality. It was a heartwarming, complete non-event.

As soon as I reached this point of the story, questions about my love life started. "When did you start dating? Did you have any serious relationships before Ken? When was the first time you fell in love?"

I went on to tell my girls about my relationships. The good, the bad and the ugly. We laughed a lot. Every time I described some ex in unflattering terms, one of the ladies would say, "Oh my God, he sounds just like my ex!"

I've had only had two real relationships. My first was with an incredible guy named Paul. We've remained good friends and he's still a part of my heart. I failed to make that one work. The second guy is Ken. I told them about how Ken and I met and how long it took for us to figure out that our feelings for each other went beyond a "friend with benefits" type of relationship. They all lectured me about taking so long to tell them about my orientation and to share my life.

It was 4:00 in the morning, and I was emotionally wrung out. As I was saying good night, Linda grabbed me and gave me a huge, long hug. She looked me in the eyes and said, "Finally! Finally my best friend shared his life with me." She was headed up the stairs when I heard her say, "Don't ever make me ask again."

I got the meaning loud and clear. Don't ever disappear from her life or hide myself from her; she would love me always. Ditto, Linda.

The next morning we saw everyone off to their appropriate destinations. Laura was the last to go. Since her parents live in NJ, and she was driving down to spend a few days with them before heading home. I was still a bit shell-shocked from our conversation that had lasted till the wee hours of the morning. We were drinking coffee on the porch when I said, "I still can't believe what happened last night. I am amazed you all were so interested in my history."

She looked at me with a smile and said, "Why?"

"Well, I just didn't think it was that interesting or important. And, to be honest, I didn't mention it last night, but I struggled telling people about my orientation for years. I was always concerned about being viewed as some diseased deviant. The AIDS epidemic was in full swing in the 80's and 90's and gays were looked at as a plagued group of men whether you were infected or not. It was scary as hell. I was afraid someone I loved would view me like that."

Laura, smiling and nodding, put down her cup, took my hand and said, "Darling, we've all known for years that you were gay and we're frustrated that you struggled to share it with us. You're dearly loved and you just couldn't let go of your own fears and tell us. We all know about each other's failed attempts at relationships. But we knew nothing about your life after high school. The sum of those experiences makes us who we are."

She continued, "Trent, Linda was so hurt that you did not come to her wedding. She was practically your sister and you were so caught up in your concerns about being gay, you didn't go to her wedding. She needed to understand the why before she could let go of that hurt. And by the way, I don't believe one of us would ever look at you like you were diseased." Tears came to my eyes.

Laura had made it crystal clear to me that I had been my own worst enemy. Trying to hold on to that secret cost my younger self more ways than I could imagine. As someone once said, "Guilt and regret are the past holding us back from our future." Whoever said that knew their stuff.

We hugged and I said, "I won't make that stupid ass mistake again!" We both laughed out loud and went back to our coffee.

I've made good on my promise. Linda and her family have stayed with Ken and me on several occasions since these fabulous ladies visited Altamont Court. I would never take their love for granted again.

OUR NIGHT WITH HUGH

"What? That queen paid how much for that T-shirt?"

- Karla Tranfield

I love New York City. I've traveled a great deal in my life and I can honestly say there is no place quite like it. Yes, London, Paris, Rome, Hong Kong and Sydney all have their unique, exciting and beautiful qualities, but NYC has a vibe and energy all its own. No matter how many times I've been there, I get a rush the moment I hit the streets.

My first trip to NYC was in 1984. I was a senior in college and I was going to The City that summer with a couple of close college friends. We stayed with a mutual college friend in New Jersey and commuted to The City. We were all theater people, so the chance to go to NYC and see "real" Broadway shows was the most exciting thing three college boys from Dallas had ever done. We had tickets to *Cats*, *Chorus Line* and *Dreamgirls*, starring Miss Jennifer Holliday.

We spent fourteen hours a day for 6 days straight in the city. This was before "the Mouse" (aka Disney) took over 42nd Street, so all of the porn palaces were still fully operational. When we stepped out of the Port Authority Bus station, we stared in wide-eyed wonder at all the merchandise that was on display in the windows on 42nd street. Since we were three sheltered boys attending a private Christian university, we'd only heard of these 'toys' in the windows, but we had never actually seen them. Dildos, harnesses, lubricants, handcuffs, vibrators—all with "buy one, get one free" signs plastered on them. I was totally fascinated. So much so, I was nearly led into one of these treasure palaces by one of the street sales solicitors.

My friend, Steve, with his jaw hanging wide open, grabbed my arm and yanked me back to reality, whispering loudly, "You can't go in there! You will end up on an express train to hell!" As we were walking away I glanced back over my shoulder. The shop seemed to be pulsating a deep red and the guy smiling at me with gold-capped teeth looked a bit like a demon. Maybe Steve had a point.

The three of us had an amazing week. On our last night in NYC we saw *Dreamgirls*. *Cats* and *Chorus Line* were both great, but *Dream Girls* was an out-of-body experience. As we walked into the Imperial Theater we quickly realized we were the minorities. In fact, we were the only white people in the balcony that night. Three lily-white boys from Texas in a sea of color. It truly was the first time I had experienced what it is like to be a minority. That experience alone was worth the price of the ticket. We had no idea what to expect, but we'd heard that the show was a must see.

Standing ovations on Broadway are more common now, but in 1984 they had to be earned. This was the first show I'd ever been to where a standing ovation took place at the end of a song. Miss Holliday belted out, "And I'm Telling You.." and when she finished, everyone, including the white boys from Texas, jumped to their feet. It was electrifying. As we were exiting the balcony during intermission, three or four wives were giving their husbands holy hell with "....Don't you ever think you can ever treat me like that!" and "...If he were my boyfriend he'd need to be sleepin' with one eye open." And my personal favorite, "First, I'd bitch slap that slut Deena Jones and then I'd be coming for your ass!"

After college, I started working for a company in Dallas, Texas, but was quickly promoted and moved to its headquarters in northern New Jersey. NYC was less than an hour away by train. I was a twenty-eight year old single man, so I went in with friends as often as possible. Every few weeks we would pick something new to explore. Art museums, The American Museum of Natural History, The Metropolitan Museum of Art, American Ballet Theater; the list was truly endless.

The first trip to the The Metropolitan Opera (the Met) took my breath away. The scene from *Moonstruck* with Cher and Nicolas Cage doesn't do it justice. The fountain and the facade of the Met with the Chagalls lit in the huge, arched windows are definitely worth the visit. I was seeing an opera for the first time with my friends Mark and CJ. Mark and I had done several musicals together when I lived in Dallas and he was staying with me for the summer. He is a skilled performer and music teacher and is an opera aficionado. CJ was my best friend in NJ and my "work wife." Her husband traveled eighty percent of the time so CJ and I were the *Will and Grace* of our time. She is an avid supporter of the American Ballet Theater and the Met. We were going to see *Tosca* with Luciano Pavarotti. As this was a last minute purchase, our seats were way, way back and very, very high in the second mezzanine.

Opera fans are not the same breed as Broadway theater fans. Never mistake the two. Those who attend opera on a regular basis take it very seriously. Any noise is frowned upon and will draw a rebuke or hiss from your seat-mates. Second, do not clap between particularly stirring arias. They have a curtain call per act, so save your applause for those individual curtain calls. I learned all this the hard way. At one point I had CJ change seats with me, as I was afraid the blue-haired matron beside me was going to put a stake in my heart for clapping at inappropriate moments.

The sets, the costuming and singing were all spectacular. My issue with opera is the extent to which it pushes the whole "willing suspension of disbelief" concept. When you attend a live theater production, opera or dance performance you must accept that you are being pulled into a different world. As an audience member you must willingly suspend your disbelief and accept what you see on stage as real. This allows your mind to accept a fifty-year-old actor or actress playing a thirty-year-old person and not let the age disparity detract from the story.

Tosca is an often-performed, famous opera by Puccini. Due to the number of dramatic twists, turns and surprises, it has been categorized by some critics as a melodrama. Tosca, the raven-haired beauty that is the opera's namesake, is described as a remarkably beautiful woman who is the inspiration for a young artist who gets himself caught up in political intrigue with tragic consequences. Pavarotti was not at his slimmest nor was he very youthful at this point in his career. So we really had to "suspend our disbelief" to see him as the young artist, Cavaradossi. But it was Pavarotti at the Met so we just went with it. The real challenge to this theatrical convention was about to walk on stage. The woman playing Tosca was a behemoth. She looked nearly 6 feet tall and had to weigh around two hundred and eighty pounds. She was a linebacker. She didn't walk onto the stage; she lumbered. She had a magnificent voice, so if you closed your eyes, you could imagine a young, raven-haired woman in her place.

It went from bad to worse. The man playing Scarpia, the evil chief of police, was about 5'9" and weighed about one hundred seventy pounds. During the part of the opera when Scarpia is trying to force himself on Tosca and ravish her, the struggle looked like she was tossing a ragdoll around the living room with Scarpia hanging on for dear life. I couldn't wait for her to stab him in the heart and put an end to it as fast as possible. During the third act, our young virile artist was facing what he and Tosca believed would be a "mock" firing squad. But our dead chief of police had betrayed them. Or, since Tosca had killed Scarpia after throwing him around the stage like a Kleenex, you could say he was just getting even. Instead of blanks, the executioners used real bullets and killed the young artist.

Up to this point I'd managed to deal with Luciano's size and age, but his death scene was beyond painful. To control his descent he had to stumble back against the proscenium and slowly slide down to one knee before lowering himself to the floor. It took nearly two minutes for him to die. In trudged Tosca hauling herself across the stage on the run from the police for the murder of the chief. Naturally, she was not actually running. It took her about a minute to kneel down to try to wake her love, whom she thinks is faking death. Surprised at his death, she slowly rises to the sound of shouting off stage. At this point in the opera, the police were supposed to run in and chase her up the balustrade to the top of the wall. In this version the shouts stayed off stage for a very long time as Tosca heaved herself up the stairs. I had lost my suspension of disbelief in the first act so by now I was just smiling and shaking my head. Once she was on top of the wall, the soldiers ran in and started climbing after her. Tosca raised her fists and sang/spat something at them in defiance and flung herself off the wall.

I gasped in horror as I watched this enormous person jump off the top of the castle wall. The blue-haired matron heard my audible gasp at Tosca's shocking choice of suicidal death. She turned to us with a smile and, whilst leaning over CJ, said, "Shocking, isn't it? Watching that poor young woman kill herself like that. I have seen this opera three times and it always gets to me."

Still staring at the stage, I said, "It wasn't her death that caused me to gasp. It was trying to imagine who or what was catching her!"

It was the blue-haired matron's turn to gasp. She only had one word for me. "Cretin!"

CJ slouched back into her seat indicating to little miss blue hair that she was not involved in this conversation. Mark gave me a look of total disgust and headed for the exit.

Mark and CJ wanted to meet Pavarotti and made a beeline for the stage door when we exited the Met; I waited by the fountain for them. I was taking in the magnificence of the Met and thinking it was one of the most beautiful places in the city, when a very large man less than twelve feet away let rip this enormous, lengthy and very loud episode of flatulence. It was so loud and so long at least two-dozen people turned to look at him. He just smiled and said, "I have been holding that back during the whole opera. It couldn't wait any longer."

I laughed out loud. The first thing that came to mind was, *'I wonder what the blue-haired matron would have thought of that?'* This was my one and only experience with opera. CJ and Mark never invited me to see one again. It was obvious this would never be my entertainment medium of choice.

Moving back to Morristown and living close to the train station meant I would get the chance to go into the city as often as we liked. It also meant wed have a lot of house guests who would invite themselves for a visit and use our home as a launch pad into NYC. It actually was amazing how many friends took advantage of our location. It gave us an excuse to go into the city and see Broadway shows. As if two queens needed an excuse. Its a cliché.

Ken and I have had more than a few unsuccessful Broadway ventures. We saw the dreadful play, *The Beauty Queen of Leenane*. A warning to all who attend Broadway plays or musicals. In my experience, if it is Irish in nature—either the writer is Irish or the play has an Irish theme—it will be depressing as hell. True to form, the *Beauty Queen of Liani* was dark and depressing. I left the theater wanting to slit my wrists. I'm more of a musical theater guy, but even *Billy Elliott* was too dark for me.

One of the biggest and longest running musicals on Broadway is *Phantom of the Opera*. I don't dislike this musical, but my taste for it has waned over the years. Every time someone visited us in NJ, they wanted to go see *Phantom*. It was hard to say no when they had already bought you a ticket. My head nearly exploded when Ashleigh, Lindsay and Erin wanted to go see it for their birthdays. Karla provided her shoulder as I wept openly. This was my seventh time seeing this musical. As the song "Point of No Return" began, I realized I had reached the point of no return and went down to the bar for a shot of vodka.

The most memorable Broadway shows Ken and I never saw were *Dame Edna: The Royal Tour* and *Dame Edna: Back with a Vengeance*. We love a good drag performer and Dame Edna is one of the most famous drag comedians in the world. Our first attempt to see Barry Humphries as Dame Edna was a disaster. We had six people joining us for the show, but when we got to the box office, there were no tickets on hold for us. I had ordered the tickets online and had my confirmation number. They had to be there. When the box office manager finally ran down our tickets, it became apparent why we had no tickets on Saturday night - I had ordered them for Friday night's performance. We all ended up at a great restaurant drinking away our disappointment. It was my first and last time ordering tickets online. Ken does all the ticket ordering for us now.

When *Dame Edna* returned to Broadway, I was excited. It was my chance to redeem myself. I surprised Ken by securing tickets and making reservations at Chez Josephine's in The City. I had put the tickets in his birthday card, which I gave him during dessert. He took one look at the tickets and let out a gasp.

"Surprise!"

Ken looked at me and said, "I can't believe you did this. We are finally going to see *Dame Edna!*"

Jean Claude, the proprietor of this fine establishment, overheard what Ken said and came over to our table. "Oh, mon ami, *Dame Edna* closed two weeks ago. He is in London now."

I said, "I don't think so Jean Claude. We have tickets for tonight."

He looked at me with a sad expression and said, "I am so sorry, my friend, but he closed early."

All I thought was, *Not again!* Sure enough, when we got to the theater, Dame Edna had closed early. Obviously, Ken and I were not meant to see Barry Humphries' amazing character.

Though Ken never got to see Dame Edna, he was able to go to a gay version of the Super Bowl – yes, he got to go to the Tony Awards. Not just *any* Tony's; the 2005 Tony Awards hosted by Hugh "I'm a Broadway God" Jackman.

Karla worships at the altar of Hugh Jackman. When she found out Ken was going with our friend, Catherine, she was ready for blood. Catherine was my friend, but she asked Ken to the Tony's instead of me. Yes, Catherine and I are still close friends. I willingly admit Ken is better eye candy in a tux, but this was the Tony Awards!

To be fair, I don't really like crowded events; in fact, I hate them. Catherine knew this so she knew I was not going to be the fun-loving date Ken would be. I happily watched it from the comfort of home. Gay men who read this are going to gasp and clutch their pearls and bitch slap the person closest to them for dramatic effect. Clearly some of them would have escorted my happy ass to the nearest HRC office to have my rainbow membership card revoked – but I digress.

Karla cornered Ken just before he left and gave him his marching orders. Come home with a piece of HJ's clothing, or don't come home at all. It was actually more precise. "Come home with a pair of his jockey shorts or I will hunt you down like a blood hound."

Catherine and Ken did it right. Limo, after party, the entire red carpet experience. When Ken got home I had to listen to stories about sitting eight rows from the stage, how he met and cheek-kissed Kathleen Turner, yada, yada, yada. Story after story about the stars he met. Okay, now I was a tiny bit jealous. Unfortunately, he did not get a pair of Hugh's jockey shorts. Karla has never forgiven him.

When Hugh Jackman came back to Broadway with Daniel Craig in *A Steady Rain*, Karla was damn well not going to miss it. With Daniel Craig and Hugh Jackman on the same stage, *I* wasn't going to miss it. American Express offered the opportunity to purchase tickets prior to them being made available to the general public, so Karla and my mother-in-law began dialing and working the online reservations like two computer geeks at a hackathon. This went on for nearly two hours. It was a limited run and it seemed that everyone with an American Express Card in the tri-state area was trying to get tickets (or should I say every queen in the tri-state area with an AMEX card). After two hours, success. We had eight tickets to *A Steady Rain*. Altamont Court was going to Broadway whether Broadway wanted us or not.

Not to be outdone by Ken and Catherine's Tony night, I hired a limo for the evening: A big stretch limo that could fit all eight of us. The Courtians were going to Broadway in style. We all gathered at our house for a glass of champagne and some noshing. I had made Gruyere cheese puffs to go with the champagne and cheese. Karla had the brilliant idea of taking all of this with us in the limo. It sounded like a great idea. There's my favorite word again, IDEA. What sounded good at first turned into a roller coaster ride of splashing champagne and flying cheese puffs.

The limo actually felt like a clown car once we were all stuffed inside. We should've ordered the next size up. We were packed in so tight that a few folks were sitting more on their hips than their butts. Getting into the city meant navigating miles of road construction work that was in progress. The words "in progress" are redundant because all the roads in NJ are always having work done, all the time. It's a lot like "Ground Hog Day;" you feel like you are in a never-ending loop with freeway construction. When we hit the first big pothole those cheese puffs exploded off the plate like popcorn and the last champagne bottle blew its cork, sending bubbly everywhere. I shouldn't have removed the wire cap. It looked like a bad adult game of twister inside the limo as we were all grabbing flying cheese puffs and avoiding the champagne stream. The carpet of that limo was going to need steam cleaning. If the ladies laughed any harder we were going to need to stop to purchase Depends.

The "less than amused" limo driver dropped us at Chez Josephine's for dinner. The look on his face said, *I do not want to pick these crazies up later tonight. I wonder how much trouble I would get into if I just left these loons in Manhattan?*

As usual, Jean Claude had everything prepared and met us at the door. With the number of times Ken and I have been there for dinner we should have our own engraved seats. The next challenge was going to be getting all ten of us to the theater after dinner. We had to walk a couple of long blocks, then two short blocks to the theater. I really felt for Ken. With all his back issues, that walk really took a real toll. Adding to the fun was a steady rain. No, not the show, but an actual steady rain. More of a heavy rain, if memory serves me correctly. The rain was so heavy there were no taxi's to be had. We were prepared with our umbrellas, but the walk to the theater left us all soaked from the knee down. Ken's back was killing him by the time we arrived. The moment we got to the theater I got Ken a shot of vodka from the bar. It was the only painkiller on hand.

The show started and I admit to being star struck. I had seen these guys in movies, but this was a whole new experience. Karla was trying hard to contain her inner high school girl and not squeal when Hugh came on stage. She was like a teenager at a concert. I was impressed with both their performances. For the record, *A Steady Rain* is not an uplifting show. It is a hardcore, heavy drama with a tad bit of comic relief in the dialog. It's about two cops who are partners and their trials and personal entanglements that end in tragedy; this was not *The Boy from Oz*. They both gave outstanding performances. Their on-stage chemistry was amazing.

The real show began after the curtain call. It was spring in NYC and *Broadway Cares, Equity Fights Aids* charity fundraiser was in full swing. Hugh and Daniel were auctioning signed photos, pictures with you and your friends and, the pièce de résistance, signed

Guinea tees they had worn in the show that night. Here was Karlas chance to own a piece of Huge Jackmans underwear. This last item caused an auctioning frenzy. They started at one thousand dollars each. The bidding was furious. There were two camps: the queens and wealthy husbands of matronly socialites. The price kept going up. $2000, $3000, $4000. We were sitting there in shock. When the bidding stopped, the price had reached $5000. Karla was beside herself. She could'nt believe she'd been outbid by two gay men with deeper pockets. To maximize the dollars to the charity, Craig and Jackman signed both t-shirts and sold each one for five thousand dollars.

Being the more grounded individual at this point in time, I asked her, "What the hell were you going to do with Hugh Jackman's sweaty T-shirt?"

She responded without missing a beat. "Sleep with it between my thighs."

PAYBACK'S A BITCH

"Look mama, I'm pretty. I'm a pretty girl, Mama."

- Gypsy Rose Lee, *Gypsy*

Transformations are amazing. We see them every day in nature. A tadpole becomes a frog. A caterpillar becomes a butterfly. Among humans, our children become young adults. That transformation is truly a miracle. I watched it happen with my stepdaughters, Ashleigh and Lindsay. One minute they were little girls playing with Barbie dolls; seemingly overnight they became women. I will never forget the moment Ken and I realized our youngest had blossomed. Lindsay wore baggy clothing everywhere. It was the style all the kids were wearing and it drove me nuts. They walked around looking like unmade beds with greasy hair poking out from under their sideways baseball caps. I would love to know who came up with this look so I could strangle them in their sleep.

Lindsay's big reveal happened while we were living on The Court. She wanted to have a slumber party at the house with all of her cousins. Our kids always wanted to have slumber parties at the house. Our nieces would schedule sleepovers even when our girls weren't home so they could have the run of Morristown. We hosted our oldest niece's twenty-first birthday at our house so she and her friends could celebrate in town and not have to drive home. When we woke up the next morning we found five girls with hangovers, trying to sleep off a night of partying in Morristown. It must have been a memorable evening, as I found a big orange traffic cone on the front porch and three different types of boots on the front lawn. I figured it was better not to ask how they got there.

For Lindsay's near-weekly sleepovers, she would invite her cousins or friends from northwest Jersey and eastern PA down for the weekend. Everyone would show up on Friday and leave sometime Sunday. The girls were either up in their 'Penthouse' rooms on the third floor or down in the basement watching movies. At one of these marathon events, the girls were having a 'Who has the Cutest Pajamas' party. It should have been called 'Who has the Skimpiest Pajamas' Party. I saw way more pierced belly buttons than I needed to. Ken and I were in the kitchen when Lindsay came bounding around the corner heading towards the basement, and instead of wearing her normal baggy sweats, she had on a cropped tank and a pair of short shorts. She stopped for thirty seconds to say they were staying home to watch movies downstairs, then continued her run down the stairs.

All Ken and I could do was stand there slacked-jawed. Overnight our youngest had expanded from a B-Cup to a D-Cup. How the hell did that happen? *When* the hell did it happen? Not saying a word, I pulled the bottle of Patron from the freezer and poured two healthy shots. We swallowed them in one gulp.

I said, "Well, Honey, its official. We no longer have a little girl. In fact, there is nothing little about what just came through this kitchen."

Ken, still stunned by his daughter's blossoming body, said, "I don't want to talk about this – ever!"

"Blame it on your mother," I said. "She's the one with the enormous..."

I stopped dead in my tracks as Ken's eyes were shooting daggers.

I continued, "...Personality. She had to pass those personalities on to someone. It seems like Lindsay hit the genetic jackpot." Ken was not amused.

When we moved to The Court, all the kids of The Court were very young. Six years later they were all becoming young men and women. I had become very close to Karla's daughter Erin, having been a part of her life since she was seven. She was pure tomboy and gave her brothers a run for their money. She was a natural athlete from birth and continued to excel at sports. Soccer, field hockey, rugby; she had an aptitude for them all.

Erin even wrestled in middle school. The boys on the opposing teams always underestimated her. They saw her as an easy target. That opinion lasted exactly fifteen seconds after the referee blew the whistle to engage. After she flipped and pinned her first opponent, they were leery. After pinning her sixth boy of the day, she had gained their respect.

I was sitting on the porch reading when Karla appeared out of nowhere, poured herself a glass of wine and collapsed in a chair. "We have a problem," she said.

All I could think was, *Oh God, what now? Who died? Is Rich back in the hospital?* I said, "What now?"

Karla gave me that *Help me Obi Wan Kenobi. You're my only hope* look before she said, "You've been talking about having a civil union and Erin doesn't have a dress."

Oh for heaven sakes. At this point our civil union was more talk than reality. Ken and I had received a "Hold the Date" card for his cousin's civil union. We knew it was only a matter of time before it became a point of conversation with his mother. But at this point, we didn't have anything planned. Of course, that was all about to change.

Not having a dress wasn't Armageddon. "Karla, I have no idea when or if we are going to have a civil union. If we do, we will get her a dress."

"No, you don't understand," Karla continued, "Erin doesn't own a dress. Hell, the only time she wore a dress was for her first communion and she only did it because I let her wear her orange sandals and bike shorts with it."

"Are you serious?" I asked.

"Yep. She refuses to even try one on. If you want her in a dress you'll have to ask her yourself."

I've always thought of Erin as my goddaughter, as we had developed a strong bond over the past six years. We joke that I am her 'fairy godfather.' Every girl should have one. That night after dinner I dropped by to tell her I wanted her to wear a dress for our potential commitment ceremony.

Her nose crinkled and she said, "Really? Do I have to?"

I said, "Yes, baby, you do. Everyone is going to be really dressed up and it is important to me that you be dressed up as well."

"Can I think about it?"

"Of course you can."

As she left the table Rich looked at me and said, "You got a better response than we did."

"Of course I did. I am her Fairy Godfather!"

As Rich, Karla and I chatted, Rich decided to add his two cents about what type of dress would be appropriate. "I think she should wear a black dress," Rich said. "Isn't that a classic? I always hear women talk about black cocktail dresses."

There it was, fashion advice from the straight father. A man who I have seen walking the kids to the bus stop wearing a Sponge Bob tee shirt and Darth Maul boxers.

I stared at him incredulously. "If she were twenty-one and going to a cocktail party in Manhattan I would agree with you. But Ken and I are thinking about having an afternoon ceremony in spring, so no, it doesn't work."

"I still say you should look for something in black."

I thought, *How funereal.* I turned to Karla and said, "Leave it to me. I will come up with something fabulous and appropriate."

Erin suddenly appeared in the kitchen and said, "Okay, I will wear a dress for your ceremony. One condition. I want it to be black."

Oh for heaven sakes! I glared at Rich and said, "Fine." But I was thinking, *Black? I will give you black! You will be drowning in black.*

Erin had grown into a beautiful woman. She just couldn't see it through her tomboy image. A girl that can shoot hoops, wrestle and gut and filet her own fish could not see a pretty princess beneath. She has amazing green eyes, perma tan skin, an Audrey Hepburn neck and eyelashes a model would kill for. On top of all of this, she's built. Truly built. I could tell from looking at her, she was the perfect size two. The first thing I had to do was put this idea of a black dress to a quick death. I had to give her exactly what she asked for in a way that screamed, *This looks like crap, I am not wearing black.*

As I went through the Mall at Short Hills I picked up a half dozen black cocktail dresses and one really hot pink dress. Erin hated the color pink so I knew that one would never make it on her body. I had to make sure they all looked good on the hanger so I wouldn't be accused of sabotage. Lets be clear, I was totally and willingly guilty of sabotage; it just couldn't seem obvious. After I had selected an acceptable group of rejects, I went on the hunt for the real dress. I found several I liked, but nothing that jumped off the rack. I was back at Neiman's, yet again, when I walked past a mannequin wearing a bejeweled Egyptian collared, apricot colored silk dress with a slightly flared skirt that fell just above the knee. BINGO. This was it. The only size two was on the mannequin so I asked the merchandizing director to pull it down and had it steamed so it would be perfect. A quick stop at one of the shoe stores netted me a plain black pair of pumps and a fantastic pair of silver strappy heels.

It was time for the unveiling, trying on and choosing of the dress. I kept the dresses in one room and gave them to Erin one at a time. Six black dresses in a row. On the fourth dress, which looked good on her, she said, "I feel like I am going to a funeral."

I nearly laughed out loud. I said, "That dress didn't come with a black veil, but if it had, it would be funeral ready." The next one I gave her was a form-fitting black dress. Once she shimmied into it she took one look and said, "I look like a slut." *Yes you do and that wasn't by accident.*

That did cause me to laugh out loud. When I brought out the pink dress all she said was, "I am not wearing pink, ever." Finally, I handed her the silver strappy heels and the Neiman's garment bag. "This is the last one, so I am crossing my fingers it works."

The first thing I heard from the bedroom was, "It's orange."

"It's not orange, it's apricot. Now put it on."

I heard a grunt and the movement of clothes, then nothing. Dead silence. Karla and I were standing in the hallway with our ears nearly pressed against the door, waiting for a reaction. Nothing. Sixty seconds later she opened the door and stepped into the hall-way. Karla started fighting back tears. Erin looked radiant. She *was* radiant. Her smile was so big it hurt to look at it. She kept walking around in her heels and new dress.

Finally she said, "I look good in this! Look at my calves, Mom! These heels make my calves look amazing."

"So, we have a winner?" I asked.

They both nodded and Erin went back in the room to change. She had her own *"Gypsy"* moment. I could almost hear the words,

"Mama, I'm pretty. I'm a pretty girl, Mama." A gay man can find a musical theater reference for just about any situation.

Karla looked at me and said, "Bitch, you orchestrated this whole thing to get her to choose that dress!"

"I am innocent," I said. "Erin and Rich wanted a black dress, so I gave her several black dresses to choose from. Can I help it if the apricot color against her tan skin and green eyes made her look stunning?"

Karla punched me.

"Ouch. What was that for?"

"How much is that dress?"

"You don't want to know," I said.

"Trent Pines, how much?"

"Four hundred and fifty dollars."

First I saw total shock in her eyes, then resignation. She said, "She looks so amazing." She paused, "I never thought I would get her into a dress."

"So are we keeping it, or am I taking it back?"

Karla glared and said, "After seeing the way she looked and seeing the look on her face, how in the world do you expect me to tell her we have to find another dress?"

"I told you I would get you to pay four hundred dollars for a dress. Payback's a bitch."

"I owe you for this, Bitch," she said with a smile.

During all of this dress shopping, Ken's cousin and his partner's formal invitation arrived for their civil union. It was now a given we would be having a civil union ceremony. There would be no escaping my mother-in-law. But I digress, this chapter is about transformations so you will have to wait until the next chapter to read about the evolution of our civil union.

My next challenge was to convince Erin that pulling her hair back in a ponytail was not an acceptable hairstyle for that dress. She lived in a ponytail. It was the only way I had ever seen her wear her hair. When she handed the dress over to her mother, I said, "Okay, sweetie, you have to trust me. With this dress and those shoes you will have to get your hair done and get a manicure and pedicure. If you are going to wear this, you have to go all the way."

She looked at me like I had just kicked her dog! She looked at the floor, shuffled her feet and finally, grudgingly said, "Okay."

I looked at Karla and said, "I just signed you up for one hundred and fifty dollars worth of beauty."

She gave me a sarcastic glare and mumbled, "Put it on my tab."

Ken's stylist Holly was up for the challenge. The big day had arrived and it was time to send her in for her make-over. She was having her 'Miss Congeniality' moment. She went in looking like a disheveled tomboy. No one was prepared for her transformation. Holly trimmed and treated her hair before she put together her up-do. While her hair was de-frizzing under the treatment, the manicurist was taking a belt sander to her feet and a machete to her cuticles. I had given them all marching orders right down to the French tips.

When she walked out of the beauty shop she bumped directly into our good friend Joe. Joe had known Erin since she was four years old. Joe said, "Excuse me, miss, I am so sorry."

Erin smiled and said, "That's okay, Joe, I was just heading home."

Joe continued to stare at this beautiful young woman who seemed to know his name. Then it hit him like a train, "Oh, my God! Erin, is that really you?"

Erin just looked at him and said, "Duh?" Now it was time to put on the dress and her silver Cha-Cha heels.

When she showed up at the ceremony, half the people who had known her most of her life didn't recognize her. Even my mother didn't know who she was. Karla and Rich were completely taken back. I had replaced their petite tomboy with a stunningly glamorous young woman. I had loaned my defibrillator paddles to Karla just in case Rich had a cardiac event. After this evening of unprecedented glamour, there was no going back.

From that moment on, every event called for a new dress. Eighth grade graduation, soccer banquet, you name it, we had to go dress shopping. Just for kicks I took her in to Dolce and Gabbana. I had seen a stunning dress in the window and wondered how it would look on her. Roman, the head stylist at the store, took one look at Erin and said, "Oh my, I have something much better in mind." Within ten minutes he had her dressed head to toe in a silk leopard print dress that fit her like it was custom made. He added a pair of black patent leather pumps and a form-fitting black leather jacket. She looked like she should be in Milan.

She was standing in front of the mirror wearing three thousand dollars worth of D&G looking every bit a runway model when I heard Karla say harshly under her breath, "DON'T EVEN THINK ABOUT IT!"

MY BIG FAB GAY WEDDING

"I can't believe it! You two have been together longer than your cousin Eddie and his partner Paul and they got married first! What's wrong with you? When are you two going to make this happen?"

– Sally Howlett, Mother-in-law

It was our sixth year on The Court when Ken's cousin Eddie and his partner Paul had their civil union. Ken and I will never live it down. As I predicted, the moment my mother-in-law got their announcement she called to raise holy hell that they were beating us to the altar. How many gay couples face this kind of pressure? Acceptance is a great thing, but now I know how single straight women feel when their sisters tie the knot first and they become the sole focus of their mother's attention.

Sally's demand for a wedding was brought about by the NJ legislature passing a law that allowed gay couples to enter into civil unions. I find the entire argument over whether or not gays should be able to marry absurd. Contrary to the beliefs of the folks on the far right, this will not destroy the traditional family or traditional marriage. The heteros have done a great job of that all on their own. Their seventy-two hour celebrity marriages, the often quoted fifty percent divorce rate, and the number of public officials caught having affairs paints a less than happily-ever-after picture. If marriage is so sacred, why is it so easy to divorce? How about a constitutional amendment that bans divorce? Or one that makes adultery a punishable offense? Do you think that those would get ratified by the states? Not a snowball's chance in hell. It would be the ultimate intrusion of the state into our private lives.

A constitutional amendment banning gays from marrying is just as offensive. You either believe in less government or you don't. Supporting government intervention in private lives because it supports your particular religious views is hypocritical. I actually applaud when so-called 'activist' judges are brave enough to do their jobs and ensure that everyone's rights and liberties are protected. The original activist judges allowed women to vote, abolished Jim Crow laws, and allowed for interracial marriage. Yes, they were thought to be activists at the time they handed down their decisions, but now? The whole idea of two people being unable to marry because of their race is absurd and embarrassing. As the current twenty and thirty somethings get older, they will look back at same sex marriage the same way we look at the ban on interracial marriage and segregated bathrooms, schools, water fountains and public transportation. It is the judiciary that protects our rights and it should be unaffected by emotionally charged ideology. Here's to Edie Windsor for challenging discrimination and winning.

Whew, that was heavy. The truth is, I hate weddings. I'd rather not be invited and if I am invited, I would prefer just to send a check. The mere fact that some families take out second mortgages to throw the wedding of a child's dreams is truly ridiculous. A bride or bride's family spending six, ten or twelve thousand dollars for a wedding dress when most of these newlyweds can barely afford a one-bedroom apartment is borderline criminal. I am sure the people at Kleinfeld's NYC are going to put a hit out on me after they read this.

I feel the same way about plated dinners. Catering is one of the most expensive line items for any wedding. Per plate costs can run fifty, sixty, seventy dollars and that doesn't include the alcohol. The food is rarely worth what you pay for it. Even worse, it usually lacks flavor and is often served lukewarm. On top of all this you have the issue of the seating chart. This is a disaster in the making. Who in the family is fighting with whom? Who refuses to talk to each other? Whose kids don't get along? The last thing you want at your wedding is your guests participating in a WWE SmackDown during dessert.

After Ken and I decided to have a ceremony, I was extremely thankful that he wanted to do upscale heavy appetizers with a couple of carving stations and, most importantly, no assigned seating.

To keep the costs down, we decided to keep the libations simple. I make a mean Margarita and Ken makes a mean Cosmo, so we had Ken's Cosmos and Trent's Texas Margaritas. With Vodka and Tequila as our base we added some mixers, beer and wine to round out our selections. If you wanted something else, you were at the wrong party. Imagine our shock at the end of the evening when every one of our massive bottles of Patron was empty and we still had four bottles of Vodka left. Somehow, it seemed appropriate.

I have been telling our daughters for years that they have a set amount for their weddings. They can A) Spend it all, B) Spend it all and any additional costs will come out of their own pocket or C) Have a modest wedding and bank the rest for a down payment on their first home. It's hard for kids today to save enough money to get their own home. Option C makes home ownership more of a possibility. I am very practical when it comes to large sums of money. I know I am going to get hate mail from the association of wedding planners so, wedding planners, please send a copy of your letter to Kleinfeld's NYC so they can add their thoughts to it.

As much as I wanted a ceremony that was really small and simple, the problems I faced were Ken's Italian background and my Italian mother-in-law. Now that Eddie and Paul had thrown down the gauntlet, I was backed into a corner. It was something Ken really wanted, and it was something my mother-in-law really wanted. I was along for the ride. So we set a budget and began the planning process.

When it comes to a wedding, a great deal of budgeting has to do with headcount. I knew that as soon as this train left the station there was no going back. At first I thought it would be around forty or fifty people. This was a foolish estimate as our combined immediate families totaled over thirty. We settled on a list of one hundred and thirty names, thinking we would get a ten to twenty percent drop-out rate; after all, this was a gay civil union and eighty percent of our invite list was straight couples. Even though we'd known most of these people for years, we both figured there'd be a few folks who might be uncomfortable and opt out. We were wrong. Oh man, were we ever wrong. We had a one hundred percent take rate and several unhappy people who were not on the original invite list. It was already giving me a headache.

Ken took over the reins and dove in headfirst. First he utilized our Altamont Court Family to book the Kellogg Club for the ceremony and reception. Most of the street belonged to this social club, as membership came with pool privileges for the summer. The Court became totally engaged in the planning and execution of our civil union. The Club president was the first one to coin the phase, "This is the first Civil Union....", which became the catch phrase used by everyone involved with this event. The caterer, the florist, the formal wear shop....the list was long. Every single one of these organizations seemed excited to be participating and could not wait to share the news that they were working on our event. Ken calls me jaded when I say, "Money is the great equalizer" and "Their interest in our ceremony was driven by the size of our checks." But even I had to admit that these folks seemed genuinely excited to be involved.

Ken and I quickly agreed on the structure of the ceremony. We wanted a formal ceremony that would be short, crisp and big on love. We asked our daughters, Ken's stepson from his first marriage and our nieces and nephews to stand up with us. All of them agreed enthusiastically. We had the guys wear tuxes but told the girls to pick dresses they felt comfortable in. The only rule was: the dresses had to be different colors. We had to get a rainbow in there somehow.

To the folks sitting in the great room it would feel like a typical wedding procession, as the eight couples made their way in to a song from *Rascal Flats*, "Bless the Broken Road." Then we decided to change things up a bit for Ken and my entrance.

I love sci-fi. *Star Wars, Star Trek, Battlestar Galactica, Doctor Who, Lord of the Rings*. It took Ken a long time to warm up to this geeky side of me. When he finally did, he embraced it totally. So as Rascal Flats faded out, the disco version of the *Star Wars* theme would come blasting from the speakers. Ken and I would walk in hand in hand to the sounds of Sci-Fi Disco.

The first minister Ken wanted was booked out so far in advance there was no way he could meet our schedule. My ever-so-helpful 'sister from another mister' had a suggestion of her own. Karla said, "You should ask Frankie. She's a minister and lives here on The Court."

I looked at her and said, "Who?"

"The tall platinum-haired lady who drives the VW Beetle that is usually parked across from your house."

"Oh, the one with the weird vanity plate that says *Een Heid?*"

Karla said, "That's the one!"

"What the hell does that mean anyway?"

Karla said, "It's Dutch for *UNITY*."

"Right, of course it does." I said. "Is she the lady with the odd accent?"

Karl punched me in the arm and said, "You idiot. She's from the Netherlands, so of course she has an accent."

"I don't know, she seems too Earth mother and hippie-ish for my taste," I said. "I'm not burning sage and doing some rite of spring spiritual dance during our ceremony. That's too weird."

"Weird? You are two gay men having a civil union commitment ceremony at a social club on the white bread side of the tracks in Morristown, New Jersey – does it get any weirder than that?" Karla asked.

She had a point.

Ken convinced me we needed to meet with Frankie and discuss how we wanted our ceremony to flow. Frankie was every bit the earth mother I thought she would be. At the same time, I found her to be warm, engaging and genuinely interested in what we wanted for our ceremony. She gave us a copy of the standard service she used for weddings and commitment ceremonies—all twelve pages of it. My first thought was, *Hell no, we need something that's no more than ten minutes long.* I expressed my concern with the length of the ceremony and Frankie said, "This is just a template. You two can change it any way you want to. I am very flexible. It is your day so it should be the type of ceremony you want."

Apparently, I had judged her too soon. She really is a wonderful person. Ours was an unconventional ceremony so it seemed only appropriate that we have this unconventional minister. We worked with her to develop a short but meaningful ceremony that was full of joy and love – exactly the kind we wanted.

The months leading up to the ceremony were a whirlwind. Ken played the role of the wedding planner, and I was along for the ride. I did enjoy the tasting preview at the caterers. I think the Head Chef was our kind of "family" and he was pulling out all the stops. He did something with asparagus wrapped with chicken and prosciutto that was nearly orgasmic. Each culinary offering he brought out for us to taste was better than the one before. Let's just say my toes curled and my eyes rolled back in my head more than once during the tasting. Ken was batting a thousand with every supplier he chose.

When we reached the end of the tasting, our chef asked us about dessert and a cake.

I said, "I will handle the cake."

He gave me a skeptical look and said, "Seriously? You're going to make a cake for one hundred and twenty people?"

I laughed and said, "I know it sounds strange, but I am known for my cakes. Ken has a huge family and I make the cakes for each party."

Still not sure I could handle it he said, "It's just a lot to take on right before your ceremony. Do you have big enough pans?"

Big enough pans? You have no idea how big my pans are. I said, "Trust me, I have 18-inch base pans for the bottom tier, 14-inch for the middle and 12-inch for the top. You can say I'm a "size queen" in the kitchen, so...do you think that will cut it?"

He laughed out loud and said, "Okay, I believe you, I believe you!"

I really liked this guy.

I started on that cake two days before the ceremony. It was huge. A vanilla cake, with custard and fresh strawberries between the layers, covered with white chocolate butter cream icing. To top that off, I applied shaved white chocolate all over the cake. It looked like it was covered in heavy snow (and in the words of Sheryl, my sister-in-law, it was F$%&ing amazing.)

Ken and I decided we would incorporate one of our special traditions into our ceremony. When I moved out on my own after college and got my first apartment, I set a tradition. The first time you were a guest in my home, we toasted your arrival with a welcoming shot of tequila. If you didn't drink, I didn't force it, but I don't remember many turn-downs. Ken and I have continued this tradition. It seemed appropriate to incorporate tequila into our ceremony.

Ken had been collecting Patron bottles over the last couple of years so we decided to incorporate them into the centerpieces. Before you judge, Patron bottles are hand blown in Mexico and when all the labels are removed, they really are beautiful. You can fill them with something like bath salts and they make a great gift. Judgment should be reserved for our consuming so much tequila that we had enough bottles to place an arrangement on every table.

The weekend before our ceremony I ran the Patron bottles over to the florist. As we unloaded all those bottles, I could see the look on the florist's face and it read, *What kind of alcoholics did we agree to build arrangements for?* Her assistant was a guy who couldn't have been more that twenty years old. He took one look at the bottles and said, "Whoa, dude! That's like some serious alcohol consumption. I wanna come to your house for Cinco De Mayo. Seriously, you dudes look like you know how to party."

I laughed and thought, *Yes. yes we do.*

The day before the big event was a blur. People coming in from all over the U.S. and friends arriving from Europe – it was a mad house. Ken and I decided the rehearsal dinner should be a backyard affair. It seemed appropriate, as most members of The Court family were involved. My mother-in-law cooked and Karla, Rich and the kids took care of setting up the back yard. We needed six banquet tables, end to end, to accommodate the crowd. I told Ken that Erin and Davin had agreed to vacuum the backyard after the party so he could relax.

The day finally arrived. We were about to stand up in front of one hundred and thirty people and say our vows. Friends, family and The Court would all be watching as Ken and I formalized our fifteen-year relationship. Ken had done a spectacular job pulling together our special day. Yes, even I, the wedding hater, was excited. From 11:00 AM right up to our walking down the aisle, it was a crazy whirlwind of activity. Ken and I were working with the caterer, the minister, the florists and so on to make sure that everything looked good and would run smoothly.

Heather took the reins at some point and said, "You two go home now! I got this." Ken tried to protest, but Heather, being Ken's version of Karla, would have none of it – she quite literally pushed us out the front door.

As Ken and I packed our stuff up to get ready at the club, Ken said, "Babe, are you ready to do this?"

"Of course I am," I replied.

"No regrets?" he asked.

"Nope, not one."

We hugged for what seemed like an eternity, took a couple deep breaths, and headed to the club. We were getting married.

I NOW PRONOUNCE YOU 'UNIONIZED'

"..... when you realize you want to spend the rest of your life with somebody, you want the rest of your life to start as soon as possible."

- Billy Crystal, in *When Harry met Sally*

Okay, not exactly married but we were having a civil union and all marriages are a type of civil union. When we arrived at the club, Heather had done a fabulous job managing the set-up. Everything looked spectacular. Heather was already in her gown, the one Ken and I had picked out for her the year before. She looked stunning. We set ourselves up in the back room and did one last sweep of the club to make sure everything was perfect.

When I got to the kitchen, the Head Chef from the catering company greeted me. He looked at me and said, "Surprised?"

I said, "Absolutely. I didn't expect you to be here doing the cooking in person."

He winked at me and said, "I wouldn't have missed this event. I want it to be perfect for you guys."

I gave that big bear of a man a big bear hug, fought back the tears and said, "Thank you."

I left the kitchen and entered the back hallway and saw all of our nieces, nephews and daughters dressed in their tuxes and dresses. They looked amazing. I watched Ken as he went from nephew to nephew, straightening ties and tightening vests. Oh for heaven's sake, again with the tears. I wish I could have blamed it on PMS (but alas, I don't have a uterus to curse!)

Ken and I watched from the back as our rainbow tribe made its way into the great room. Our two closest friends, Will and Scott, a couple we've known for fifteen years, flew in from Switzerland to be our best men. We watched as they escorted our daughters down the aisle. We stood there holding hands tightly until we heard our cue and as the disco theme from Star Wars blasted out of the speakers, we squeezed hands and walked gallantly down the hall and into the great room where one hundred and thirty people were waiting for us to "unionize." Lots of giggles, laughs and applause rose from our friends and family as we approached the alcove in the great room of the Kellogg Club.

Frankie was wonderful. She delivered a truly touching ceremony that brought forth smiles and tears. She slipped at one point and said, "wed," which caused a lot of chuckling from the room. She giggled, apologized and used the word "commit" the second time around.

We were in NJ, so instead of 'wed' I would have gone with "unionized" though I am not sure how the AFL-CIO would have reacted.

Most comments we received about our ceremony actually revolved around the kids. Everyone seemed touched to see all the kids in our family standing up with us. At some point during the party, my sister-in-law Heidi cornered me and told me something truly astounding. Her three kids had attended three gay commitment ceremonies and had never been to a heterosexual wedding. All I could think was, *Wow, there must have been a lot of pent up demand. I had no idea she had so many gay friends.*

Scott has a beautiful singing voice and agreed to sing "Someone Like You" from *Jekyll and Hyde*. Ken and I had seen this show together and fell in love with the song; so much so, we had the works "if someone like you..."engraved on the inside of our rings. It seemed the perfect song for him to sing after we completed our vows. His partner Will, who I have known for more years than either of us care to admit, agreed to do the toast. After the ceremony was complete, I took a moment to thank everyone for being part of our milestone event. Friends and family had come in from all over the country: aunts and uncles from Texas, many of our gay friends from Atlanta, our very close friend Paul from North Carolina. Laura, who came in from Arizona, represented the high school girls gone wild group and Linda sent her husband Jerry and their daughter Emily over from Ohio. It was an eclectic crowd. Linda was at her goddaughter's graduation in California, so she was not able to attend. She was not amused that we all were sending pictures of the party to her cell phone.

Sadly, my father was not able to attend. His health at the time would not allow him to travel. He called the house right before we left for the ceremony to say, "I am so proud of you and Ken, you know that, right?"

I said, "Yes, Dad, I do know that."

"Make sure you bring that family of yours for Christmas. It's been too long since I've seen my granddaughters."

"I will, Daddy." Waterworks again.

During my welcome and Scott's song, the catering team was passing out libations for Will's toast. Ken and I offered our guests a choice in toasting beverages. We offered the entire place a shot of silver Patron tequila or a glass of prosecco. Yes, a tequila toast. You should have known that was coming. The catering staff had pre-poured the toast so they could ensure everyone would have a glass by the time Scott finished his song. What I hadn't prepared them for (nor had I anticipated) was the number of people who chose tequila. Seventy percent of the people in that room wanted tequila. Ken and I could see the staff scrambling; we just didn't know why. During his toast, Will saw the catering staff darting and dashing around trying to get everyone a glass. He turned his toast into a stand-up comedy routine to buy time.

At some point during his monologue he told people we had drag queens in the audience and that part of the evening festivities would be identifying who they were. There were no drag queens in attendance. Ken's ex-dating partner, the Barbie dressing drag queen, was not in the room. However, I did like the idea of having 6' 5" glamazon drag queens on hand, so I made a mental note to keep them in mind if we renew our vows. I did feel sorry for our close friend Lauren. She's a 5'9", 6 foot in heels, truly stunning blond who spent the entire evening being asked if she was the drag queen. I believe she started saying yes so people would leave her alone. Bless her heart.

Right after the ceremony we did the customary pictures: the people in the ceremony, family, all the boys from Atlanta, our best men. It was a long list. The last one we took was of Ken and me with all the members of our Altamont Court family. As we were setting up for the photo I thought, *These people are so much more than friends and neighbors. They truly are family.* It remains one of my favorite pictures. My brother kept calling our Altamont Court family, *The Others,* as if the residents of The Court were members of some secret island community from the show, *Lost.*

We were setting up for the Altamont Court Family shot when I saw my garage-sharing neighbor Pat grab Karla by the arm and whisper something in her ear. The color drained from Karla's face and they both scurried toward the back of the porch. The last thing I wanted on our special day was drama. I couldn't imagine what in the world was so urgent. They quickly returned, smiling, no stress on their faces. I thought, 'whatever' and we went on with the photos.

I cornered them after our photo and asked, "What the hell was going on with you two?"

Karla, who calls Pat "PP" for "Prissy Pat," a name she earned on a 'Just Us Girls (JUG's) Weekend, said, "PP was unhappy with my choice of undergarments."

Pat looked at her in utter disbelief and said, "Unhappy? You had the worst case of VPL I have ever seen. It was so bad it would have shown up in the photo."

"VPL?" I asked.

"Visible Panty Line," Pat whispered.

I glared at Karla and said, "You have lived next to two gays for six years. Have you learned nothing?"

Karla, who almost never wears formal wear, lamely defended herself, saying, "I couldn't find my Spanx so I thought a pair of control top granny panties would help suck in my tummy bulge."- Wrong!

I looked at her dress and said, "Well your VPL is gone. What did you do?"

Karla told me that Pat, being a good friend and neighbor, shielded her while she shed her offending panties and tucked them into her clutch.

I started laughing. "So you have Karla's granny panties in that clutch you're carrying?"

Pat giggled and nodded.

"Way too much information. Pat, you get the best neighbor and best friend award. Keeping Karla's offensive panties in your purse goes way beyond the call of duty."

Vows said, pictures taken, it was time for the party to begin. Ken and I did the customary first dance to the song "At Last" sung by Miss Etta James. It was the perfect way to start the evening. Our ravenous guests were keeping the servers and bartenders hopping while the DJ started the music. He opened with selections from the

'60s and quickly moved to something more appropriate for a gay commitment reception: '80s dance music.

After my fourth shot of tequila, I no longer cared who had VPL, unless it was me.

As the dancing moved into high gear I got a big kick out of my brother's four-year-old twin boys. Both are blondes and we'd bought them matching white suits. Those two little boys never left the dance floor. They jumped, shimmied, shook and jived the entire evening. My brother walked up to me as I was watching them get their groove on, and I said, "Tod, your boys are having a ball. Everyone is enjoying their dancing."

Tod said, "Yeah, I know. By the way, who's the chick over there in the blue jacket?"

I looked across the room and saw my step sister-in-law Sheryl. I said, "That's Ken's stepbrother's wife Sheryl. Why?"

Tod stood quietly for a second and then said, "She's a hardcore Jersey girl, isn't she?"

"You could say that," I said.

Tod continued, "She came up to me and asked me if those little blond boys were my sons. Of course I said yes."

Giving him a questioning look I said, "And?"

Continuing to stare in her direction, Tod said, "Well she told me they were adorable."

I knew there was more. "And?"

"And that they were 'F#$%ing delicious'."

There it was. My step-sister-in-law's trademark word.

Tod continued, "She just kept repeating how F#$%ing delicious they were and that she could eat them with a F$%&ing spoon."

Ah, the Jersey vernacular. A thing of true beauty.

"Every time I see her she just smiles and says, "F#$%ing delicious."

"It's a compliment."

Tod just laughed and joined his boys on the dance floor. My brother dances like a straight white man. He looks like the dancing gopher in *Caddyshack*.

Since our daughters and nieces had entertained us over the years with so many memorable Broadway performances, we had a surprise for them. Ken and I both love country music and Ken loves to line dance. So Ken selected a line dance he could teach the girls and made them learn it in a weekend. If we had to sit through their performances, they were going to have to take part in one of ours and in front of all our guests. Thus was born the "Ken and Trent's Dizzy Dance." So in front of one hundred people, Ken, our nieces, the boys from Atlanta and I did the "Dizzy" line dance. It brought down the house.

The evening was half over and I had yet to taste any of the food. The caterers were serving the cake when I finally broke away from the crowd to get a bite to eat. As I came into the grand dining room to get some food and a slice of cake, I could see all the boys from Atlanta gathered at one table. There was only one woman at that table. It was my mother-in-law. It looked like the queen holding court. In this case it was the queen holding court with a bunch of queens. There was a lot of royalty at that table. She was eating up every moment of their attention. As I walked back toward the grand salon with a slice of cake and a plate full of nibbles, I could hear her laughter all the way down the hall.

Our party was in full swing when I re-entered the great room. All the tables and chairs had been pulled back to make way for dancing. Serious, unrestrained dancing. The DJ was spinning Donna Summer, The Village People, Thelma Houston, and Madonna. There were so many people dancing under the lights with their arms in the air you would think you were watching a gay circuit party that had been crashed by a bunch of straight people. It was Studio 54 minus the cocaine. At some point in the evening Ken got so overheated Heather thought he was going to pass out. The Altamont Court Boys Club obligingly dragged him outside onto the back porch and poured a pitcher of ice water down his back. Good friends are hard to find.

Since the club was in a residential neighborhood, we had a hard stop at 10:30 PM. At 10:25 PM the DJ played the ultimate closing song. There was a collective sigh when our dancing horde heard the familiar sounds of Donna Summers' "Last Dance." Couples swayed in the arms of their significant others as the music slowly built to that familiar disco beat. When the music changed, the room exploded with people jumping, whirling and spinning. There was a feeling in the room that something special had taken place. Something that no one wanted to end. At the very end of the song there was a cheer so loud it shook the hall.

Ken and I stood near the door so we could thank everyone for being a part of our special day. Even I, Mr. Trent-Who-Hates-Weddings-Pines, had to admit this had been an amazing event.

Ken escorted my family back to the house so Karla and I could stay to make sure the caterers cleared and cleaned the club. We were sitting in a couple of foldout chairs when she took my hand and said, "This was one hell of a party. The Kellogg Club will never be the same."

Smiling, happy but exhausted, I said, "I guess we didn't over-hype it when we said it would be the social event of the season."

Karla said, "I have to tell you something about a couple of your guests."

I immediately thought, *Did she find a couple of drag queens at the party?*

She continued, "Two different men I spoke to said basically the same thing. They came because their wives, who are your friends, made them come, and they weren't thrilled to be at a gay wedding. They didn't believe gays should marry.'"

I looked at her a bit stunned and said, "They just came right out and said that to you?"

"That's the interesting part," she said. "They both started off that way and ended with, 'But after watching Ken and Trent, I have to admit I've changed my mind.'"

"Really? " I said incredulously. "One event changed their minds?"

Karla said, "They both seemed very sincere that this event changed the way they view same-sex marriage. And isn't that what it is all about? Changing people's minds and hearts one person at time."

Karla was right. When something is personal, we view it differently. We reflect on it, soul search, and try to understand on a deeper level. A personal connection brings you into the fray. It's easy to judge from the sidelines and take hard line positions. But when it's personal—a son, a daughter, a best friend—we seek to understand and accept.

I squeezed her hand and said, "Okay, sister mine, time to go home. I am sure they are all at the house having a nightcap and we are missing out."

With that, we got ourselves together and headed home. When we got back to the house, our porch was filled with members of our families: Ken's, The Court's and mine. It was eleven-thirty and no one showed signs of going to sleep.

By twelve-thirty people had started heading home and just Karla, Ken, my family and my good friend Laura remained on the porch. We brewed some coffee and tea and started talking about the evening. My mother had tucked away a couple pieces of cake and was judiciously guarding each forkful. Mom has a thing for baked goods and she was not about to share her cake with anyone. Later I found out she had two more pieces hidden up in her room. She was turning into an Altamont Court squirrel.

At one-thirty AM, a police car came driving down our road and stopped just short of the house. We were all watching as the policeman stepped out of his car and started walking toward our porch. None of us realized as he approached that he was here at the request of one of our neighbors who was not impressed with the amount of noise we were making. I'm sure it was one of the neighbors we didn't invite. If this man hadn't been driving a real police car, I would have thought he was a stripper in a cop-uniform. This was one very attractive, very built, very young Morristown cop.

He took one look at the motley crew of old folks on the porch, smiled, lowered his head and shook it back and forth saying, "This is not what I expected."

"Are we in trouble officer?" I asked. I was thinking to myself, *There are worse ways for Ken and me to end our wedding night than being handcuffed by a Chippendale dancer.*

He said, "Well, sir . . ."

Damn, that ruined everything. The 'well, sir' reminded me I was an old guy.

"We've had a complaint about the noise level. I was expecting a bunch of drunken college kids. I never expected..." he stopped mid-sentence as if he was choosing his words carefully, "...I never expected to find a mature group of adults drinking coffee."

Mature? I thought. *Well, I guess that's better than "A bunch of old farts.."*

I said, "I am so sorry, officer, we'll take this inside."

He immediately said, "No, that's not necessary, just keep it down. If I get another call I will have to ticket you. I really don't want to do that."

About that time a second squad car pulled up. As the officer stepped out of the car he looked up toward the porch and saw that same group of 'mature' people his fellow officer did when he arrived. He looked confused.

The officer on our porch just waved him off and said, "It's okay. They are just drinking coffee." The second officer let out a grunt of disapproval, got back into his car and drove away. Officer Chip – I named him that due to his Chippendale Dancer looks – said his goodbyes and we all waved as he left The Court. I'm sure he was thinking, *What a F#$%ing crazy bunch of old geezers – bless their hearts.*

The next morning we were all dealing with mild hangovers, when our good friends Tom and CJ (the CJ who refuses to ever take me to another opera) showed up to drop off a gift to commemorate our civil union. Ken and I were surprised, as we really weren't expecting gifts. CJ asked us to sit down in the living room and placed a rather heavy box on my lap. I couldn't imagine what she had come up with.

As I unwrapped the gift, I stared at a large box of Godiva chocolate – four pounds of it! I looked up at her and said, "Seriously? Why in the world would you buy us a giant box of chocolate?"

CJ said, "Just open the box!"

Okay, I thought. *I am dealing with a hangover and she is playing "disguise the gift as a sugar coma."*

I lifted the lid, removed the tissue and found myself speechless. I was staring at a pair of candlesticks CJ and Tom had inherited from CJ's Great-uncle Arthur. I knew the candlesticks well. They were Greco Roman in design. Miniature figures, carved of marble, kneeling on brass pedestals that supported the base for the candle. The detail on these small statues is nothing short of amazing. When I first saw them at CJ and Tom's house, I teasingly told CJ that if she didn't leave them to me in her will, I was going to break into her house and steal them! It had been a running joke for years and here they were sitting on my lap. Ken knew all about these treasured pieces and neither one of use could find words to express our gratitude.

I finally looked up at CJ with tears in my eyes and said, "Why?"

CJ said, "Tom and I talked about it a lot. We wanted you to have something truly special to commemorate this milestone in your life."

"CJ, this is a wonderful gift, but it's just too much."

"No, it's not, Trent; it's perfect. I have told you a few stories about Arthur and his partner Karl over the years, but I haven't shared everything. Arthur was an Oxford Rhodes Scholar, which was a huge achievement, especially for a boy from Montana. He met Karl when he returned from the UK in the late 1920's. Karl was an extremely successful and sought-after interior designer for socialites on the upper east side of New York; he was actually listed in the New York Social Register. They traveled the globe for Karl's clients, often picking up pieces for their home as well."

Ken and I were mesmerized by this story.

"They purchased these candlesticks in the 1950's while traveling in Italy. When we had the estate appraised, they were estimated to be approximately three hundred years old."

I just sat there shaking my head. CJ reached out and took my hand and said, "Karl and Arthur lived an amazing life. They were a gay couple in a committed relationship during a period of time when you didn't talk about such things. They were together sixty years. Tom and I felt this gift best represented their relationship together. We are giving them to you and Ken and wishing you sixty years of happiness together. We think Arthur and Karl would approve if they were here."

All I could think was, *they are here with us right now.*

Ken and I did our best to hold back tears. These candlesticks were far more than their aesthetic beauty. They represent a sixty-year commitment of two very special men. I prayed Ken and I would live up to their standard and that someday, after sixty years together, we would find a committed gay couple to pass them on to.

TRANSITIONS

"Life isn't about waiting for the storm to pass; it's about learning to dance in the rain."

– Anonymous

Change is never easy. The fact is, no one really likes change but it is often necessary for growth. Most of us do not go willingly. We are pushed and forced into change to survive and mature. Life is not always kind, so we have to learn to adapt.

My career has always been based on change. Taking on new and challenging projects has allowed me to expand both personally and professionally, and almost always came with a promotion. I had been in the same assignment for several years and wanted to venture into another part of the business. I knew this would mean we needed to move back to Atlanta. Leaving NJ this time would not be easy. Although our girls were out of high school and moving on with their lives, our family had grown. We were now an integral part of the fabric that made up Altamont Court.

The first thing I thought when this opportunity presented itself was, *How in the world am I going to break this news to Karla?* It was bad enough that I'd have to explain this to our kids and Ken's mother, but Karla and I are so painfully alike, I knew she would not make it easy for me.

I had completed a couple of interviews but had managed to keep it quiet. Ken agreed that we should not share any details with members of the family until we had some certainty around the opportunity. When I was asked for references, I provided my list. It included peers, key senior officers and a couple of outside references. One was my uncle; the other was my mother-in-law. She's a Senior VP outside of my company so I figured she would serve as a good personal reference. She was number twelve, so I figured she would be the last person anyone would contact.

Imagine Ken's dismay when his mother called and said, "So, you have something you want to tell me?"

Ken said, "I don't think so, Ma, why?"

With an edge to her voice Sally said, "Really? So I find out you're moving to Atlanta when I get a reference call from someone Trent interviewed with?"

Ken was stunned. When he called me, I was speechless.

Due to the strategic nature of this job opportunity, the hiring senior executive had called all twelve of my references. Now it was my turn to genuflect in front of my mother-in-law. I called her immediately and fell on my sword. She was remarkably understanding. I had come to NJ for Ken's career and our daughters; now it was my turn for a career move. We loved Atlanta, so going back would be like going home.

Unexpectedly, my mother was very unhappy about our move. When I called her to let her know we were heading back to Atlanta, her reaction was immediate and disapproving.

"What do you mean you're going back to Atlanta? How can you leave that nice town you live in and all your wonderful neighbors?" She continued to lament, "Well, I guess this means I will never get to see The City again or go to another Broadway show."

Oh, brother, she had just elevated herself to drama queen status.

I said, "Mother, get a grip. You can go to The City anytime you want. Ken and I go up once a year to see shows so you can join us."

"It won't be the same. I won't be able to walk around town and go into The City when I want to."

"You'll live," I said. My mother should know better. I don't do guilt.

I had to face Karla before the rumor mill made it to the street. After a shot of the old stand-by in the freezer, I went next door. Karla took one look at my face and said, "Oh, no. No, no, no! Whatever you are about to tell me, I know I am not going to like it so turn your ass around and go back next door."

She seemed to know what was coming and was not going to make this easy. I took a breath and said, "Pull out the Tequila, we need to talk." She grabbed it from the freezer and poured two shots. We clinked our shot glasses and downed their contents in one gulp. Looking at each other, our eyes began to tear up.

She spoke first. "You're leaving me."

I swallowed hard. "Yes."

"Bitch."

"Back at you."

"When?" she asked.

"Three months."

We sat there for a few more minutes. Finally, we stood up and hugged. A fierce, I-am-never-letting-go, type of hug.

When we finally released she said, "I am not going to be able to talk to you for a few days so don't take it personally. Just give me time. On the other hand, I have no idea how the kids will react. You have to tell them yourself. You're on your own, baby."

Erin's reaction was to be expected. She was truly unhappy with me. Her fairy godfather was leaving and in her mind that was not acceptable. For weeks she would just glare at me and walk away muttering something that sounded remarkably like "Bitch." Before you judge, she has heard her mother and me call each other bitch for the last six years. To us it's a catty term of endearment.

Davin was more reserved. He just stood there staring at me. He blinked a few times and said, "Seriously?"

I said, "Yes, seriously."

"That sucks." As he started to walk away, he turned and said, "You never made me a cake for my birthday."

For some reason his parting comment hurt more than it should have. Davin is not one to be overly emotional. In his mind, as long as I lived next door there would be a birthday cake at some point. His realization that there would be no cake was his way of telling me this move upset him. I knew I had to make this boy his own cake before I left.

The day the house went up for sale a shock wave blasted down The Court. Nearly everyone on the street dropped by to ask questions. Every time I turned onto our street and saw the "For Sale" sign in our yard, my heart skipped a beat. Selecting the realtor was an interesting process. Casey, my mother-in-law's friend who sold us the house, had moved to the Jersey Shore so we had to scratch her off our list. New Jersey has an excess of realty mavens who formed a line outside our house to pitch their wares. It looked like the scene from *Mary Poppins* with all the nannies in line for an interview sporting the same style of clothing and hair. We selected our realtor like everyone else does; we based our decision on the quality of their wardrobe, shoes and jewelry. If you can't sell your own image, how on earth are you going to sell a house! Of course a kick-ass marketing plan doesn't hurt either.

Houses like ours – a completely renovated, center hall Queen Anne colonial, in town, on a cul-de-sac - don't come on the market very often in Morristown. However, I was concerned because we were selling at the worst possible time. The house went on the market between Christmas and New Year's with our first open house happened during an ice storm. I spent the entire day cleaning and salting the walks. I figured the traffic would be light, but I didn't want anyone slipping on my walkway and procuring the house through a lawsuit.

I was wrong about the traffic. Our realtor became overwhelmed in the first hour. She had to call in reinforcements from the office to help manage the flow. Over a four-hour period we had thirty-six couples and ten single people tour our home. It was a insane. By the end of the night we had three offers. We were in the middle of the Great Recession in a bottomed-out housing market in the middle of winter. Ken and I were shell-shocked. The next thing we knew our house was in the middle of a bidding war. The three interested couples all scheduled second visits and that's when the fun really began.

Each time a couple visited, I went next door and worked remotely from Karla's dining room. I could see into our house from her living room windows, which allowed me to know when the prospective buyers left. As soon as I saw their car leave, I'd pack up and head home.

When I am shopping for a home I am in and out of a house in no time. The first two couples set up camp for the afternoon. Couple number one spent two and a half hours in our home. I am not talking about a home inspection; this was a second visit to see if they wanted to increase their offer. I couldn't imagine what they talked about for two and a half hours while looking at our home. It was like watching Mime Theater through the windows. The husband really wanted the house. The wife was not so sure. He was pacing, waving his arms and pulling at his hair during the last thirty minutes.

Finally, my realtor pushed them out the door because couple number two had arrived. This couple stayed for an hour and a half. Ninety minutes. As I watched the semi-comedic happenings through Karla's window, my nervous energy took over. I was staring up at her chandelier and wondering what in the world was taking these people so long when I noticed it was dirty. Not just dirty, but really dirty. Cobwebs, dust, film on the crystals. I couldn't take sitting there anymore. Her chandelier was the diversion I needed.

I went out to the kitchen and started pulling out cleaning supplies. Swiffer dusters (which I had given Karla as a Christmas gift),

Windex wipes, brass cleaner. I dragged all of this stuff into the dining room and started cleaning the chandelier. I was standing in stocking feet in the middle of the dining room table and wiping down crystals when Karla walked into the room. She looked at me and said, "Should I ask?"

"No."

She looked at me for another second and said, "Okay," turned and headed back up to her office.

By the time couple number two had left I had cleaned and polished the chandelier and paste-waxed the dining room table. As I was leaving to go home Karla yelled down, "I have some grout you can clean the next time you get bored."

In my most mature voice, I yelled back, "Bite me."

Once The Court accepted the inevitable, requests for contract addendums began appearing on our doorstep: Buyer must allow access to their backyard for movie night, buyer must make quality leftovers available to neighbors, buyer must make their front porch available for weekend happy hours, buyer must participate in Halloween fest...the list was long and quirky.

When couple number three came back for their second look, I ran next door to tell Karla I was there to clean her grout. I figured I had at least an hour to kill. Since it was close to 5:00 PM, we pulled out a bottle of wine, grabbed a couple of glasses and some munchies and sat down by the fireplace. Okay, 3:15 PM is not close to 5:00 PM, but as Alan Jackson sings, "*It's Five o'clock Somewhere.*"

Karla looked at me and said, "This sucks."

"I got that the first one hundred times you told me," I said.

Changing the subject, I told her, "I really like this last couple. They're young, they're planning a family and seem like they would fit in with the rest of the crazies on The Court."

"Who you calling crazy?" Karla asked.

"I could have said mentally unbalanced."

She smiled. "You have a point."

I had a good feeling about couple number three. They just seemed to 'fit' with the house and with the neighborhood, but they only stayed twenty minutes. I wasn't sure what to make of that after the marathon runs of couples one and two. Within two days we had revised offers from each of the interested buyers. Couple number three, the ones who stayed the shortest amount of time, submitted the highest bid.

Ken and I agreed to accept the contract. On that following Saturday we saw couple number three, Karla and Kennedy (yes, another Karla, who we dubbed K2) standing on the sidewalk looking up at the house. I quickly waved them in so we could be properly introduced. "Of the three buyers, you were truly our favorites. This street is kinda special. We're very close to all of our neighbors so it was important to find someone who we thought would fit in. So where are you guys from?"

Kennedy said, "Well, we are renting a condo in the building at the front of the street." I couldn't believe it. They were already members of The Court, and now they were making it official.

K2 looked at us and said, "I can't tell you how much we love this house. I know it may sound a little crazy, but your home has an amazing energy. It just feels good when we're in here."

Ken said, "We have an eclectic group of friends; some are even self-proclaimed psychics. All of them say the same thing, 'Your house has an amazing energy.' So no, we don't think that sounds weird at all. It's a compliment."

Places do take on energy over time, absorbing the emotions of the people who inhabit them or the events that transpire in them. You can feel it when you enter a place where terrible things have happened. Even if you don't know the history of a place, you can often feel its energy. I know it sounds a bit 'new age, tree hugger, hippie-esque,' but Ken and I both believe it. This home raised several happy families before ours. We simply added our own brand of energy to the place. And add we did. Birthday parties, Thanksgivings, Christmases, slumber parties, backyard barbeques... you name it, we hosted it. All that love and joy had left a permanent mark on our home.

I asked them to sit down so we could tell them a bit about their new neighbors. K2 and Kennedy stayed for nearly two hours listening to stories of Altamont Court. They laughed, gasped and generally shook their heads in disbelief. Kennedy laughed and said, "You two are making this stuff up. You just want to make sure we buy your home."

"I am not making this up, I swear. In fact, let me show you some mock addendums to your contract." I shared with them all the various handwritten notes we had received.

K2 asked, "Can I keep these?"

"Of course. You're the ones that have to live up to them."

As they said good-bye, they shared one last thing with us. K2 was pregnant with twins. Ken and I were so excited. There would be new babies on The Court. Kennedy said, "And one more thing. We are having a girl and a boy."

K2 continued, "When we saw the pale green guest room we both thought it was perfect for a 'gender neutral' nursery. But the icing on the cake were the two rooms on the top floor."

I stared at her for a minute, not sure where she was going and then it hit me. Ashleigh had painted her room a light pink and Lindsay had painted hers blue. The house was ready for a boy and a girl. I knew immediately the house had chosen its next occupants just as it had chosen Ken and me. They were goners the moment they crossed the threshold.

SAYING GOODBYE

"Where there is love, there is life"

– Mahatna Ghandi

With the house sold and moving day imminent, the realization that we were leaving The Court had set in. Ken and I were mopey. Karla and the kids were mopey. The whole street was mopey. The two gay guys that helped add to the reputation of The Court were actually leaving. We decided to throw one last party for the street and invited everyone. The Court had prepared a going away gift. Jane had created a board with pictures on it and a Forever Honorary Altamont Courtian certificate that everyone signed, including the pets on The Court. After a lot of love, laughter and tears, everyone made their way home.

Ken looked and me and asked, "Having second thoughts?"

I said, "No, but if I were it is too late now."

We both laughed.

"Tomorrow we have to move you into Warren and Heidi's. I guess it's fitting that we started there and we're ending there." Ken still had physical therapy to complete and couldn't help with the move. Actually, I mandated he not be around when the movers started packing because it would drive him crazy. He would, in turn, drive me crazy. So his absence was in both of our best interests.

It took the movers four full days to pack four floors full of stuff. How can two people possibly have so much stuff? As the boxes piled up, the house, once again, began to look like an episode of "Hoarders," only this time it was the "Extreme Edition." In the middle of all this chaos, it was Davin's birthday and I was on the hook for a cake. I gave Karla the list of ingredients.

She took one look at it and said, "What the hell is this? This is what you put into your chocolate cake? I should've never seen this."

This from a woman who puts lard in her pie crust.

"Just get me those things so I can get his cake made before he comes home from school."

After Karla's quick run to the grocery, I started putting the cake together. Usually I decimate my kitchen; this time I decimated Karla's. Cake mix, pudding boxes, cocoa powder, condensed milk... the kitchen was covered in a light dust of flavorful mayhem. Stacked in the sink were a half dozen bowls and three used cake pans.

"Trent Pines, you are never again cooking in my kitchen."

"Liar," I said. "Erin's sixteenth birthday is next year and you know she is going to want this exact same cake. You have a year to recover before I swoop in and make another mess."

"You know Davin's been sick. His stomach has been awful. I don't know if he will be able to eat that."

I said, "It doesn't matter whether he can eat it or not; what matters is that I made it for him."

Karla got a lump caught in her throat and said, "You're right. I hate you."

With a lump in my throat, I smiled at her and said, "I hate you back."

I ran home to see how the army of packers was doing with the house. They had five guys working non-stop, but due to the amount of stemware, collectables and artwork, it was slow going. No one wanted to be responsible for breaking the Murano stemware. In the mood I was in, I would have made one of them fly to Venice to buy new ones. I was so busy with the movers, I hadn't realized the kids were home from school. I'd left the cake in the center of the island for Davin so it would be the first thing he saw when he came home. I couldn't believe Karla hadn't called.

I walked back over to see if the kids were home and as I came up the back steps I saw Davin sitting at the island staring at the cake. I asked him, "You like?"

He just kept looking at the cake. He finally raised his eyes to look at me and said, "I can't believe you did this. I can't believe you made me my own cake."

"I had to," was all I could say.

Davin jumped up from his bar stool and gave me a big, long hug, said thank you, and ran up the stairs. I stood there for a minute and thought, *Most kids would have been hacking into the cake as soon as they saw it.* I had to remind myself Davin was not the average kid.

With tears in my eyes, I walked back across to our house thinking, *I have never felt more like a yo-yo.* As soon as I walked in the back door the phone rang. It was Karla. *What now?* "Yes?" I said as I answered.

"Davin was blown away by the cake."

"I wasn't sure. It seemed that way, but then he went upstairs."

Karla said, "I had to ask him. He was in his room, lying on the bed, tossing a ball in the air, not really saying anything, so I asked, "What did you think of your cake?" He said, "I can't believe he did that. They're really leaving, aren't they?" "Yeah, baby, they are." After a moment he said, "It sucks." I told him "Yes, it does.'"

As Karla told me this, tears were running down my face. Davin had it right; this sucked.

After four days of packing, the loaders arrived. Five new guys began to empty our house into a truck, a giant truck that took up most of the street, further distressing our neighbors and friends. During this entire packaging and loading process, I had to manage our four cats. I moved them from room to room and finally isolated them in the master bedroom after it was completely empty. I posted a ROOM CLEAR - DO NOT ENTER sign on the door. The last thing I needed to deal with was a rogue cat.

The eighteen wheeler was finally loaded and my truck was crammed full of everything except me, the kitties, and a sleeping bag. I ran back up to "Walton's Mountain" to have one last dinner with Ken and my in-laws and say goodbye.

I had the most difficult time saying goodbye to Ken. We were going to be separated for four weeks. Though I travel a lot for business, we had never been apart for four weeks. It was going to be a challenge for both of us. I had the added challenge of living with four cats at a Residence Inn while I had the floors refinished and the walls painted in our new house.

We said our tearful goodbyes and I headed back to the house. As I pulled into the driveway it hit me, *This is it.* This would be my last night on Altamont Court. I got out of my car and started walking toward the front of our home, but I couldn't bring myself to go in just yet. I walked past the front of our house and down the street. The night was cold and clear and there was a bright full moon. I stopped in front of each house for just a moment, said a small prayer for the family inside, and moved on to the next.

As I walked down the street I realized for the first time that Ken and I had lived a very "heterosexual" life while we were members of The Court family. Two kids, a house, backyard barbeques, children's birthday parties, holiday family events. Everything most gay couples struggle to obtain. Many of our close gay friends didn't understand it at all. When they visited, they noted that all of our closest friends were straight couples. It would be easy to say it all happened by accident, but I don't believe that.

I made it back to the front of our house and stood there, my breath making little clouds of vapor. As I stared at the house, I realized just how remarkable our lives had been on The Court. I slowly climbed the front stairs and, before I entered the house, put my hand on the doorframe. I thanked God for our time on The Court and for the wonderful memories we created while living here. I asked the house to protect and care for its next family with as much love and warmth as it had cared for us. Then I entered our home for the last time.

I called Karla to let her know I was home. "We'll be right over," she said, and hung up the phone. Davin and Erin wanted to see the kitties before I left. I was leaving for Atlanta at five AM and no one was getting up that early to say goodbye. I was looking around our totally empty house when I heard the front door open.

I hadn't seen Erin in five days. She had disappeared once the movers arrived. All the kitties appeared out of nowhere when they heard the kids. With no furniture, we all just sat down on the foyer floor with the kitties. Alexander ran right over to Davin and climbed in his lap and pawed up his chest so he could rub his face on Davin's chin. Those two always had a close connection and Alex seemed to know Davin was upset. He sat in Davin's lap for the next thirty minutes. Erin played with the rest of the kitty horde, but never looked me in the eye.

Karla said, "Are you ready?"

"Ready? Ready is relative. My truck is packed to the brim and I have a fourteen-hour drive ahead with John and four cats. I am as ready as I'm gonna get. The Scooby Doo gang had the mystery machine, and I have the rolling pussy palace."

Karla and Erin laughed out loud. Aha, a crack in the armor! Erin finally looked my way and said, "Are you going to make them stay in their carriers the entire trip?"

I am sure everyone at the ASPCA let out a collective gasp when I said, "No, no, no – that is too long for them to be caged. I have their kitty stands in the back, food, water and a litter box. Once I start rolling they usually settle in quickly."

She said, "Good. I was going to be really mad at you if you kept them caged for fourteen hours."

Fourteen hours with four kitties crying in their carry-alls would have landed me in the psych ward of some hospital.

The kids each gave me big, long hugs and ran out the door. Karla and I stood in the foyer and watched them leave.

Karla said, "I am not saying goodbye, bitch."

I looked at her and said, "Back at you. You know we really can't be separated at this point no matter where we live."

She smiled and said, "Easy for you to say; you're the one moving."

I laughed with tears in my eyes.

After a big hug she said, "Hate you."

I smiled and said, "Hate you more."

One more quick hug and she was gone.

I didn't get much sleep that night as the kitties were completely unnerved by all the changes in the house. They walked the halls meowing like cats in heat. When they finally settled down, all four decided to sleep on top of me. This was not conducive to a sound sleep. I got up at 5:00 AM on the dot, pulled together my few remaining things, loaded the kitties in their carriers to transport them to the truck, and then loaded my remaining things into the Yukon.

As I came around the front of the truck I saw a piece of poster board on my windshield. In big bold letters it said, "I will miss you, bitch! Love you, Erin – aka, Bufanaquishria (the nickname the girls on the field hockey team gave her for developing an exceptional pair of glutes). I stood there staring at that poster in the twenty-degree morning air, laughing and crying at the same time. She had forgiven me just enough to say good-bye.

I backed out of the driveway and drove down the street one last time. I stopped in front of our home and said thank you to that lovely Queen Ann center hall colonial for all she had given us. It was time to start a new adventure in our old hometown of Atlanta. As I drove away I realized that this home and the extraordinary people of Altamont Court had left their imprints on our hearts forever.

EPILOGUE

"Just when I thought I was out....they pull me back in!"

- Al Pacino in The Godfather

It's been a few years since we left The Court. To be honest, it often feels like we never left. You may move from The Court, but you never really leave The Court. Sort of like *Hotel California*.

Karla's husband Rich frequently finds himself in Atlanta on business. We forbid him to stay in a hotel so he stays with us, giving us a chance to catch up. On one of these visits he reminded me that Erin's 16th birthday party was just around the corner. I looked at him quizzically and said, "And?"

"And you convinced her she needed to have a big Sweet Sixteen Party since its a NJ rite of passage and because so many of her friends were inviting her to their parties."

I wasn't following. What did this have to do with me? I repeated, "And?"

"And if you think Karla is going to throw this party without you, then your brain has atrophied over the last year. Karla would rather just buy her a used car and be done with it."

Oh God, I *was* totally guilty of convincing Erin she needed a Sweet Sixteen Party and I'd completely forgotten I had guilted Karla into throwing this party. Even worse, I had committed myself to spearheading the event and making the cake. Which explains why that cute little ditty by Eileen Barton started to flood my mind, "If I'd known *this* was coming, I'd have baked a cake..."

With Rich clearing up my confusion, back to The Court I went to mastermind Erin's Sweet Sixteen Party. Erin wanted her party at the Kellogg Club, the same place Ken and I held our commitment ceremony. I wasn't sure the club was going to survive another Court hosted event. I made a trip back for the planning, selecting a caterer and the all-important trip to help Erin pick out a dress. Four months later I returned for a long weekend to bake a cake and help Karla manage the party.

In my mind a sweet sixteen party is a coming-of-age event; the Yankee version of a debutante ball. At least that was how June Cleaver and I envisioned it. Wrong. This sweet sixteen was nothing like the Neil Sedaka song. On the day of the event, I went up to the club early to help Erin get dressed and into her make-up. What's the good of having a Fairy godfather if he can't do flawless makeup? I then joined the other adults for chaperone duty.

Throughout the evening we confiscated water bottles filled with "iced tea" (really kids, if you're going to spike a water bottle, at least use a clear liquor). No one had warned Rich he should have enlist his friend Mike, a former Newark police investigator, for security duty. Instead Rich had drafted Jim to police the grounds, ensuring kids didn't leave the party to sneak a drink or smoke off site. During Jim's "walk-abouts" he found well-stashed bottles of vodka buried in the snow with just the caps showing. Clever. Jim emptied them out and put them back in the snow, leaving the "clever ones" empty handed. As the night progressed we were doing our best to keep the single toilet bathroom to single use. I scared half a dozen teenagers by pounding on the door and yelling, "One at a time."

As the guests arrived, it seemed that each successive girl had on a shorter, tighter dress. I thought I was at a hookers' convention. I couldn't imagine letting either of my daughters leave the house in these dresses and they were six years older than these girls. I kept thinking, *Did either of her parents see her leave the house looking like a two dollar whore?*

Erin was definitely not sporting hooker attire! I had selected a white halter-neck dress that had silver and gold lamé woven into the chiffon fabric. It was a tea-length gown that I paired with a set of gold beaded shoes to complete the look. She was stunning and elicited a collective gasp from her crowd of friends when she made her entrance. The best part? She stood out because she wasnt wearing black spandex.

The kids danced most of the night (if you could call what they were doing dancing). They were packed in the grand salon and the DJ was blasting bad techno dance music. What I was happening on the dance floor looked more like an episode of *Animal Planet* than *American Bandstand*. By the end of the evening I had sworn off ever planning or attending another sweet sixteen party.

During Rich's next visit, we were just starting dinner when Karla called to say Erin was struck by a car after lacrosse practice and was in the ER. I told Rich to please stop visiting as his visits brought unwelcome news. We were getting frequent texts from Karla about Erin's condition when I noticed Karla had sent me a private note. It said, "Erin is miserable and very scared. Can you send her a personal note to cheer her up and distract her?" Erin loves our cats so I thought I would send her kitty pictures. They had just gotten their summer lion cuts so they had tiny bodies and big heads.

I sent her a text that said, "The kitties heard you were in an accident and wanted me to send you their pictures to cheer you up."

The next text I got was, "Stop sending pictures. She is laughing too hard and it is making her head hurt!"

There is just no pleasing some people. I do suppose it is hard to belly laugh strapped to a backboard, wearing a neck brace. Erin is well on her way to college now and I hope she keeps her crazy. Never hide it, sweetie. It is part of who you are and it's what makes you fabulous.

The Sweet Sixteen Party was just the start of several events that led us back to The Court. We've continued to return on occasion for Friday in the Driveway and that event continues to grow. At some point they're going to have to get a permit to close the street and make it a block party. Ditto for Cinco de Mayo. Ken and I had turned the entire court into Tequila addicts before we left so it was no surprise to Karla when I called to insist that she host a reunion party for us when we happen to be in town on May 5th. My mother-in-law provided exceptional tequila she'd picked up from a duty free shop in Mexico. In a weak moment I insisted that

Karla and our friend John, who has continued to attend events on The Court long after we left, try a shot. Next thing I knew they had set up Karla's forty-two inch kitchen ladder for trust falls. I walked into her kitchen to find people climbing up just to drop back into John and Karla's waiting arms. They were yelling, "FALL, FALL, FALL," as they caught people. Neither of these two partners in crime cared that this activity was ripe for a lawsuit. Joe, the neighborhood sommelier, was not impressed and hid the ladder before anyone had to call 911.

I noticed on this trip back that Davin had grown up. No, he hadn't just grown up, he had turned into an Abercrombie and Fitch model. He's six feet tall, has an eight-pack set of abs you could grate cheese on, smoldering good looks and of course those killer Tranfield eyelashes. Hell, even his name screams male super model: DAVIN. I find that I can handle aging. I can handle aging as long as I don't have to see the children I met when they were five years old grow into adults. It was bad enough watching our daughters turn into women, but to see the youngest member of The Court family become a young man makes me feel really, really old. I finally convinced Karla to get a trifold-modeling card done for this kid. Between his face and his body, he should be walking a runway somewhere. Preferably Milan. I love Milan. I need a reason to go to Milan.

Davin finds this whole modeling thing amusing. His take is, "If it helps me pay for college, I'm in. It has to be easier than earning a wrestling scholarship."

If Erin is my faux goddaughter, this boy is my faux godson. No matter how popular or good looking he has become, he's remained grounded and honest to himself. Don't ever lose that, Davin. It makes you truly special.

After moving off The Court, I figured my days of managing oversized, over-the-top parties was over. That was before my mother-in-law decided she wanted to throw herself a huge 70th birthday party. Not just huge, it was ginormous. The guest list was over two hundred and fifty people, including several privileged members of The Court. It felt like the size of a royal wedding. Ken and his siblings started preparations for this event a year in advance. When the four of them were teenagers, they formed a band and to this day they play at all of the big family events. "Mustang Sally" has become a staple and was certainly on the play list for this birthday extravaganza.

Listening to their weekly conference calls always gave me a headache. Ken and his siblings each have to give their opinions and views on everything. This sounds fine until you're actually listening to what they are saying. They all say the same thing. You have to listen to the exact same idea explained four different ways. No one can just say, "That's a great idea," and move on.

Sally had rented the banquet hall for four hours. They were so busy adding songs for the family band, guest speakers, video presentations and so on, they hadn't noticed they had added six hours of content. In desperation my lovely husband wrangled me into the process. Having run very large corporate events, I knew exactly what it would take to make this party a success.

The first thing I did was to map out the evening timeline, proving to everyone that they could not do twelve songs, have four speakers and three video segments and expect anyone to eat and dance. Sally (the birthday girl) had her own list of special requests. Meanwhile she was telling everyone she wanted lots of dancing and mingling and nothing formal or scheduled but she never told anyone in the family the same thing twice. It's the Italian Matriarch in her. She wanted it to be a surprise and for us to do whatever we wanted as long as we managed to do everything on her list. Her list was endless and ever changing.

The night of the event I ran the evening like a field commander under fire. Thank God for Fabio, the head event planner at the facility. He was family, so to speak, and seemed to appear out of nowhere every time I needed him. He was a real flirt, which added some much needed levity to my situation. Between his skills as an event planner and his willingness to mix me special margaritas (from liquor not on Sally's approved list), I made sure his tip was commensurate.

I believe Sally invited some members of The Court to provide comic relief throughout the evening. Heather and Karla kept my mom dancing almost non-stop. Even in New Jersey it is acceptable for three white women of a certain age to dance together in a social situation. When the DJ Played "Piano Man" all eyes turned to Todd, Heather's husband, who is a dead ringer for Billy Joel. The Court table, which was down in front next to the dance floor, felt it was time to give Todd the recognition he deserved.

They coerced Todd into lip-synching the song and they formed their own doo-wop group to back him up. With no microphone in sight, Karla improvised with a dinner fork. All was going well until the finale when Todd dipped forward in great passion and Karla lifted the fork to catch his final words. Todd's head and Karla's forked collided, leaving Todd with four tiny bleeding holes right in the center of his forehead. He spent the rest of the night wearing a bandana, which made him look more like Brett Michaels. He had some explaining to do on Monday morning when his division president wondered why he was giving his presentation with tine marks on his forehead.

Sally's party was a smash; her own version of a Sweet Sixteen Party, which I dubbed her "At least I'm not Seventy-Five Party." It was wonderful to see how happy she was to be the queen of the night, surrounded by friends and family; I tipped my crown to her. By the end of the weekend, I had once more sworn off trips to New Jersey.

That is, I had sworn off trips to New Jersey until an unexpected miracle forever changed the way I view my life. A year after we moved, our oldest daughter called with some big news. She had something very important and very unexpected to share. Ashleigh was pregnant with our first grandchild. This pregnancy was a miracle.

You see, I was there when Ashleigh went through chemotherapy just prior to puberty. We were all told there was a good chance she would never be able to have children. Her odds of ever becoming pregnant were less than fifty percent. She and her partner Kenny may not have been ready for it, but the fact that she could have a child was a welcome blessing. Nine months later a beautiful and brilliant little girl, Paiton Marie, was born. To say we are proud grandfathers is an understatement. I started buying her a complete wardrobe before she was even born. I've already bought her so many designer dresses, it's embarrassing. Now we had an even bigger reason to visit

New Jersey. You'd think after all these years I would learn to "never say never." Every time I do, it bites me in the ass.

As a rule, life is messy. Ken has heard me preach this point on numerous occasions. It's messy when we enter the world and messy when we leave it. The same can be said about the parts in between, whether literally or figuratively. Regardless the hand you are dealt, you make the most of it. Nothing's truly predictable and the harder we try to control things, the less control we actually have. To get the most out of life we have to accept that time with those we love is limited. If we face each day understanding that our time and our love are the only things we truly own, it allows us to embrace each day or event as a single, non-repeatable moment in time. To be wholly in that moment we must share our hearts openly and without fear. There is a wonderful line from musical *Les Miserables* that touched my heart when I heard it; *"To love another person is to see the face of God."* To me, that one line captures the truth of love completely.

I think back over my life and smile. We have such grand plans when we're young. I was one of those people who mapped out everything. Every step was choreographed. I had no interest in a home with a white picket fence. No interest in a spouse. No interest in ever having children. I remember vividly telling my dad all of these things when he asked which side of the fence I preferred, and yet I am blessed with an amazing husband, two wonderful daughters and a miracle of a granddaughter. I have my family, my in-laws and my family from The Court, who accept and love me in spite of my flaws and will forever be part of my life. Most of us spend our lives looking for and seeking acceptance and love. I found all of that and more on a little cul-de-sac named Altamont Court.

So to my father I say, "It wasn't what I'd planned or wanted, nor could I have possibly predicted my life would turn out this way. But, Daddy, I love it all and I wouldn't change it for anything in the world."

Thank you for taking the time to travel down my memory lane. I'm nowhere near being done with this journey called life, and I hope that you can say the same while enjoying the many blessings that you are afforded. William Purkey, a professor at the University of North Carolina, Greensboro closes out each of his speeches with the same quote and I think you'll agree its a great way to close out this book. These are words we should all live by:

> "You've got to dance like there's nobody watching,
> Love like you'll never get hurt,
> Sing like there's nobody listening.
> Live like it's heaven on earth
> and speak from the heart to be heard."

I would add, don't be afraid to let your crazy out, and remember, if you don't have anything nice to say – come sit by me. Bless your hearts.

PS - Yes, my mother has made several trips back to NJ with us to see her friends on The Court and attend Broadway shows. Mom and Karla wouldn't have it any other way.

XOXO Trent

ACKNOWLEDGEMENTS

There would be no book without my amazing partner Ken and the wonderful crazies that make up The Court. They are the reason I chose to share this incredible story so that you could be part of the love and the laughter.

There are several others I need to thank as well.

When I called my Aunt Vicki in Texas (a prolific writer herself) and asked if she knew a witty gay editor, Vicki's first response was, "Is their any other kind?" And "yes, I do." She introduced me to Jeromy Thompson, a truly gifted writer who helped me add additional wit for your enjoyment. Vicki also served as a part-time editor by challenging the consistency of the narrative and flow of the story line. Their input was invaluable.

Ken and Karla helped me fill in the blanks when my memory failed. As they shared their insights, I began to wonder if my memory had, in fact, failed or whether I had purposely chosen to forget.

Laura and Linda, my high school buddies, and Erick, John, Bobby, Peter and Suzanne, my work buddies, who contributed story line improvements and helped me identify and fix a mountain of punctuation errors. My niece Erika who organized and formatted all the photos and Cynthia Crombie, a dear lady with a sardonic wit who found ever more creative ways to challenge my grammar skills.

A very special thank you to Beth Bruno, my editor. Beth took a grammatically challenged rough draft and helped me shape it into the book you have just read. She continually challenged me to improve the narrative while maintaining my voice throughout the story. I am truly grateful for her sharp eye and keen insights.

And last but not least, the great state of New York and New York City for facilitating our marriage on October 4, 2013. As expected, we celebrated our formalized nuptials that night on The Court.

PICTURES

THE HOUSE

WELCOME TO OUR HOME

The original boys of Altamont Court (Rich, Jim and Todd)

The original boys of Altamont Court as they are usually photographed

The Rich who stole Christmas and Karla, my sister from another mister

Saturday night at the movies: "*Grease* is the word..."
Lindsay's 16th Grease themed birthday party

Ken and our daughter Lindsay's 16th birthday party

My mother-in-law, Karla, and Lindsay as Rizzo,
Beauty School Drop-out, and Sandy

Manilla: She loved Neiman's as much as I do!

Paisley Ann getting her party on as Cosmo Kitty

From the top: Alexander the Great, Pricilla the Queen
of the Desert, and Princess Anastasia

Mimi: My baby doll – I still miss her.

Buddy's philosophy: "No problem is so big that a
roll in the grass won't make it better."

Heather in her
"Eldin the painter" drag

Heather all dolled up

Ken, my mother-in-law, me and my mother on the Grand Canal
in Venice (I told you our mothers were mismatched)

Ken, Sally, and Sally on the "real" Spanish Steps

The Sallys storm the Colosseum

Ken and Trent in Greece...without our mothers

The new kitchen

48 people doing the Thanksgiving Conga

Pugsly the Terrible, the toast of Morristown and cat chaser extraordinaire

Nephews, nieces and daughters recreating "A Christmas Story" with the Festivus Pole

Our last Christmas in Morristown

Mother Christmas

"I made a pot of sauce, you'll come to dinner!"

George and Pat after 10 hours of laborious yard work

Ashleigh at 13: This is the dress that caused Ken's cardiac arrest.

Girls Gone Wild Weekend: Trent and Ken with the honorary
Altamont Court girls (Laura, Sue, Tracey, Linda, and Anita)

SSheryl as a F$%#ing Fabulous Valkyrie at the Nancy Whiskey Pub

Ken on his way to the "gay super bowl" — The Tony Awards

Erin in her WWF Smack Down couture

Erin's transformation to glamour goddess complete

Davin should have read the sign.

Davin at 17 - Hello Abercrombie and Fitch – Courtesy
of Roger Spiess, Spiess Studio, Denville NJ

Ken with the all the ladies of the Court

Our Nephews -These boys are delicious!

Studio 54 minus the cocaine

All the gentlemen of The Court

The Cake

The boys of Atlanta

Ken and Ashleigh at our commitment ceremony, she's all grown up

Lindsay and Ken, she grew up too fast, seems
like she was just "sweet 16" yesterday

Our Altamont Court family (or as my brother calls them THE OTHERS)

The new caretakers of that fabulous Queen Anne
Colonial – Kennedy, Karla and the twins

Paiton Marie, the most fabulous and perfect granddaughter in the
world! (Courtesy of Roger Spiess, Spiess Studio, Denville NJ)

COOKING
ON ALTAMONT COURT

ALTAMONT COURT CAFÉ – DELICIOUS IS SERVED

Admit it. Reading this book made you hungry. It's OK; we're only human and food is an essential part of our happiness. Hell, writing the book made me hungry! So much so that before I wrote down these recipes (as you recall, I don't write anything down I make them up as I go) I had to make, bake and sauté them all again just to make sure you got what you came for: The Recipes from The Court. Whether it was Thanksgiving, Christmas, family dinners, my Sunday cooking marathons or dinner parties, I've had the privilege of creating and tasting many wonderful dishes that were brought to the table. Food is friendship and keeps us close (especially when the food is incredible) and since this book has a vast presence of culinary creations, I thought it only appropriate to share some of the recipes with you. As you will notice, the names of the recipes represent events from the book: 'Trent's Divine Balls,' 'Made a Pot-a-Sauce, You'll Come to Dinner,' 'Karla's Forgotten Twice Baked Potatoes' and, of course, 'The NOG' (you are very welcome). Feel free to add or take ingredients away from the recipes, but if you do then you won't be experiencing what we experienced at The Court – so if you do, I say, Bless YOUR Heart.

MANGIA!

MADE A POT OF SAUCE,
YOU'LL COME TO DINNER

Ken and I both grew up with the "Sunday pot of sauce." As long as I can remember, my mother made a huge pot of sauce with every kind of meat imaginable (chicken legs, Italian sausage, pork chops – all fried up in olive oil and then dropped into the sauce to finish cooking). Her sauce was delicious.

My mother-in-law is the queen of the meatball. She also makes an incredible pot of sauce, but her specialty is the meatball itself. I combined what I learned from these two amazing women and added a few of my own choices of ingredients. It is the perfect meal to make for Sunday dinner or any large get together.

PS – you should make sure you have a few Mason Jars, lids and rings to bottle the leftovers. This recipe makes a lot of sauce!

Meatballs/Sauce
No holiday with Italians is ever celebrated without a pot of sauce, meatballs and a half dozen assorted pasta dishes – shells and sauce anyone?

The Sauce:
> 2 X 28 ounce cans of Cento Tomato Puree
> 3 X 28 ounce cans of whole San Marzano tomatoes (You will puree these in a food processor.)*
> 1 X 28 ounce can of tomato sauce

2 X 28 ounce cans of crushed tomatoes

1 X 28 ounce can of finely diced tomatoes

1 X 12 ounce can of tomato paste

1 X 32 ounce bottle of tomato juice

1 sweet onion finely diced

2 tablespoons of minced garlic

1 tablespoon of dried basil

2 teaspoons of dried oregano

2 cups of red wine (Keep the bottle handy for medicinal purposes.)

1 tablespoon of garlic powder

1 tablespoon of onion powder

1 tablespoon of sea salt (Add additional salt to taste.)

1 teaspoon of finely ground black pepper

1 teaspoon of finely ground white pepper

* Select the lowest sodium can tomatoes you can find and salt to taste.

First step, pour yourself a glass of red wine. As Alan Jackson sings, "it's 5 0'clock somewhere." Now, sauté diced onion and minced garlic in three tablespoons of olive oil until onions are soft.

In a food processor or a blender, puree whole tomatoes and pour the content into a large saucepot, the larger the better (in this case, size does matter!) Add all cans of tomatoes as well as tomato juice and wine to the pot. Put the sauce on medium heat and stir until all the tomato products are well mixed. Add the cooked onions and garlic mixture and stir into the sauce. Now add all dry ingredients and stir them into the sauce until they are well incorporated. Stir frequently until it boils, then reduce the heat to low. You will need to stir frequently to reduce the risk of the sauce burning to the bottom of the pot. If you feel the spoon sticking, <u>do not</u> try to scrape the bottom of the pot. If you do, burnt black stuff will float up and make your sauce taste like an ashtray.

Personally, I believe a good sauce is a daylong project. That bottle of medicinal wine will make the time fly. Remember to have a second bottle on hand for guests. Start it at 10 AM and it will be ready by 5 PM – remember, all good things come to those who wait!

The Meatballs:
  1 loaf of bakery Italian bread (Don't worry, all you carb watchers, you will be gutting your loaf of bread like a fish – aka, pulling out the insides.)
  4 pounds of ground beef (80% lean). Even better if you can get Wagyu ground beef.
  1 cup of finely grated or Parmigiano-Reggiano cheese
  1 cup of finely grated Locatelli Romano
  2 teaspoons of oregano
  2 teaspoons of onion powder
  2 teaspoons of garlic powder
  1 teaspoon Italian Parsley
  1 tablespoon of finely ground sea salt
  Pepper to taste (I grind in a mix of white and black pepper.)
  3 large eggs

2 pints of heavy cream
1/2 cup of Italian breadcrumbs
2 tablespoons of olive oil

If you like your meatballs spicy, add a tablespoon of red pepper flakes.

Night before Prep:
Cut the loaf of bread in half and hollow it out. Put the shell of the bread aside in a zip-lock bag and use it for testing your sauce later. Tear your bread guts into small pieces and put on a cookie sheet to dry overnight.

Place all meat in a large mixing bowl and add cheese and dry ingredients. In a food processor with a cutting blade, place dried breadcrumbs and the 2 pints of heavy cream. Puree this mixture – it will look a bit like ricotta cheese or a very wet dough. Pour contents in with meat and mix by hand. Once the wet bread mixture is incorporated, add eggs and olive oil and mix them in by hand. If your hands can't handle this or you don't like getting your hands dirty, you can use the dough hook or paddle attachment on a Kitchen Aid mixer to blend the meat mixture.

Warning, Warning! Danger, Will Robinson! You are now at a critical stage in the meatball making process: rolling the balls. I do not like overly rolled, tight balls. It makes them seem tough when they are cooked. I roll the balls lightly until well formed and drop them raw into the sauce. Make sure the sauce is nearly at a boil. Do not crank up the heat to high as you can achieve a boil at medium heat. You do not want to burn your sauce. Once all the meatballs are in the pot, reduce heat and cover with lid. Do not stir until the meatballs are firm. This takes about 50 to 60 minutes. Once they are firm, remove lid and continue to cook. The meatballs should be at the perfect consistency and thoroughly cooked after 2 hours of simmering in the sauce. I leave mine cooking in the pot all day. They come out amazingly tender and full of flavor.

I also like to pan sear sweet and spicy Italian sausage and drop it in the pot to cook with the meatballs. It's amazing.

I skim the excess oil that comes from the meatballs and sausage off the top of my sauce to reduce the grease.

Mangia!

TRENT'S DIVINE BALLS

First dubbed "DI-VINE" by our good friend Pat, I'm sure she won't be the last to compliment these balls. The Italian name for rice balls is **Arancini.** They are best served with a side of Marinara. You could make your own sauce, but for something like this I have a cheat: Bertolli's Vineyard Marinara! For a jarred sauce, it's wonderful. Soon you will have your guests telling you how divine your balls are!

You will need:

2 cups of risotto rice (Arborio)

1 cup finely of grated Grand Padano cheese

1/2 cup finely of grated Locatelli romano cheese. Must be Locatelli – Do Not Waiver

1 onion

4-5 cups of chicken broth or chicken stock (stock has a richer flavor)

1 cup of white wine (again, keep the bottle handy for medicinal purposes)

4 eggs

2 cups of white flour

2 cups of Italian bread crumbs (separate out 1/2 cup)

1 teaspoon of minced garlic

stick of salted butter

cup of olive oil

1 teaspoon of sea salt

teaspoon of ground black pepper

teaspoon of onion powder

teaspoon of garlic powder

8 ounces of Fontina cheese (cut into cubes for stuffing inside the balls)

Salt and pepper to taste (Chicken broth can have a lot of salt so before you add more make sure you taste it first.)

4 cups of peanut oil or for those who have an allergy, canola oil or shortening or, even better, Extra Virgin Olive Oil.

Prep:

Sauté Pan I like a wide-mouth pan with a deep lip (I mean, who doesn't, right?)

Cookie sheet with an edge, lined with parchment paper. If your cookie sheet is non-stick, you can skip the paper.

Pre-cut Fontina cheese into 1/2 inch cubes

Dice half of the onion

Beat up one egg – show no mercy folks

Set oven temp at 350

Cookie sheet with wire cooling rack sitting inside

The Rice:

Melt butter in sauté pan and add olive oil. Bring pan to medium heat. Add diced onion and minced garlic. Cook until onion is soft but not brown. If the heat is too high the garlic will pop like popcorn – trust me when I say it's not cute and clean-up is messy! Medium heat is more than enough. When the onions are soft, add butter. Once melted, add rice and sauté for 2-3 minutes. At this point stir in white wine and cover 2 to 3 minutes. Pour yourself a glass of that medicinal wine and enjoy it while your wait. Remove lid and stir often until liquid is absorbed. Begin adding broth (or stock) one cup at a time. This may be time consuming but it is an all-important part of the process. That glass if wine you're sipping makes the time pass faster. You must stir frequently throughout the cooking process – stop complaining, you can stir and sip your vino so you are multitasking!

As the liquid from the first cup of broth is absorbed, add the second and so on. For risotto balls, you want the rice more firm than creamy so start testing it when the 4 cups of broth have been absorbed. Keep adding broth until you reach an al dente texture. Each cup will take 5-10 minutes to absorb. When the rice is ready, pour it out on a baking sheet to cool. Let cool 15-20 minutes.

Once it is cool enough to handle, put rice in a mixing bowl and fold in the grated Romano and Grand Padano cheeses, 1 cup of Italian breadcrumbs and that egg you beat with reckless abandon. Mix thoroughly.

For those who like to cook in advance, you can make the risotto mixture a couple of days ahead of time and keep it in the refrigerator. Just remember to let it warm up at room temperature for 30 to 45 minutes before you use it.

If you were making a risotto dish you would continue to add broth until you reached a creamy texture and the rice is more tender – but we aren't doing that so don't go overboard with the broth.

Now it is time to assemble and shape the balls!

You need three bowls. One bowl with 1 cup white flour, one bowl with remaining 3 eggs (well-beaten) and one bowl with 1 cup of white flour, 1 cup of Italian bread crumbs, 1 teaspoon of salt, teaspoon of finely ground pepper, teaspoon of garlic powder, teaspoon of onion powder. Use a fork to mix it up to incorporate the spices.

Take a cube of cheese and approximately three tablespoons of the rice (balls will be about 1 inch in diameter), put the cheese in the center and form the ball around the cheese. I treat these like meatballs, rolling them in my palms. If it is too sticky, wet your hands. I hate sticky balls. Once you have the balls neatly rolled, it's time to get fryin'!

The only pan I consider worthy for frying food in is a cast iron skillet or pot. Fill skillet with inch of olive oil or the oil of your choice and heat. Take the balls and roll them in flour, then the beaten eggs, and then the spiced flour and breadcrumbs, before dropping them in the hot oil. Roll them around in the hot oil until they are golden brown. Remove and place on cooling rack/cookie sheet.

Once you have fried all of the balls, pop them in the oven to ensure the cheese is thoroughly melted inside, about 12 minutes. Serve with a side of marinara sauce and enjoy as these balls melt in your mouth and disappear from the tray.

Mangia!

THE NOG

The base of this recipe came from Catherine's kitchen. Over the years I have tweaked it to make it my own. I am not responsible for the condition of your guests after they have consumed two or more cups of this libation. In fact, I guarantee you will have overnight houseguests after just one taste!

The fermenting process takes three to four weeks so make sure you do this over Thanksgiving weekend so its ready for Christmas and New Year's Eve.

You will need:
  18 large eggs
  3 cups of sugar (Caster Sugar or Super Fine Sugar is the best)
  3 cups of heavy cream
  5 cups of whole milk
  3 cups of Maker's Mark Bourbon
  3 cups of Myers Dark Rum
  2 cups of good cognac
  1 cup of brandy
  2 tablespoons of Tahitian vanilla
  teaspoon of vanilla bean paste
  1 pinch of fine sea salt

Separate the yolks and save the whites for later.

Using a mixer at medium speed, blend yolks, sugar, vanilla, vanilla bean paste and sea salt. Mix at least 2 minutes. Blend in the heavy cream. Once it is incorporated, pour contents into a large saucepot that fits in your fridge. Using a long wooden spoon, stir in whole milk. Once incorporated, add assorted liquors and stir this heavenly mix to blend it all together. Once this is complete, I put the lid on the pot and place it in my basement refrigerator for 3 weeks. The 20-quart pot I use can hold a double batch.

Your other option is to buy glass bottles (I get mine from Sur La Table. You can also use Mason jars used for canning) and a funnel and bottle your brew for fermentation. Store them in the refrigerator for three weeks and you are ready to go.

You thought I forgot to tell you what to do with the egg whites, didn't you? If you're health conscious, use the egg whites for omelets. I freeze mine until I am ready to serve the eggnog. When you serve The Nog, defrost the egg whites, whip them with some sugar and place a couple of spoonfuls on top of my cup of Nog, grind some nutmeg on the foam and violà! Ready to serve.

Make sure you have clean sheets on the extra beds for guests who cannot drive home after enjoying this festive concoction. Of course if you have a couple glasses of Nog you won't care about clean sheets.

PS – I let my guests know this is a "creeper cocktail" because it will sneak up on you fast.

Cheers!

THE PASTA

For me, fresh pasta is one of those luxuries in life everyone can afford. I am not talking about the "supposedly" fresh pasta located in the cheese aisle at the supermarket. I mean the stuff you make from scratch. When the girls were young, they loved making fresh pasta with me and fought over who got to turn the hand-crank on the pasta machine. I always made it a family affair – you should as well. You'll be making amazing memories while you're making amazing food. You will also be making a mess of your kitchen but it's totally worth it.

You will need:
    4 cups of double zero flour "00" (You can usually get this at an Italian Deli or specialty store or you can locate it online.)
    6 whole eggs
    1 teaspoon salt
    1 teaspoon extra virgin olive oil
    Warm water, if needed (You will see below when and why.)

Beat the 6 eggs, salt and olive oil in a bowl with a fork until completely blended.

I like the convenience of a food processor with a dough blade to make my pasta. The purists among you will not use a food processor. You can use your hands or a fork if you do not have a food processor and work the dough until it is smooth.

Put all flour in the processor. Pulse processor blade as you add the egg mixture. Do this until it becomes a ball. You may need a bit of warm water if the dough is not coming together. I am a big fan of Double "00" Flour – it is the perfect flour for pasta and pizza. If you live in the south, White Lily flour will work. Depending on the size of your food processor, you may need to split this recipe into two batches. Just cut the recipe in half: 2 cups flour, 3 eggs, teaspoon salt, teaspoon olive oil – for you lazy folks who don't want to do simple math (you know who you are and you are thanking me right now), bless your hearts.

Once you have a dough ball, place it on a well-floured surface. You will need to add flour to the surface during this entire process. Knead until dough becomes smooth. Do not over knead, as it will make the dough tough. Shape the dough into a log. Now for the fun part - rolling your dough! You can roll the dough out with a rolling pin – this takes some real skill, time and effort. (not to mention patience – pray you still have a bottle of wine on hand.)

You can buy a hand crank pasta roller; this works well but also takes time and a little practice to feed the dough and crank the handle at the same time. My favorite way to roll pasta is to use a KitchenAid mixer with the pasta rolling and cutting attachments. Wham, bam, thank you Ma'am – rolling made easy! Purists are rolling their eyes.

Rolling the pasta is part of the kneading process. You will start with your roller on the first setting. Cut an inch wide piece of the pasta log, pat it flat on the floured surface and feed it through the rollers. If the dough is too wet, it will pull apart. Pat the dough in additional flour, fold in in half and place it through the roller again. I pass dough through at least 3 times on the widest setting to further smooth the dough before I move the setting to the next number. For pasta sheets, roll them down to a 5 or 6 on your pasta roller making sheets thinner with each past through. You only need to past the dough through each new setting 1 time.

Lightly flour between the sheets as you lay them out or they will stick. Once you have your pasta sheets you are ready to fill with cheese or meat or you can put these sheets of pasta through the pasta cutter for linguini or fettuccini or spaghetti or layer them for lasagna. If you are making linguini, fettuccini or spaghetti, let the noodles air dry for about an hour.

Just remember if you are making anything in a baking dish to spray it with a non-stick baking spray and put a layer of sauce on the bottom before placing your food in the dish. The spray and layer of sauce helps keep the pasta from sticking and the sauce on the bottom marinates the noodles as they bakes so that every bit pops with flavor.

The texture of this pasta is tender and firm – hey, hey people, we are taking about the pasta here!

Mangia!

CHEESE FILLING FOR SHELLS, MANICOTTI, RAVIOLI

Fresh pasta is fabulous. Fresh pasta filled with this cheese mixture is orgasmic. While Ken and I were struggling to get our kitchen built, we ate out several days a week. One of our favorite restaurants in Morristown is Guerriero's. Jack, the owner, head chef and consummate host, opened his restaurant during our renovation. He saw us a couple times a week for six months. His ravioli is divine. Although he wouldn't tell me everything he put in his cheese mixture, he did tell me to add Fontina Cheese to mine. It was an outstanding addition. Thank you, Jack!

You will need:
>   1 quart of whole milk Ricotta
>   1 cup of finely grated Grand Padano
>   1 cup of grated whole milk Mozzarella
>   1 cup of grated Fontina cheese
>   2 eggs
>   1 teaspoon of sea salt

Use a hand mixer on low to blend all the cheeses and eggs together. If you enjoy cheese filling with more seasoning, add garlic powder, onion powder and pepper to taste. Spoon mixture into a piping bag or if you don't have one use a zip lock baggie and cut off a bottom corner. I prefer a piping bag as the zip locks can pop open while you are squeezing out your cheese mixture and can get very messy!

Fill your shells, manicotti or ravioli with this mixture. It can be layered into a lasagna as well. Don't forget the important rule of spraying and saucing the bottom of your baking dish or you will be using a crowbar remove your food from the dish.

If you are boiling fresh ravioli, DO NOT use a rapid boil or your ravioli will explode – it is a sensitive little stuffed pasta and if you aren't careful, your hard work will be ruined. I bring my water to a boil, back it off to a light boil then add the ravioli. Fresh pasta cooks quickly. 3 to 5 minutes and you're ready to serve.

Mangia!

KARLA'S FORGOTTEN TWICE BAKED POTATOES

Those marvelous creations that sadly never made it to the dinner table, bless their baked hearts.

You will need:
   4 large baking potatoes
   4 ounces of sour cream
   pint of heavy cream
   stick of butter (4 tablespoons)
   Salt and pepper to taste
   White extra sharp cheddar, cut into thin strips (easier for melting, but if you are a size queen and need them thicker – knock yourself out!)
   4 strips of cooked crispy bacon

Wash and scrub potatoes with skins on them and gently pierce each potato with a fork 4 or 5 times to avoid potato explosions. Bake for 45 – 60 minutes at 375 degrees (or reduce cooking time by inserting cooking nails). Let baked potatoes cool 10-15 minutes before starting the next steps.

Once cooled, cut potatoes in half (length-wise) and gently scoop out the cooked potato into a mixing bowl, reserving the potato skins for later.

Add melted butter, milk, sour cream and salt and pepper to taste. Whip ingredients together. Baked potatoes are stiffer than boiled potatoes and may require extra liquid ingredients (sour cream, butter or cream or all three – these potatoes won't judge you so it will be our little secret!).

Place reserved potato skins on a shallow baking sheet. Spoon in whipped potatoes, making a channel in the center. Add cheddar cheese to the center and sprinkle with crumbled bacon.

Return to the 375 degree oven until the cheddar cheese melts.

Left over potatoes refrigerate and freeze well.

Mangia! (I had to say it even though this is not an Italian dish.)

PASTA CARBONARA

As my mother-in-law often says, "Pasta Carbonara makes Fettuccini Alfredo look dietetic!" It's Davin's absolute favorite recipe. I have seen him wolf down an entire pound of pasta covered in carbonara sauce. Oh, to have the metabolism of a seventeen-year-old athlete.

You will need:

Pancetta – a minimum of 8-10 oz. I get the pieces cut at the deli in 1/8 inch slices. If you are a bacon lover, substitute a pound of extra thick cut bacon.

sweet onion, diced finely

1 cup of heavy cream

2 tablespoons of extra virgin olive oil

1 pound of pasta – spaghetti, linguini or fettuccini

6 large egg yolks

cup of finely grated Parmigiano-Reggianno cheese

cup of finely grated Pecorino Roman cheese

1 teaspoon of ground black pepper

1 teaspoon of ground white pepper

Grand Padano for grating over finished dish

Carbonara is simple to make but easy to screw up – so pay close attention to the details of this recipe.

Using a mixer on low, beat together yolks, cream, pepper, and grated cheeses and let stand. Cube and fry up the Pancetta in two tablespoons of olive oil. I prefer mine a little on the crispy side. Add onions, cook until soft, and set aside.

Boil pasta in well-salted water and a good splash of olive oil. Cook until it's al dente.

Drain pasta and add back to pot; leave heat off. Do Not rinse your pasta! You need to keep the heat and the starch. Pour in onion and pancetta and toss with tongs. Pour egg mixture over **hot** pasta, toss with tongs and serve immediately. The room temperature egg mixture cooks from the heat of the pasta and metal of the hot pot. If you keep the heat on, you will end up with pasta and scrambled eggs! Serve immediately.

Mangia!

THE SALAD

When I was growing up, my mother always made her own Italian dressing. This was before ready-made packets of seasoning. Using olive oil, red wine vinegar and half a dozen seasonings from the pantry she created a fabulous Italian salad dressing. I cheat a bit and use a packet of Good Seasonings Italian dry mix as it makes it a hell of a lot easier. Our girls and nieces dubbed this salad "Candy" because this dressing makes you want to eat salad...Wait for it... like CANDY. Ashleigh and Lindsay demand this dressing every time they visit.

You will need:
  2/3 cup of Colovita extra virgin olive oil
  cup of Colovita white balsamic vinegar
  1 packet Good Seasonings Italian dressing mix
  1/2 teaspoon sugar
  Pinch of finely ground sea salt.

Dissolve packet of seasoning, sugar and salt in the vinegar. Wisk until sugar has dissolved. Add extra virgin olive oil. Wisk until dressing develops a syrupy thickness.

Dump in salad, tomatoes, carrots, celery and toss.

Mangia!

HOW DO YOU SAY "I NEED YOUR CHEESECAKE RECIPE," IN ITALIAN?

This is the recipe I attempted to pick up from a chef in the hills of Italy outside of Florence. It's easy and always gets comments like, "Oh my God, this is delicious! What's in it?" Below is my attempt at recreating it – it's pretty damn close.

Filling:

2 packages of Philly Cream Cheese - 8 Ounce rectangles (room temp)

3 tubs of mascarpone cheese (room temp)

2 cups of Caster sugar (Dominos super fine sugar will work for a less sweet version, reduce sugar by cup)

1 teaspoon Tahitian vanilla

1/4 teaspoon of vanilla Powder

Crust:

1 package Stella Dora Breakfast cookies (If you can't find these, try vanilla wafers.)

6 tablespoons of unsalted butter, melted

2 tablespoons of sugar

1/2 teaspoon of vanilla

Blueberry Compote:

1 16-ounce package of frozen blueberries

1/2 cup of sugar

For crust, pre-heat oven to 350 degrees.

Place the cookies in your food processor with the cutting blade and pulse until you have a consistent crumbled mix. Add melted butter and pulse until well mixed. Pour crumble mixture into a 9-inch pie plate. Using your fingers, press the mixture firmly and evenly on the bottom and up the sides of the pie plate. Place in the oven to bake for 10 to 12 minutes. Remove and let cool.

In a Kitchen Aid mixer with a paddle attachment, add Philly and mascarpone cheeses to the mixing bowl. Turn mixer on setting 5 or 6 to blend the cheeses. Add sugar, Tahitian vanilla and vanilla powder and mix until well dissolved. DO NOT over blend or the cream cheese will break down and look like cottage cheese. Slow and steady is the way to go. Use a rubber spatula to clean the blade and blend cream cheese from the bottom of the bowl. Remove bowl from mixer and use spatula to mix ingredients for another 30 seconds.

Put mixture into cooled piecrust. Place plastic wrap over pie and place in the refrigerator overnight.

Blueberry compote:
Pour bag of frozen blueberries into a skillet. Use medium heat to thaw. Once the juices begin to puddle, add sugar. Cook mixture down until it becomes syrupy. This can take about 20-30 minutes. Pour into a glass bowl and let cool before placing it on top of the cheesecake.

I prefer to serve this cheesecake with a couple of spoonfuls of blue-berry compote drizzled on top when serving, versus topping the entire cheesecake and then serving. It's a nicer presentation. If you want to go super fancy, add a sprig of mint to garnish.

Mangia!

KARLA'S ARTERY CLOGGING APPLE PIE

Every year, Karla, Rich and the kids would go apple picking and return from this adventure with bags and bags of apples. The first year I saw them unloading their bounty I thought, *What the hell are they going to do with all those apples?* I soon learned the answer to that question when an apple pie showed up at our back door. Karla makes several dozen pies in the fall. She freezes some and sends others out to the neighbors to curry favor. I love apple pie. I adore it. I could live on it – Hell, make one big enough and I would live in it! Yes, I love apple pie. Karla makes one of the best apple pies I have ever laid on my tongue, my arteries clogging with every sinfully delicious bite.

10" double crust dough
   2 cups of sifted flour
   1 teaspoon of salt
   teaspoon of baking powder
   2/3 cups of lard – don't judge, just trust
   Prepare 1 cup of ice water with 1.5 tablespoons vinegar – you
   will only use 6-7 TBSP water in the recipe

Combine flour, salt and baking powder. Cut in lard. Add 6-7 tablespoons of ice water. Mix with fork. Form ball. Let stand in refrigerator for several minutes while you prepare the filling.

Apple pie filling

6-7 cups tart apples, cored, partially peeled and thinly sliced. I prefer Jonathan apples but they are difficult to find – just make sure the ones you choose are tart.

2 tablespoons lemon juice

cup of white sugar

cup of light brown sugar

2 tablespoons of flour (if using freshly picked apples use extra flour)

1 teaspoon of ground cinnamon

Dash of nutmeg

1 tablespoons of butter, cut into chunks

Combine apples with lemon juice. In a separate bowl, combine all dry ingredients then add dry ingredients to apples and toss to coat.

Roll out 2/3 of the pie dough on a floured counter or board. Place in ceramic or glass pie pan so the crust hangs over the edge approximately inch. Add apple mixture mounding the apples and dot with butter. Roll out remaining crust and place over apples. Roll up the bottom crust over the top crust. Crimp with a fork along the top edge of the pie pan, then flute with your fingers. Cut vent holes into the top crust. Your pie is now ready to go into the oven.

I put my pie on a cookie sheet to avoid drippage hitting the bottom of the oven and setting off smoke detectors. Place the pie in the oven and bake at 375 degrees for 50-60 minutes until crust is golden. Take care to rotate the pie midway if your oven heat is uneven so the crust edges don't burn. The juice bubbling out of the vent holes should look like it is beginning to thicken – grab a plate, a fork, your cholesterol and heart medications and DIG IN!

Mangia!

"WHAT DO YOU MEAN HE WON'T GIVE ME THE RECIPE?", CHICKEN SALAD

After one bite, I had to go see the chef to learn his secret. He wouldn't share his recipe, but he shared one of the keys to its delicious flavor – Apple Juice Marinade! I developed this recipe using his trade secret. Enjoy!

You will need:
  4 large boneless, skinless chicken breasts
  1 32-ounce bottle of apple juice
  2 cups of mayonnaise
  1 teaspoon of sweet pickle relish
  1 tablespoon of horseradish cream sauce
  1 teaspoon of fine sea salt
  1 teaspoons of ground white pepper
  1 teaspoon of super fine sugar
  1 red delicious apple
  2 stalks of celery

Boil, cool and rinse chicken breasts. Pull breasts apart and place in bowl. Fill bowl with apple juice. Cover and marinade overnight. Yes, over night. You know the saying, "good things come to those who wait." This is no exception.

After 12 plus hours soaking in the apple juice, pour contents into colander to drain. Before returning chicken to bowl, squeeze out excess apple juice by hand. If you don't do this, your chicken salad will be too wet, leaving a soggy impression.

In a separate bowl, mix wet ingredients (mayonnaise, horseradish sauce, and pickle relish). Stir to combine. Add salt and pepper and stir.

Dice celery and apple (small chop, not fine). Add to wet ingredients and mix well. Pour dressing over the pulled chicken and mix thoroughly. You can always add additional mayo if you like your chicken salad on the wet side. Serve it however you see fit, but once you do, you'll be the one getting the question "Can I have your recipe for this chicken salad?" To save you the hassle, just tell them to buy my book.

Mangia!

MOLTEN CHOCOLATE CAKE IS THE BASE OF THE FOOD PYRAMID

According to Erin Tranfield, chocolate is the single most important food group – ever. She has declared it the base of the food pyramid. After trying this recipe, you may believe this as well.

You will need:

6 ounces of semi-sweet chocolate* (Valrhona, Lindt or Ghiradelli)

2 ounces of bitter sweet chocolate* (Valrhona, Lindt or Ghiradelli)

3/4 cup of unsalted butter

3/4 cup of unsalted butter for greasing ramekins

3 egg yolks

3 whole eggs

1 cup of sugar

 cup of all-purpose flour (I prefer a finely milled flour like White Lily.)

*you can play with the chocolate balance if you like darker chocolate, just change the ratio of Semi Sweet and Bitter Sweet

Grease the inside of 8 ramekins or other oven safe 8 ounce dish, with butter and dust lightly with flour. In a double boiler or bowl over a pot of boiling water, melt butter and chocolate. Once melted, set aside until mixture cools to under 100 degrees.

In a mixing bowl, use an electric mixer at medium speed to combine the 3 egg yolks, 3 whole eggs and sugar until a batter begins to form ribbons on the beaters. This will take 3 to 4 minutes.

Pour in melted chocolate mixture with while mixing. Once incorporated, mix for 2 minutes. Pour in 3/4 cup of flour and mix for another 3 minutes. Pour finished batter into ramekins, cover and refrigerate for 1 hour. These can be made a day in advance and chilled overnight.

Preheat oven to 475 degrees. Put ramekins on a cookie sheet and place in the oven for 10 to 12 minutes until they have puffed up and jiggle when moved. Do not over bake or the center will set up like an ordinary cake (which has happened to me on more than one occasion and defeats the purpose of this recipe's namesake).

Remove from oven and serve. I prefer to serve them in the ramekin on a plate with vanilla ice cream on the side. Add fresh berries for presentation and enjoy this recipe from the single most important food group.

Mangia!

FLYING LIMOUSINE CHEESE PUFFS

These are the little gems that went flying all over the limo when The Court went to Broadway. They are so good, the entire group declared the 5-second rule and ate them anyway. 6-second plus cheese puffs were chased with a swig of champagne.

You will need:
  1 cup of all-purpose flour
  teaspoon of salt
  1 cup of whole milk
  4 ounces of unsalted butter
  5 extra large eggs (room temp)
  1/3 cup of finely grated Parmesan cheese
  2/3 cup of finely grated Gruyere cheese

Prep:
Mix salt and flour together and set aside.
Beat 1 egg in a small bowl.
Cookie sheet with silicone baking mat placed on top or insulated cookie sheet.
Pastry brush
Set oven at 425 degrees.

In a 3-quart saucepan, combine the milk and butter, stir and bring to a boil. Once butter is melted, remove from heat and dump all the flour in at once and stir with a wooden spoon until a dough ball forms. (I'm starting to see a pattern in my recipes – BALLS!)

At this point I use my Kitchen Aid with the paddle attachment, but a hand mixer works just fine on its low or medium setting. Transfer dough ball to large mixing bowl. Beat in the 4 remaining eggs, one at a time until completely blended into the dough. It should look smooth and shiny. For those of you distracted by smooth and shiny things – LOOK AWAY! We still have work to do! Add the grated cheeses and blend thoroughly.

At this point I like to use a piping bag with an attachment to pipe them on to the baking mat. You want the dough balls to be around 1 inch in diameter. You can use a spoon to do this as well. Place the dough balls about 2 inches apart. Use a pastry brush to lightly brush the tops of the cheese puffs with the beaten egg – careful shiny people – this will make them shinier.

Place baking sheet in the middle of the oven. Bake for 9 to 11 minutes depending on your oven. Rotate the sheet at 5 minutes for even baking. They will reach a golden brown.

Once again you will have the pleasure of talking about my balls. I do not recommend consumption of these balls in a moving limousine. You've been warned.

Bon Appétit (I had to say Bon Appétit this time because these puffs are French)

TRENT'S TEXAS MARGARITAS

My Motto: Start with good booze or don't bother. Life's too short to drink cheap liquor.

   2.5 ounces Patron Silver
   1 ounce Grand Marnier
   1 ounce fresh lime juice from fresh limes
   1.5 ounces orange juice from fresh oranges
   3 ounces Margaretville mix
   coarse kosher salt for rims
   fresh lime juice for rims

Pour all your liquids into a cocktail shaker and shake! Dip the rim of your glass in lime juice then into a plate of coarse kosher salt. Add ice to your glass and pour contents of the shaker into a glass full of ice and enjoy.

Cheers!

KEN'S COSMOS

Good Vodka! If you aren't going to use the good stuff, you might as well use lighter fluid or anti-freeze.

3 ounces of Vodka, Ketel One or Grey Goose or equivalent
1 teaspoon Rose's Lime Juice
3/4 ounce Cointreau
3 ounces Ocean Spray Cranberry Juice Cocktail

Pour all your liquids into a cocktail shaker and shake! Pour contents into a martini glass and enjoy.

Cheers!

ONLY BECAUSE KARLA'S INSISTED, LAST MINUTE QUESO

Perfect after a grueling workweek. Must be served with an adult beverage – any kind. Everybody will love it, but know one should know what's in it.

    1 12 ounce can of Hormel beef chili, no beans
    1 8 ounce can of Rotel tomatoes
    1 16 ounce block of Velveeta cheese (regular) My youngest daughter calls Velveeta "faux cheese" since it doesn't have to be refrigerated.

Open cans of chili and Rotel tomatoes and pour them into a sauce-pot and heat to a boil. Turn back to a medium low heat. Cube the Velveeta cheese and drop pieces into the chili, Rotel mix. Stir until they cubes are entirely melted.

Serve with white Tostitos tortilla chips....and that adult beverage.

Trent was born in Columbus, Ohio and grew up in a small town (cornfields of the Midwest as he would say) just east of the city. After graduating from Pickerington High School (Go Tigers!) he attended college at Abilene Christian University in West Texas and earned his degree in communications. Trent went on to further his education and completed his MBA at Emory University in 2003. Although he has a love for the performing arts and has performed on various stages in Texas, New Jersey and Georgia (never in drag, mind you), his desire for a stable paycheck with medical coverage outweighed his desire to pursue his theatrical dream and become the next Broadway phenom. It was then, at the age of twenty-four, that he started his career with his current employer;

an international communications company, and learned that he had an aptitude for business. Thirty years later he still enjoys going to work and is pleased to present to you his latest artistic endeavor and first literary piece, *Life on Altamont Court*. Trent can be contacted at:

lifeonaltamontcourt@gmail.com

Made in the USA
Middletown, DE
17 April 2020

89280115R00205